Dark Bayou

Dark Bayou

Infamous Louisiana Homicides

ALAN G. GAUTHREAUX *and*
D.G. HIPPENSTEEL

Foreword by CHARLES C. FOTI, JR.

McFarland & Company, Inc., Publishers
Jefferson, North Carolina

Library of Congress Cataloguing-in-Publication Data

Names: Gauthreaux, Alan G. | Hippensteel, D.G.
Title: Dark bayou : infamous Louisiana homicides / Alan G. Gauthreaux and D.G. Hippensteel ; foreword by Charles C. Foti, Jr.
Description: Jefferson, N.C. : McFarland & Company, Inc., Publishers, 2016. | Includes bibliographical references and index.
Identifiers: LCCN 2015043439 | ISBN 9781476662954 (softcover : acid free paper) ♾
Subjects: LCSH: Homicide—Louisiana—History.
Classification: LCC HV6533.L8 G38 2016 | DDC 364.15209763—dc23
LC record available at http://lccn.loc.gov/2015043439

British Library cataloguing data are available

ISBN (print) 978-1-4766-6295-4
ISBN (ebook) 978-1-4766-2296-5

Manufactured in the United States of America

McFarland & Company, Inc., Publishers
Box 611, Jefferson, North Carolina 28640
www.mcfarlandpub.com

So the victims will not be forgotten…

Table of Contents

Acknowledgments

The authors would like to acknowledge the following individuals who selflessly assisted with the production of this work:

The Honorable Charles C. Foti, Jr., for his insight and the foreword; the Rev. Dr. Craig W. Rinker, for his constant "loving life" posture, his ability to make the heart and spirit of Scripture come alive, and his ever-present talent in giving comfort to others; Dr. Edward P. St. John, for his lifetime example of believing in students, the process of education, and continued research; Dr. Florent Hardy, Louisiana State archivist, for his inspiration, tutelage, and assistance with primary materials; Bill Stafford, assistant archivist with the State of Louisiana; John Fowler, assistant archivist with the State of Louisiana; Dr. Florence Jumonville, archivist at the University of New Orleans, Earl K. Long Library; Connie Phelps, librarian in Special Collections at the University of New Orleans, Earl K. Long Library; Al Barron, director of the Washington Parish Public Library and fellow East Jefferson High School alumnus; Mary Wenet, archivist, Northwestern State University; Winola Holliday, whose recollections of Bogalusa's past helped put the history of Washington Parish in a humanistic perspective; Irene Wainwright, former chief archivist at the New Orleans Public Library, Special Collections Division, who never ceases to amaze with her research acumen; Yvonne Loiselle, current chief archivist of the Special Collections Division of the New Orleans Public Library, whose special assistance with the photograph collection proved extremely helpful; Randy "Country" Seal, sheriff of Washington Parish, whose professionalism, candor, and assistance with parts of this work proved instrumental; W. J. LeBlanc, attorney at law, for his insight into the workings of the criminal justice system as they pertained to one of the most bizarre murder trials in recent local memory; Col. Joseph D. Passalaqua (ret.), Jefferson Parish Sheriff's Office, former chief of the Crime Scene Division; John Fox, historian with the Federal Bureau of Investigation; Patricia L. Lloyd, whose interesting and intelligent viewpoints kept our historical assumptions honest; Shelley Fairbanks, a formidable student and intellectually honest supporter; Allison J. Pitcher, a friend, supporter, and admirer of literature who left this world too soon, and who encouraged not only literary works, but other artistic endeavors in and around the city of New Orleans; and Lisa Gauthreaux, for her patience with research trips to strange destinations on a limited budget.

Foreword by Charles C. Foti, Jr.

In the United States as a whole, the murder rate has been cut nearly in half in the last four decades, falling from 7.9 murders per 100,000 people in 1970 to 4.5 murders per 100,000 in 2013. Louisiana has been part of this trend—the state's homicide rate fell from 17.5 per 100,000 in 1996 to 10.8 per 100,000 in 2013—but it continues to be plagued by the highest homicide rate in the country.

Murder harms society in many ways. Not only do the victims suffer directly, but their families, friends, and the community also bear the indirect burden of such crimes. Fear swells and people begin to feel unsafe, threatened, and hopeless. The justice system moves at a slow and deliberate pace. Further, the process of reaching a conviction and doling out a sentence, at least when the proceedings are hampered by weak, circumstantial, or tainted evidence and poor or questionable witnesses, does not always lend itself to an outcome that seems equitable, for either the justice system or the victim.

The cases highlighted by Alan G. Gauthreaux and D. G. Hippensteel in this book illustrate the elements of killing, though the perceived gain or justification for the assailant differs in each case. The cases portray numerous murders that occurred in New Orleans, Crowley, Bogalusa, Varnado, Metairie, and as far north as Lake Charles. Gauthreaux and Hippensteel take the reader on a journey of history and criminology through a myriad of murders across time and place: the origins of the first *Mafia* "don"; the sinister assassinations of police chiefs that began in the late 1800s; the tragic case of a notorious madam whose paramour sought to relieve her of her fortune; ritual murders influenced by a teen-aged cult leader; a "cold, calculating, methodical personality with sociopathic traits" accused of using morphine to kill a close family member in a case motivated by greed; an enlightening reassessment of the assassination of Sen. Huey P. Long; racially charged murders that defined a volatile period in Louisiana (and U.S.) history; the true case of a Jefferson Parish housewife who succumbed to one of the most brutal deaths in Louisiana history; and the truly inexplicable case of a well-known local television personality whose ego convinced him he would be spared from life imprisonment for the murder of his wife. All of these cases keenly illustrate the history, culture, and written law of the time, and they provide insightful historical views of criminal justice procedure and development. Perhaps even more importantly, these cases are truly intriguing—but perhaps little remembered—events that beg for a more complete and unbiased assessment.

In *Dark Bayou*, Gauthreaux and Hippensteel offer readers of this genre a fascinating peek not only into time, and not only into the criminal justice system, but into the dark side of the primal psyche. As the criminal sheriff in New Orleans for more than 30 years, the former attorney general of the State of Louisiana, a prosecutor, and defense counsel, I well realize some of the underlying motivations for murder are emotional, social, religious, economic, educational, political, greed, anger, self-defense, alcohol and drugs, revenge, jealousy, and domestic abuse. Gauthreaux and Hippensteel chose cases that illustrate some of these core causes of murder, and they integrate an unbiased historical precision in describing these cases with their desire to appeal to a mass audience in accomplishing that objective. *Dark Bayou* deservedly belongs among the most important works within the shadowy realm of true crime.

The Honorable Mr. Charles C. Foti, Jr., is a partner with the law firm of Kahn, Swick, & Foti, LLC, in Madisonville, Louisiana, and an advocate for humanitarian causes. He was the sheriff of the Orleans Parish Criminal Sheriff's Office from 1974 to 2003 and was elected Louisiana attorney general in 2004, serving until 2008.

Preface

Dark Bayou began as an historical interest in the peculiar and ghastly, but evolved into an historical and social study of serious crimes in the annals of Louisiana history. The authors realized that a fascination existed with humans' dark imagination and its relation with the unknown, unsolved, or controversial. In Louisiana, there have been several incidents where "Truth is stranger than fiction"—and the cases profiled in *Dark Bayou* well demonstrate that adage.

Although some of the homicides mentioned in *Dark Bayou* might seem familiar to some readers, they have not been very well publicized in the remembrance of Louisiana history. Other cases documented here have received very little attention throughout history but were selected because of their controversy, misrepresentation of justice, or ambiguous documentation. A few of them have been written about in passing, but not as part of a historical record. *Dark Bayou* seeks to correct this oversight by recounting these crimes in a popular history format, instead of consigning them to the droll recitations of authors past.

Serial killers were not included in this work because their crimes can contain volumes of psychological analysis that would detract from the telling of these stories. Also, we felt that the victims should have been treated with far more dignity than they received—an aspect of each case that we made one of the primary missions of this work. However, this omission does not detract from perhaps a later volume, where the crimes committed by serial killers will be the primary area of concentration.

The motives of the perpetrators profiled in this book run the gamut from greed, to jealousy, to religious fanaticism, to racial motives that even the most seasoned psychiatrist would struggle to comprehend. Given the varied rationales of the criminals, *Dark Bayou* seeks to recount the history of the crimes based on the documentation available, focusing on giving a factual perspective rather than a psychological profile.

The cases contained within *Dark Bayou* are strange and bizarre, and stand alone in their own right. The reader will take a journey through Louisiana's dark history—a journey filled with shadowy corners and dark figures who invade people's nightmares. When perusing these pages, the reader is advised to remember that the crimes documented actually occurred and the perpetrators of these crimes are no figment of the authors' imaginations. The monsters depicted here actually existed.

Introduction

"The thin line between good and evil does not go through states or ideologies, but through the heart of every man and woman."—Alexander Solzhenitsyn

Murder is one tragedy of humanity that simultaneously repulses and fascinates us, both as individuals and as societies. Since Cain murdered Abel, religious thinkers, philosophers, novelists, playwrights, and social scientists have tried to identify, comprehend, explain, and predict this act in the human experience. Theories abound.

The authors have not written *Dark Bayou* to provide support, speculation, or proof of any particular theory, as a criminologist might be tempted to do. Nor should this book be taken as simply a "flat" and lifeless historical narrative. Rather, our first hope is that readers will find these cases not just fascinating, but instructive as to human behavior.

Just as American jurisprudence judges each case individually on its own merits and evidence, so our hope is that readers employ their own worldviews to assess the cases of murder in Louisiana history presented in this book. In the preface, we outline several general premises that interested us and prompted us to create this work. More specifically, we began our research by selecting more than 30 cases for possible inclusion into the book that we thought readers might find interesting. As part of the necessary winnowing process, we developed the following criteria for selecting cases: (1) unknown in the literature or reporting, (2) little known in the literature or reporting, (3) misrepresented in the literature or reporting, (4) involved a variety of murderous human behavior, and (5) appealed to a variety of readers.

Although the cases presented here are taken from Louisiana history, each state likely has similar cases embedded in its history and in its present. In the final analysis, these Louisiana cases and similar cases across the American landscape reveal the base characteristics we find so repulsive and fascinating.

The research demonstrated that the boundary between good and evil may not be as clear as one would think, especially when complicated with human desires and emotions. These are the more primitive traits that move evil hearts to sinister action. Yet these same primitive traits may also render those individuals with pure hearts willing to sacrifice themselves to rid the world of a perceived evil. In our modern society, the efforts to overcome nefarious designs for murder and mayhem rarely garner much notice. Rather, serious societal fascination with the macabre invades our lives with such abandon as to desensitize our personal belief systems and ignite an abhorrent character within us all. The cases within *Dark Bayou* will whet this morbid appetite and satisfy the maddening addiction to the opaqueness of the human soul.

Today, murder and mystery dominate the American public sphere—at least in terms of entertainment. Some estimates note that perhaps as much as 70 percent of television programming, movies, and video games deals with crime, murder, and the "mystery" behind such evil behavior. Certainly, local and national news organizations know that "if it bleeds, it leads." This approach to grabbing viewers' attention works because we are fascinated by murder and evil. Usually ignored are the truths behind such human behavior: Murder creates a ripple of evil that changes lives beyond family and friends, beyond the investigators who respond to the calls, beyond the costs to the community and the taxpayer. The ripple of evil is not an abstract, static, inanimate, opposite of good. Evil is alive. It is a virus, a parasite that relentlessly eats away at good. Good and Evil, as Solzhenitsyn knew, resides not in a specific time or place, or in the choice of weapon or strategy, but in the human heart.

Small wonder we are so simultaneously repulsed and fascinated.

The First Godfather

"Three people can keep a secret ... if two of them are dead!"—Sign above the doorway at the "headquarters" of Carlos Marcello

Many historical documents, and just as many legends, have been cited as proof of exactly which individual may have established the Mafia within the United States and the exact point in time when that group's founding occurred on U.S. shores. The American quest for the first Godfather includes legends throughout the South, and especially in Louisiana, where a rich cultural folklore and dark legacies concerning the "underworld of crime" hold sway not only among Louisianans but also among Americans in general. Historians attempting to conclude who may be the first Godfather must be prepared to make suppositions based upon documented materials that may not unequivocally define the Mafia's role in American history or precisely pinpoint its growth or origin.

However, interest in the "don of dons" still exists in Louisiana, in the United States, and within the Mafia itself. The Mafia, though certainly a covert organization, could not fully hide its existence. Indeed, it is common knowledge it has roots intertwined with the reams of police corruption and graft among politicians in the Pelican State. One of the individuals credited with becoming the patriarch of the southern "dons" whose emergence led to the beginning and eventual thriving of La Cosa Nostra, both in Louisiana and the rest of the country, was a Sicilian named Joseph P. Macheca.

According to sources, Macheca was born as Peter J. Cervanna, Jr., in Sicily in 1843. His humble beginnings and eventual death led to his immortalization in history as the First American "Godfather."[1]

In Sicily, two years after Peter's father went to prison, Peter's mother, who was unable to care for Peter on her own, left the two-year-old at an orphanage. Peter's mother later remarried, and she reclaimed her son from the orphanage with the stepfather who gave young Peter his name, Joseph P. Macheca. After journeying to Louisiana, young Joseph grew into manhood while rising steadily through the ranks as a Mafiosi. Macheca's rise to underworld power began when, while still in his teens, he established several legitimate successful businesses in New Orleans. He also dabbled in politics and made a reputation for himself as a "mover and shaker." The more successful his businesses became, the more power Macheca sought through whatever means were available to him. Several historians agree that Macheca—the orphaned son of a Sicilian convict—structured much of the Louisiana criminal organization, thereby becoming the "father of the American Mafia."

Prior to Macheca's rise, there were very few references to the Mafia. Local newspapers described most crimes involving Italians as vendettas, acts of revenge to settle offenses against either a person or a family member. Moreover, successful Italian or Sicilian immigrants suffered from rumors that they gained their wealth through underworld alliances and unsolved homicides, a path that was all too common in the Old Country. Macheca was also the subject of those whispered rumors, although no documentary proof exists to establish any of these accusations. Successful and influential in his own right, Macheca faced the wrath of a corrupt business community. But as a true businessman, Macheca became adept to the "Louisiana way" and successfully navigated his way through the "Anglo" world.

In February 1861, at the age of 17, when Louisiana seceded from the Union and entered the war on the Confederate side, Macheca served in the 22nd Louisiana Regiment, but for only nine months. According to some incomplete yet decipherable sources, the young Macheca initially enlisted in the Confederate Army for 90 days. Because of the expected invasion by Union forces, however, the state government lengthened the terms of soldiers' enlistment to nine months.[2]

After his enlistment ended, Macheca moved the family businesses to Houston, Texas, where he allegedly entered into smuggling for the Confederacy. When the war ended in 1865, he returned to New Orleans with the wealth he garnered from his illegal enterprises and purchased real estate. Macheca's businesses grew quickly, and he formed a steamship company that began a fruit trade with Central and South America.[3]

With his lucrative business ventures as backing, Macheca sought to try his hand at Reconstruction politics, but soon realized that Louisiana was not the state he had left a few years earlier. In 1867, Republicans in the U.S. Congress were tagged with the moniker of "Radical" because of their commitment to advocating for blacks' rights as well as punishing the South for making war. White Democrats within Louisiana, in turn, sought ways to rebel without actually igniting another war.

In March 1867, the federal government divided the former Confederacy, excluding Tennessee, into five military districts, with a major general of the army as each district's governor. The military governors of each district were given the mandate of registering as voters only those adults who demonstrated loyalty to the Union.[4] Likewise, all citizens of the affected states had to swear an oath of allegiance. Despite the active leadership and the advancement toward more diverse and equitable treatment of blacks in Louisiana, the federal troops who remained in the city when the war ended took up the cause of the Republican Party and fervently sought to limit the rights of former secessionists. These were the capricious conditions that Macheca would encounter in his new pursuit of the political power in Louisiana.

In 1868, in a concerted effort to combat the rising tide of Republican rule in Louisiana, the "Knights of the White Camellia" formed, with intentions similar to those of the Ku Klux Klan, which had organized in Pulaski, Tennessee, the year before. The Knights of the White Camellia terrorized both blacks and their allies, the Republicans, forcing voters to choose between the "right" political party or beatings—or worse.[5]

In the fall of 1868, Macheca got involved with the Democratic Party in Louisiana. Thanks to the renown he enjoyed from his successful business enterprises, he was welcomed into the party leadership in New Orleans.[6] He campaigned for the Democratic candidate for president in that year, Horatio Seymour. In turn, for the first time, local newspapers alleged Macheca to be the head of the Sicilian Mafia entrenched in the city of New Orleans because of the influence he seemed to wield in both business and politics.[7]

The sudden publicity brought Macheca to the forefront of underworld notoriety. Newspapers and law enforcement at the time contended that the Macheca "family" fought with another faction led by Raffaelo Agnello for control of both the New Orleans docks and any and all "business" that may have been conducted clandestinely beneath the noses of local law enforcement for well over a year. In an effort to seize control of these businesses, and in typical Mafia fashion, Macheca ordered the murder of Agnello. On April 1, 1869, Agnello allegedly suffered several gunshot wounds while walking to meet with Macheca at the latter's business in the present warehouse district. Several years later, Agnello's brother, Joseph, suffered the same fate. With his power consolidated and despite the fact that he had been accused of several, if not most, gangland murders in the state, Macheca still sought some level of anonymity, yet wanted to be recognized as a "legitimate" businessman and a warrior for the American ideals of democracy.

By 1869, Louisiana had become overrun with "scalawags," homegrown supporters of the Republican Party, and "carpetbaggers," Reconstruction-era migrants from the North seeking financial opportunities. The new state Constitution of 1868 provided civil rights for blacks and school integration. At the same time as pro–Republican forces sought ratification of the new constitution, the state held a gubernatorial election that Republican Henry Clay Warmoth won. Governor Warmoth subsequently used his executive position to increase his wealth and to exact substantial measures intended to garner equality for the freed people. Once elected, however, Warmoth felt the hatred of many Democrats in Louisiana—a wrath so intense that some openly threatened his life.[8]

When Warmoth took office, factions of the Ku Klux Klan—more specifically, the Knights of the White Camellia—engaged in intimidation of Republican voters through violence. Warmoth retaliated by pushing through the legislature a law enacting his "Returning Board." This legislation disavowed any vote deemed to be cast through illegal means or through intimidation. White Democrats in Louisiana viewed Warmoth's actions as an attempt to thwart their influence over voters within the state. In the 1870s, as a result of the ongoing uncertainty over the rightful victors in elections, the Republican Party in Louisiana splintered into several factional groups. Soon, Democrats saw their terror campaign against blacks and Republicans failing; subsequently, the Democratic Party did not have enough support to claim a victory over the Radicals. After first concentrating their efforts in mostly rural areas, the white Democratic leadership concluded that urban areas such as New Orleans were ripe for more intense concentration.

Governor Warmoth's tenure in office was marked by a period of enormous corruption never before seen in Louisiana. Fortunately, his power in his short term deteriorated rapidly when he refused to back a candidate for the Senate from Louisiana, Casey Dent, President Ulysses S. Grant's brother-in-law. In addition to advocating for his provocative Returning Board, Warmoth continued to alienate Democrats when he claimed he uncovered a self-congratulatory plot to keep Republican officeholders in the state senate from taking their seats after the 1870 election. Warmoth issued an arrest order for the putative offenders, claiming "an illegal and revolutionary attempt was made to eject certain members of the House of Representatives and seat others in their stead." This show of executive blustering set the standard for the actions of other Republicans who demanded power over a perceived conquered southern populace.[9]

The growing list of Governor Warmoth's enemies did not deter his supporters from advocating a handpicked successor for the next gubernatorial race. In the election of 1872, Warmoth endorsed John McEnery, a Democrat, for governor, while the Republicans nominated William P. Kellogg, a tax collector and master at self-promotion. In the statewide elections of 1872, McEnery received the majority of votes, but Governor Warmoth, as one of his last acts before leaving office, split the Returning Board in two. One Returning Board certified McEnery as the new governor, and the other board certified Kellogg as governor.[10] For a time Louisiana had dual governments whose competing political loyalties caused ferocious animosity between the factions.

Democrats and Kellogg opponents concerned themselves with this "usurpation" of the chief executive and President Grant's advocacy in enforcing the civil rights legislation pertaining to both the state and national constitutions. Because of his refusal to recognize the forces against him, Governor Kellogg operated primarily from New Orleans and did not concern himself with the violence and racial counterinsurgency occurring throughout the rest of Louisiana. This violence soon increased in severity and took on a more tactical dynamic, one dedicated to the forceful expulsion of the "foreign" government from Louisiana.

Historians and researchers have produced volumes of scholarship and the debates continue regarding this tumultuous period in Louisiana history. Although this violent and lengthy episode shaped political attitudes in the state for generations, for the sake of the Italians' legacy, Macheca's involvement deserves attention, as it demonstrates his firm belief in the American Dream. During the Reconstruction period, Macheca sought to stabilize his business interests and gain acceptance into congenial white society by organizing a group of Sicilians into a paramilitary force ready to fight for the Democratic ideals of the South. Macheca became the commander of the Innocenti ("The Innocents"), a paramilitary, anti–Republican group of pro–Democrat Italians. He used this command to assist southern whites in their conflict with the Radical Republican government of Louisiana in one of the most openly racial battles in state history. Macheca believed that helping the white Democrats regain control over the state's political structure would enhance his status as a business leader in a blossoming community and as a member of the city's elite.

After the Republican sanctioning of Governor Kellogg's victory, violence toward and impatience with the state government and Republicans in general increased. Republicans all over Louisiana feared for their lives as marauding armies of conservative whites combed the state looking for Republican officeholders and blacks, using their tactic of "bulldozing" to eliminate enemies of the white resurgence. After a lengthy standoff, approximately 59 blacks died at the hands of a small army of whites gathered around the small hamlet of Colfax in Grant Parish on Easter Sunday, April 13, 1873.

In early 1874, marauding bands of whites organized themselves into the "White League" in Opelousas, Louisiana, and demanded a return to the antebellum racial castes that dictated politics in the state. Members of the White League and their sympathizers felt Louisiana would experience an "Africanization" of the state if they did not act.[11] This new organization formalized its platform and membership grew, especially in the southwest portion of the state. The *Louisiana Sugar Bowl*, the official journal of the White League, announced on July 19, 1874:

> Love of liberty, honor, and honesty, a proper respect for ourselves, families, and friends, and the hope of retrieving the fortunes of our State and people, physically and morally, demand in tones that no true man can disregard, that our sloth and

> indifference be cast aside—that we be up and doing. The experience of past years has demonstrated that those who now hold the government are incompetent to rule; that their administration can but result in oppression and desolation; that their rule can come but corruption demoralization, and degradation in every department of life ... the White League has in view no violation of law, State or Federal.... It does propose by compact and legal action on the part of whites, to force the government of the State from the hands of that villainy and ignorance which are ruining and disgracing both whites and blacks.

The strength of the White League depended on a decentralized plan in which the masked marauders galloped throughout Louisiana communities and demonstrated their ruthlessness; their abilities to organize quickly and then disappear before they could be apprehended were key to their success.[12]

Concern among other groups ran high as tensions grew. The Italian Association met on July 23, 1874, to discuss its members' position within the Louisiana political and racial landscape. The Italian Association concurred with the direction taken by the White Leaguers and the Democratic Party. A Mr. Sperecho stood in front of the group and made an impromptu speech at the meeting:

> We, Italians, but true naturalized citizens of this great country, mean and intended to be that we have always been, Democrats, but in the true sense and significance of the word, that is, we mean to say that we are true lovers of self-government, the government of the people, by the people.[13]

With the declarations by both Italians and pro–Republican whites being publicized within the existing media of the time, Macheca made a decision about which side he would support: He chose to lend his allegiance to the anti–Republicans and readied his small force for action.

The *New Orleans Times* (a Republican-oriented newspaper) portrayed the White League as a fringe movement that did not represent the true feelings of southern whites. An editorial commentator averred that the White League would fold before the first of October 1874, due to the fact that "The Negro has become tired of his mentors and tormentors; he is attempting to do that which the white fraud has only pretended to do—he is attempting to rid himself of the scalawag and carpetbagger to do the State or the city harm." The writer stressed that the White League did not represent the whites who wanted blacks to benefit from the new policies of freedom and advocacy for civil rights. As the *New Orleans Times* proclaimed the tenets of the Republican Party in New Orleans and Louisiana, it made sense that its standard party line would benefit the ruling party of the state at the time. In contrast, newspapers such as the *Daily Picayune* and the *Daily Crescent* reflected the thoughts and feelings of the "other" white population in Louisiana, even going as far as to incite riots and advocate in favor of racial bias and retribution.[14]

On August 29, 1874, the White League began a concerted enterprise to take over the state government when group members stormed into Coushatta and demanded the resignation and expulsion of several Republican office-holders. Blacks living in the area, it seems, had threatened several esteemed whites of the parish. When a duly commissioned posse arrived at the cabins where the blacks resided, gunfire rang out, killing one of the white deputies and two of the blacks who ran from their cabins and into the woods. "The next day, Friday ... a large body of Negroes, between 300 and 400 in number, assembled near Brownsville, swearing vengeance against the whole white race, and declaring they would not leave a white man, woman, or child alive in the parish." Sensing that a White League rampage was headed their way, white and black Republicans of Coushatta requested the protection of the local sheriff. Law enforcement authorities in the small town swore in a posse, formed a defensive perimeter, and waited for an anticipated attack. The White Leaguers let the posse surrender, "conditioned upon the departure of the more prominent Republicans and the resignation of the six officeholders." On Sunday, August 30, men from the posse led the resignees from their previous night's accommodations to Shreveport. While on the road to a train station, a group of White Leaguers set upon the small party and shot them in cold blood, murdering seven whites and six blacks. Republicans around the state condemned the actions and Governor Kellogg notified federal authorities in Washington, D.C., of the massacre. The events seemed a harbinger of worse things to come, as the White League planned an even greater show of force against Reconstruction rule.[15]

Clinging to the ideology of avenging Republican oppression, the White League descended upon New Orleans in September 1874. The League engaged in clandestine dealings to supply its members with arms and ammunition. Receiving a tip from an unknown informant, on September 10, 1874, at approximately noon, members of the Metropolitan Police, the so-called violent arm of the Radical Republicans in Louisiana, and city detectives gathered in plain-clothes near the end of Canal Street and reconnoitered the area. The police officers noticed workers unloading several large boxes and bringing them into a local hardware store known as Oliver's Gas Station. The officers then "entered Oliver's Gas Station and presented him [the owner] with a search warrant and writ of arrest. No resistance to these proceedings was made on the part of the proprietor of the store." When the police opened the boxes, they discovered Prussian combat rifles. Officers from the Sixth District Police Station arrested Mr. Oliver (along with Messieurs Guyol and Fremaux) and expressed suspicion, as this was the second shipment of weapons to the store within a week's time. The police suspected the White League had plans for a major offensive against the Republican government of the state. After the seizure, the state attorney general, Simeon Bolden, issued an alert for troops to mass near New Orleans.[16]

The monument dedicated to the Battle of Liberty Place, where Macheca and his "Innocents" actively took a role in eliminating the Radical Republicans from Louisiana.

Governor Kellogg saw nothing wrong with the arrests made in connection with the seizure. He steadfastly maintained, "The pretense that this action is a violation of any constitutional or legal right of any citizen of the commonwealth is absurd, and is only defended by those who defend the conspirators against whom the officers of the law are proceeding." When asked about the actions taken by the police during the arrests and the potential infringement of the right to bear arms guaranteed by the Second Amendment to the Constitution, Governor Kellogg claimed that political organizations that sought to destroy his rule within the state had misconstrued the article. He stated, "It is preposterous to suppose for a moment that the government can allow political bodies to arm themselves in defiance of State laws while openly avowing their intention of making war upon the constituted authorities."[17] Despite Kellogg's defense of the Republican actions, the White League proceeded with their plans, unaware of the supporters whom they would encounter when the time came for action.

Even though he did not concern himself with the other events occurring around the state, Macheca saw an opportunity for himself to gain some political clout and involve the Innocents in subsequent events related to the ongoing conflict. The events that led to what became known as the "Battle of Liberty Place," commenced on September 12, 1874, as members of the Metropolitan Police seized the schooner *Mississippi* as she docked with a shipload of weapons for the White League. The shipments continued for the next two days, however, with White Leaguers protesting loudly about the restriction of their rights under the Second Amendment. White Leaguers considered using Macheca's fruit shipments as a cover for the contraband, but opted against it as they suspected the Metropolitan Police would eventually ascertain how the shipments got past them.

On September 14, 1874, the local newspapers announced that prominent businessmen in the city were calling other citizens to a mass meeting at the Clay statue on Canal Street. At the meeting, Judge Robert H. Marr, Jr., a respected jurist in Orleans Parish, presented a resolution to avoid violence by strongly suggesting to Governor William P. Kellogg that he resign. Later that night, several Metropolitans. wearing different uniforms to conceal their real affiliation, gathered at the corner of Toulouse and Royal streets. The attempted ruse fooled no one.[18]

Macheca sensed a major conflict was about to erupt and wanted to be at the forefront of the struggle. The Innocents sprang into action as the mass meeting adjourned. Macheca sent word to his lieutenants in the Innocents to organize a small force and meet in Lafayette Square at 2:00 p.m. Subsequent to calling his men to arms, Macheca walked up Poydras Street and noticed the barricades already constructed on the streets. Members of the White League had previously turned streetcars on their sides to create a defensive line that appeared impenetrable, but Macheca made his way through to meet his men at the preappointed meeting point. The group assembled at the appointed time and place after taking an alternative route to the staging area around assembling Metropolitan forces. Macheca prepared his men for the upcoming fight.[19] White League members then spread the word through the ranks that Kellogg would not resign.

On September 14, 1874, at approximately 3:00 p.m., anti–Republicans and White Leaguers' barricades stood at the ready. Metropolitans began firing down Tchoupitoulas Street and created a dangerous crossfire. According to eyewitness accounts, one of the Metropolitan divisions under the command of Gen. Algernon S. Badger, some 250 men strong, marched toward the levee at approximately 4:00 p.m. White Leaguers fired on Badger's troops, seriously wounding the general. Macheca, watching from a short distance away, rescued Badger. While some Leaguers demanded his summary execution, some of the instigators assisted Macheca in getting the general first to safety and then to the Charity Hospital to treat his wounds. In the span of an hour, Metropolitan Police broke ranks and made their way to the French

Quarter, where Macheca's men waited for them. The Innocents surrounded the Metropolitans, and the latter surrendered en masse to the Italians. Subsequently, as the White League established firm control over the city, Macheca and his men seized the arms on the *Mississippi*.[20]

On the following day, September 15, 1874, Macheca noticed in the morning newspaper that his exploits and those of his men had gone unreported. He wrote a letter to the *New Orleans Bulletin* in which he documented the Innocents' efforts during the Battle of Liberty Place. He described the rescue of General Badger, the capture of the Arsenal and the Stationhouse a full "fifteen minutes before any officer made their appearance," and the seizure of the weapons on the *Mississippi*. As part of the generally self-congratulatory atmosphere after the battle, no one questioned Macheca's claims of his group's contributions on the 14th and 15th of September. Later, as the city calmed down and Macheca's involvement was nearly forgotten, Lt. Gov. D. B. Penn, acting governor on behalf of the missing Democratic governor McEnery, sent a telegram message to President Grant that outlined the White League's (and the Democratic Party's) position. Unlike Governor McEnery's telegram of two days before, which had practically begged the president to recognize the Democrats' claim to the executive office of the state, Lt. Gov. Penn's telegram assumed a bold and unapologetic tone:

> Hopeless of all other relief, the people of this State have taken up arms to maintain the legal authority of the persons elected by them to the government of the State against the usurpers who have heaped upon them innumerable insults, burdens and wrongs. In doing so they are supported by the great body of intelligent and honest people of the State. They declare sincere loyalty and respect for the United States Government and its officers. They were only against the usurpers and enemies of the people.... We ask of you to withhold any aid or protection from our enemies of republican rights, and of peace and liberties of the people.[21]

President Grant responded swiftly and without mercy. On September 15, 1874, the president issued a cease and desist order, telling the White League and their supporters they had five days to acquiesce to the authority of the Kellogg government. Subsequently, Republicans reestablished order within the state at the five-day limit imposed by President Grant. A year later, White Democrats attempted once again to seize power and compel the Kellogg government to relinquish power to what they believed was the legally elected Democratic government. There is no doubt that the Battle of Liberty Place and the subsequent Democratic White League agitation provided the underpinnings of the process that led to the failure of Radical Republicanism in Louisiana.[22]

Despite his disappointment at the lack of accord given to his accomplishments during the Battle of Liberty Place, Macheca continued with his business interests and even survived a rift between him and his brothers. In fact, Macheca's businesses grew as Reconstruction finally ended in Louisiana.

Even though he did not receive much good publicity for his services to the Democratic Party, Macheca continued to both function as a legitimate businessman and receive the respect of his peers when it came to his underworld dealings. He thrived in his life in the shadows, but later incidents proved to be more life-threatening and would forever cement his reputation as a *Mafia* don.

In 1879, a Sicilian banditto, Guiseppe Esposito, made his way to New Orleans after escaping from the island of Sicily following the failed kidnapping and mutilation of George Rose, an English adventurer who wandered too far away from the accepted tourist traps. Although Rose survived, he returned to England missing both of his ears. After Esposito arrived in the Crescent City, he sought refuge among the large Italian population of the French Quarter of the city. Allegedly, Macheca took the young brigand into his "organization."

The fugitive's identity stayed safe for a time until police recognized Esposito and arrested him. Unfortunately, detectives in New York had claim to the "made man." In fact, New York law enforcement sent two detectives to New Orleans to apprehend the bandit after they learned he resided in the New Orleans area. Eventually, despite protestations that he was not the Esposito the detectives were looking for, the New York detectives helped with the extradition back to that city. Sicilian officials returned him to the island of his birth, where the criminal later died in prison.

Charles Matranga, heir to the Mafia after the death of Joseph Macheca in March 1891 (*Illustrated Weekly*, April 4, 1891).

Immediately after Esposito's departure, Macheca's organization split into two factions. One faction was led by Charles Matranga, with Macheca as a consigliere (advisor), also serving as a co-don. The other family was led by Joseph Provenzano. This parting of the ways signified a struggle for control over the Louisiana Mafia underworld. With the two factions locked in a mortal control for the underworld, the exploits of everyday Italians became fodder for the media.

Macheca and his fellow Italians could not foresee the torrent of racial hatred against Italians that would permeate Louisiana in the years to come, as many citizens throughout the state—and throughout the nation for that matter—assumed anyone with an Italian surname to be a member of the criminal organization, a myth in and of itself. As time went on, the stereotype of the "Dago" would reach fever pitch 14 years after Macheca's Innocents stood against Republican rule in Louisiana. Despite his public stance agreeing with the Democratic forces that tried to maintain a racist air within the state, Macheca's dedication to the principles of democracy within his adopted country would prove to be his mortal undoing. Even as tales of the mysterious Mafia circulated through the press, Macheca tried to maintain an appearance of legitimacy as a businessman. This reputation appeared more difficult to maintain as anti-foreign fervor swept the nation and, more importantly, the South.

After the departure of Esposito to a prison in his native Sicily, the Provenzano and Matranga factions fought for control of the New Orleans docks from 1888 to 1890. The attraction was obvious: As the lucrative fruit importation business grew, it expanded the New Orleans economy and created an avenue for aggressive underworld figures to make money illegally through graft and extortion. The Matrangas allegedly became the victims of a "turf" war that ultimately involved the New Orleans chief of police, David C. Hennessy. One of the instigators of this war, according to Chief Hennessy, was Antonio (Tony) Matranga, Charles's brother.

Charles and Antonio Matranga, together with suspected Mafia don Joseph Macheca, convinced stevedores and dockworkers to work for their fruit importing concerns, even though the Provenzano family already employed these workers. The Matranga/Macheca faction established a monopoly over the docks, and in the underworld circles, declared war against the other rival families, specifically the Provenzanos. Chief Hennessy tried to smooth things out between the two families, but this effort simply fueled rumors that the police department had reverted to its corrupt ways and that Chief Hennessy solicited bribes for protection of the Provenzanos. (After careful examination of Hennessy's past as documented through local media and interviews with Italian descendants, it came as no surprise to those close to the case to learn that the motive for Hennessy's murder resulted from his interfering with the warring factions and attempting to profit from their conflict.)

On May 5, 1890, after a long day of emptying the hold of a large steamer named *Foxhall*, dock workers Gerolamo "Jim" Caruso, Salvatore Sunzeri, Antonio "Tony" Matranga, Sebastiano Incardona, Tony and Frank Locascio, and Vincent Caruso (Jim's brother and the Matranga and Locascio foreman) piled into Matranga's wagon for a ride to their respective homes. Lumbering toward the French Quarter, Jim Caruso exited the wagon, bidding the other riders goodnight, and entered his home. As the wagon reached the corner of Ursuline and Dorgenois Streets, one of the men began to sing in Italian and, despite their exhausted conditions, the others joined in. The last intersection at Claiborne and Esplanade meant the men had finally approached their homes. Incardona noticed six men at the corner who, he surmised, were waiting for a streetcar. The waiting men yelled something in Italian, then raised shotguns and fired at the wagon. Tony Matranga took a shot to the right thigh, but Incardona remained unharmed as he dove under the wagon's front seat to avoid the barrage. The incident took only a few seconds to unfold; Matranga was the lone casualty. Later that same day, Jim and Vincent Caruso, Sunzeri, Matranga, Incardona, and the Locasios identified Joseph and Peter Provenzano, Tony Pellegrini, Nick Guillio, Tony Gianforcaro, and Gaspardo Lombardo as the men who fired on their wagon. It seemed the Provenzano–Matranga struggle for control of the docks had bubbled to the surface, leading many New Orleans residents to suspect a blood vendetta had been executed that May evening. At first, it appeared that the Provenzanos' arrest signified the police were taking a stand against the seething criminal element, but opponents of Mayor Joseph A. Shakspeare and Chief Hennessy saw the ambush and the subsequent arrests of the identified suspects as Hennessy's way of demonstrating his power to the Provenzanos.[23]

A few months later, the Provenzanos' trial took place. After its conclusion, because of a technicality, Judge Joshua Baker granted the convicted men a new trial set for October 22, 1890. The Matrangas were angered that a new trial had been granted, and the "family" began to think that Chief Hennessy played a part in getting the retrial granted. Additionally, rumors circulated that Hennessy would testify at the trial himself, exposing all the secrets about the *Mafia* he had learned through his attempts to secure a truce between the two factions.[24]

But Hennessy would not get the chance to testify at the Provenzano trial. On the evening October 15, 1890, alleged Mafia gunmen ambushed the police chief outside his home on Girod Street, near where the present-day Superdome is situated. Chief Hennessy died the next day. Immediately, Mayor Shakspeare called for the arrest of all known Italian criminals within the city limits. After the multitudes of small-time hoodlums had been brought to police stations around the city and questioned, 19 men were held and charged for the murder of Police Chief David C. Hennessy; among the incarcerated suspects were Charles and Anthony Matranga and Joseph Macheca.

On March 13, 1891, after a six-week trial that produced some of the finest legal arguments in the history of Louisiana jurisprudence, a jury of 12 men found the defendants not guilty. After the trial, Macheca and his fellow inmates were returned to the Old Orleans Parish Prison located near Treme and N. Claiborne, where presently the Treme Housing Development stands. Early the next morning, an article appeared in the local newspaper that called for all "good citizens" to meet at the Clay statue at the head of the city's famous Canal Street. After approximately an hour of speeches by some of the city's most esteemed business leaders, speakers called for the crowd that had gathered there over the course of the assembly (some estimates state they numbered at approximately 10,000) to march to the Old Parish Prison and exact justice (revenge) for the failure of the Hennessy jury to convict the 19 men. The frenzied crowd made their way to the prison and broke down the gates. Soon, Joseph Macheca stood over the dead body of one of his comrades. A shot rang out, striking Macheca squarely in the forehead and killing him instantly. When the crowd had finished their murderous work, they left the scene a bloody mess. Charles Matranga managed to survive the attack by pulling one of the bodies of one of the Italians killed that day over him as he lay flat in the courtyard of the prison.

MASS MEETING!

All good citizens are invited to attend a mass meeting on SATURDAY, March 14, at 10 o'clock a. m. at Clay Statue, to take steps to remedy the failure of justice in the HENNESSY CASE. Come prepared for action.

John C. Wickliffe,	W. S. Parkerson,
B. F. Glover,	Henry Dickson Bruns,
J. G. Pepper,	Wm. H. Deeves,
C. E. Rogers,	Richard S. Venables,
F. E. Hawes,	Samuel B. Merwin,
Raymond Hayes,	Omer Villere,
L. E. Cenas,	H. L. Favrot,
John M. Parker, Jr.,	T. D. Mather,
Harris R. Lewis,	James P. Mulvey,
Septime Villere,	Emile Dupre,
Wm. M. Railey,	W. P. Curtis,
Lee McMillan,	Chas. J. Ranlett,
C. E. Jones,	T. S. Barton,
J. F. Queeny,	O. J. Forstall,
D. R. Calder,	J. Moore Wilson,
Thomas Henry,	Hugh W. Brown,
James Lea McLean,	C. Harrison Parker,
Felix Couturie,	Edgar H. Farrar,
T. D. Wharton,	J. C. Aby,
Frank B. Hayne,	Rud. Hahne,
J. G. Flower,	C. A. Walsche,
James Clarke,	W. Mosby,
Thomas H. Kelley,	Chas. M. Barnwell,
H. B. Ogden,	H. R. Labouisse,
Ulric Atkinson,	Walter D. Denegre,
A. Baldwin, Jr.,	George Denegre,
A. E. Blackmar,	B. H. Hornbeck,
John V. Moore,	S. P. Walmsley,
Wm. T. Pierson,	E. H. Pierson,
C. L. Stewart,	James D. Houston,
E. T. Leche.	

"Mass Meeting" announcement that appeared in the *Daily Picayune*; the gathering led to the storming of the Orleans Parish Prison where Joseph Macheca and 10 other Italians awaited their fate (*The Daily Picayune*, March 14, 1891).

Joseph P. Macheca made a name for himself in the underworld circles of New Orleans as well as founding several successful business ventures that continue to operate today. After his death, Macheca was laid to rest in St. Patrick's Cemetery on the outskirts of downtown New Orleans. The incident in which he saw his demise created a wave of nativism throughout the United States and even reverberated overseas—the United States and Italy almost went to war over the murder of the Italian Americans. But with Macheca's death, the foundation was laid for other dons to rule the mysterious and deadly domain of the Louisiana Mafia.

After Macheca's death, Charles Matranga took over the daily running of the local Mafia family. He turned the family operation over to another Sicilian, Sylvestro "Silver Dollar Sam" Carollo in the 1920s prior to Prohibition. Matranga lived until 1941, when he "retired" of natural causes. In 1934, Carollo allegedly brokered a deal between New York mobsters Frank Costello and Phillip Kastel and then Louisiana governor, Huey P. Long, to bring slot machines to the Pelican State.

Carollo had many run-ins with the law as a result of his status as Mafia don and shuttled in and out of jail for the next 30 years. After an attempt to deport him failed in the early 1970s, Carollo died in New Orleans in 1972. One of Carollo's lieutenants, Carlos Marcello, succeeded him in 1947. Marcello ran the New Orleans mob like a dictator and by Mafia custom. He successfully maintained a tomato business while at the same time building an underworld empire of the likes seen only in New York and Chicago in the 1930s and 1940s. Marcello had his own troubles with the law; in fact, U.S. Attorney General Robert F. Kennedy illegally deported Marcello in 1961 to Guatemala. Marcello vowed to get even with Kennedy for the move. When President John F. Kennedy fell victim to an assassin's bullet in 1963, law enforcement officials believed, but could not prove, that Marcello arranged the murder to bring Robert Kennedy down from his ivory tower. Marcello remained an object of fear and suspicion until 1984, when he was indicted, convicted, and sentenced to federal prison for bribery. He died at his home in Metairie, Louisiana, in 1993.

The Other Assassinated Chiefs

"Assassination is the extreme form of censorship."
—George Bernard Shaw

On October 15, 1890, at approximately 11:00 p.m., New Orleans Police Superintendent David C. Hennessy walked to the home he shared with his elderly mother located at 275 Girod Street near downtown New Orleans. He approached his porch and reached into his pocket, grabbing his keys. When he went to unlock the door, he heard a whistle. As he turned toward the street, shotgun blasts broke the night silence. Chief Hennessy sustained wounds to his upper body and his elbow shattered with the force of the small pellets. Chief Hennessy tried to return fire, but his rounds missed their mark. In the early morning hours of October 16, 1890, Chief Hennessy succumbed to his wounds at New Orleans Charity Hospital.[1]

Various theories surfaced regarding his execution-style murder. A massive manhunt ensued in which eventually 19 Italians, who allegedly belonged to the local crime syndicate in the city, were arrested and later stood trial for the chief's homicide.

Although the assassination of Chief Hennessy will be popularly remembered as an international incident (most New Orleans residents, especially Italians, remember the maxim "Who Killa Da Chief?"), Hennessy was not the first—and certainly not the last—New Orleans Police Department chief law enforcement officer to die at the hands of an assassin. Whether the motives were political or personal, the city has seen its share of extra-legal justice dispensed to law enforcement at the hands of a lone disgruntled assassin.

Patrick Mealey

In the post-Reconstruction South, political parties struggled to regain control of their respective local governments. Since the end of the Civil War, Democrat politicians had sought a return to the antebellum mindset of a racially biased society. However, with the Radical Reconstruction Republicans invading the South after the war, Republicans forcefully bestowed equality on a society that neither wanted freedom for blacks nor desired to suffer any further for that belief. The Democrats in Louisiana began fighting a new war. Well into the 20th century, Louisiana became the bloody battleground for factional disputes based on individuals' racial beliefs. In the post–Civil War South, those beliefs ran deeply.

Throughout its long history, Louisiana has been a land of political machinations. Careers made in politics were determined by personal affiliations that could prove deadly in many instances. In the case of one beloved public servant, Patrick Mealey, his death was the result of such an affiliation and brought the dangers of opposing political ideologies to the forefront for occupants of adversarial elective offices.

One of the more volatile elections in Louisiana political history took place in 1888. Running for governor in that election year, former Confederate officer Francis T. Nicholls received heavy Democratic support for his platform, which called for finally relieving Louisiana of the "scalawags" and "carpetbaggers." One faction of the Democratic Party in Louisiana, the "Bourbons," was a reactionary rural faction that supported the other Democrat in the race that year as well as the Republican incumbent, Samuel D. McEnery. Governor McEnery wielded a Republican scepter in coercing and cajoling state legislators into forcing Reconstruction legislation through to enactment. For example, the Bourbons supported the Louisiana Lottery—an agency where graft and corruption ran rampant among politicians and nepotistic Lottery officials. The Bourbons also aggressively lobbied for lower taxes on property owners and balanced the state budget by refusing to invest money where the dividends would have benefited the people of the state, primarily through public works projects. Although the Bourbon policies led to very few deficits for the state, the general population of Louisiana remained poor because of McEnery's corrupt policies.

In addition to running only small deficits and balancing the budget through non-action for the benefit of those who held public office, the Bourbons sought to limit the voting rights of newly arrived immigrants to Louisiana and, most of all, freed blacks. The law that the Bourbon Democrats proposed would make literacy tests a part of the voting process.

In the 1888 election, Bourbon Democrats sensed the beginning of the end of their reign in Louisiana and their tempers flared against those in favor of Nicholls. One of those people who supported Nicholls in his bid for the state's executive office was Patrick Mealey, who had dedicated his life to public service and believed that Nicholls stood for the ideals of the Democratic Party in Louisiana.

Known as "Pat," Mealey was born in Galway County, Ireland, on December 14, 1844. He traveled with his parents to New Orleans at the age of six. As a youngster, he began working in a cotton pressing concern. After Louisiana seceded from the Union in February 1861, Mealey joined the Confederate Army when he reached the age of 18 and served with distinction as a private with the 6th Louisiana Infantry, "The Violet Guards," under then Colonel Francis T. Nicholls. During his time in the army, he was taken prisoner no less than twice. After the surrender of Robert E. Lee and the Army of Northern Virginia on April 9, 1865, Mealey returned to New Orleans as a paroled prisoner of war. Seeking employment in his former vocation, he became a cotton roller. In 1866, Mayor John T. Monroe appointed the young, capable man to the city's police force. When General Philip Sheridan was appointed the military governor of the state, however, he fired all former Confederates from any positions within the state or local governments.[2]

After losing his job to a Sheridan appointee, Mealey again sought employment in his former vocation. Although out of city government, Mealey took an active role within his community and received an appointment as the captain of a city workhouse in 1874. After that point, Mealey's political future seemed assured. He rose to become a major leader in the New Orleans Democratic Party and Superintendent of the Bureau of Streets, before finally winning an election as the city's Administrator of Police in 1879. The city administrators also placed Mealey in charge of creating a cemetery for indigent persons, known as the Holt Cemetery (now located next to the present-day Delgado Community College on City Park Avenue). By the mid–1880s, Mealey had become a political operative and it appeared he was destined for a higher political calling. Then, in late 1887, Mayor Joseph A. Shakspeare appointed Mealey to head the New Orleans Police Department.

After midnight on January 1, 1888, new Commissioner of Police Mealey invited a few friends for some drinks at a local bar named Johnson's located at #21 St. Charles Avenue. Mealey, along with former Congressman Nat Wallace; C. H. Parker, editor of the New Orleans newspaper, *The Daily Picayune*; and police captain John McCaffrey met at Johnson's and indulged in conversation and some alcoholic spirits. Since Johnson's had the reputation of being a friendly environment, especially to those who were pro–Nicholls, the Mealey party enjoyed being among friends and political allies.

At approximately 1:00 a.m. on January 1, 1888, as the revelers continued to partake of their beverages, Mealey noticed two men walk into the bar. Mealey led his faction in a cheer for Nicholls. The two men, Louis Claire and John Gibson, along with three other gentlemen, settled at the bar and ordered drinks. When their drinks arrived, the five men raised their glasses and toasted former governor McEnery. One of the men, Louis Claire, moved near the Mealey party and began a conversation with Mealey that quickly escalated into an altercation. Suddenly, gunfire rang out—at least 25 shots were heard.

After the smoke cleared, Mealey lay on the floor mortally wounded with a bullet hole right above his navel. Another man who was present at the time of the shooting, Mike Walsh, received two gunshot wounds to his right side. Claire and his party fled the scene. Mealey and Walsh were immediately rushed to Charity Hospital. The police later arrested Claire and Gibson for committing battery on Mealey and Walsh.

Upon his arrival at the hospital, doctors dressed Mealey's wounds. Instead of bringing him to one of the wards, they set up a visiting area in reception for people who wanted to wish the wounded public servant glad tidings. Adjacent to the reception area stood a porch where Mealey's wife and two eldest daughters, Mamie, aged 17, and Adele, aged 15, waited for news from the family physician. Dr. J. C. Beard arrived at the hospital at virtually the same time as Mealey and examined him thoroughly before dressing his wounds and administering morphine to dull Mealey's excruciating pain. Dr. Beard made his way to the porch to speak with Mealey's wife and two daughters, who appeared to have been crying incessantly since hearing of the wounding of the husband and father.

Mrs. Mealey looked to Dr. Beard to relieve her grief, but all the physician could do was to offer the woman "words of hope and encouragement." Despite the severity of his wounds, Mealey rested comfortably after doctors administered pain medicine to ease his suffering. Numerous visitors came to pay their respects to the wounded man despite his drugged state. Even Governor Nicholls, along with other state and local officials, visited the dying man in the hospital. The Attorney General for the State of Louisiana, the Honorable Walter H. Rogers, managed to sit next to Mealey's bed and listen as Mealey stated, "That fellow Louis Claire, he shot me for nothing."

With friends and family surrounding his bedside, at 11:50 a.m. on January 2, 1888, Mealey's condition worsened and he slipped into a coma. As the day wore on, his breathing became more shallow. Finally, at approximately 2:00 p.m., Patrick Mealey, so well respected and loved by all who knew him, died.[3] Mike Walsh, though badly wounded and not expected to survive, recovered; for the rest of his life, though, he experienced pain from the wounds he received that January morning.

At a preliminary coroner's inquest held on January 2, 1888, the assistant coroner, Dr. Stanhope Jones, stated that Mealey had succumbed to a gunshot wound to the stomach that bled internally (until the autopsy had been performed, more details would have to wait). After the autopsy, Mealey's body was transported to Johnson's Undertaking Services (not the same proprietor as the bar where Mealey had been shot), where the corpse was prepared for viewing and burial. As the Mealey family prepared for mourning, eyewitness accounts of what had occurred to cause the death of the much-loved public servant began to surface.[4]

The accounts stated that Louis Claire, John Gibson, Ed McCabe, "Lucky" White, William "Billy" Feehan, John McCormick, and Dick Behan entered Johnson's Saloon located at #21 St. Charles Avenue in uptown New Orleans, at approximately 1:00 a.m. on the morning of January 1, 1888. The group had been drinking heavily when they entered the saloon and made their way to the back corner of the bar to resume their night of revelry. At the front corner of the bar stood Mealey, Wallace, Parker, James Donovan, Captain McCaffrey, Lee Peyton, Tom Fannin, and other unidentified friends and acquaintances of the police chief. Immediately upon entering, Claire's party shouted jibes and insults at the men in Mealey's party. Mealey and his friends ignored the rantings and excused their drunken obnoxiousness. Claire's group continued their unruly behavior, obviously intending to provoke Mealey and his friends into an altercation. Mealey recognized Feehan and the two struck up a conversation. When asked to join the Mealey party for a drink, Feehan declined, "saying he had some friends with him, referring to Claire, Gibson, and the others."[5] Mealey stated he could drink with Feehan, but not with his friends. Feehan politely excused himself and rejoined his party.

After a few moments, subsequent to the conversation with Feehan, Mealey made his way into the adjoining yard of the saloon, perhaps to enjoy a cigar in the crisp January air. When he returned, walking from the back corner of the saloon, Gibson stepped in front of Mealey and blocked his advance. Mealey and Gibson exchanged words, with the two men standing toe-to-toe, speaking in low tones so no one around them could hear their conversation. Mealey then made his way around Gibson and proceeded to walk in the direction of where Claire was standing at the far corner of the back of the bar. "As he [Mealey] approached, Claire stepped out and accosted Mealey and some words passed, which soon waxed into a dispute."[6] Claire took a rugged stance in front of Mealey as if to prepare himself for a physical altercation. Claire, being the larger of the two men, felt sure that Mealey would back down from a fight. But Mealey just stood there before Claire. Before any punches could be exchanged between the two, men from both of their parties stepped in to separate them. Suddenly, as Mealey backed away, Claire pulled a Smith & Wesson revolver from beneath his topcoat and pressed the barrel of the weapon against Mealey's stomach and fired at point-blank range. Then Claire pulled the weapon away from Mealey's body and fired four more rounds without any target in mind.[7]

When the first shots were fired, Gibson drew his revolver and sent a shot into Mike Walsh's back. As Walsh turned to see his assailant, Gibson fired again, striking Walsh in the midsection. Gibson's subsequent rounds went astray, with one of them striking one of the saloon's other patrons in the mouth. Claire and Gibson then tried to escape into the street, but Mealey's friends were close in pursuit. Lee Peyton captured Claire with a few swings from his umbrella, knocking the assassin to the ground after Claire tried to dispose of the weapon he carried. Captain McCaffrey immediately placed the disabled Claire under arrest and brought him to his headquarters. Assistant Engineer Donovan captured Gibson later that morning with the assistance of police officer John Vigers. Authorities later discovered that Mealey had no weapon on him at the time Claire shot him.

On January 2, 1888, the Mealey family mourned their patriarch. The body of the dead chief lay in state in the front parlor of his home on Annunciation Street from the early morning hours until approximately 2:45 p.m. During his wake, notable local and state dignitaries visited to pay their respects to the Mealey family and say their final goodbyes to their much-beloved friend and colleague. Governor Nicholls as well as a future U.S. Supreme Court justice, the Honorable E. D. White, were in attendance. Outside of the home, the mourners congregated to say farewell:

> Crowds of people were on the sidewalks, and for a block on either side of the house passage on the sidewalks was attended with great discomfort and no little jostling and pushing. In front of the house the crowd was so dense that it was impossible to pass through, and to get in or out of the house required time and patience.[8]

In the afternoon, three priests—Fathers Massadiers, Footte, and Heslin—administered the last rites. The pallbearers lifted the coffin from its catafalque and made their way out of the parlor, down the front steps of the house, and into the waiting hearse. The funeral procession then moved down Annunciation Street, toward Calliope, to Magazine, to Jena, to Camp Street, then finally down the long stretch of Canal Street where Patrick Mealey was laid to rest in Metairie Cemetery.[9]

Knowing that Mrs. Mealey and her six children would need financial assistance following the death of her husband, a group of concerned citizens formed a committee to raise money; they were "[i]nspired by high personal regard for [Mealey's] sterling qualities, as well as a profound sympathy with his surviving family in their irreparable bereavement so lamentable and unexpected."[10] This Fund-in-Aid Committee, under the direction of Mr. Maurice C. Hart, solicited donations for the Mealey family from the citizens of New Orleans. The outpouring of grief and charity proved tremendous and demonstrated respect for the character of the dead police chief.

Whereas Patrick Mealey represented the pride of New Orleans public service, Louis Claire demonstrated the other side of the coin—the scourge of the New Orleans underworld. Claire worked as a special officer for the New Orleans Police Department at the time he killed Patrick Mealey. From all historical indications, it appears that Claire, even "from early boyhood, was a malicious and murderous urchin." Claire's father worked diligently as a cab driver—he owned his own service—and tried to instill good morals and hard-working values in his son. The elder Claire tried to discipline his son, but though he "strove to make a good man of his son," the incorrigible youth continued his hoodlum ways; even marriage could not settle the young man down from his felonious behavior.[11]

As an adult, police arrested Claire more than 30 times for drunk and disorderly conduct, disturbing the peace, fighting, and other assorted mischievous instances. Three months before he killed Patrick Mealey, New Orleans Mayor J. Valsin Guillotte appointed Claire as a special officer and assigned him to the 6th Precinct. Prior to the reforms instituted by later city administrations, Claire's criminal record would have been of no consequence; however, his continued run-ins with the law cast aspersions on Claire's character, especially after he became involved with Mealey's murder. Two weeks prior to Mealey's murder, police arrested Claire for being drunk, fighting, and disturbing the peace. Given that Claire faced disciplinary action for his arrests, departmental protocols dictated that the brigand should have been suspended. Yet, at the time of the murder, Claire still fully enjoyed the rank and privileges of his position. Mayor Guillotte knew or should have known that he had appointed someone with a clear criminal mindset to his police force. Claire's accomplice in the murder, John Gibson, shared the same type of upbringing and likewise experienced difficulties with authority. The two ran in the same corrupt circles.[12]

When information became available about the pedigrees of the men arrested for Mealey's murder, suspicions arose as to the true motive for the killing. Was it a run-of-the-mill homicide like that experienced every day in such a lawless town as New Orleans, or was it an actual political assassination? Claire's loyalties lay with Nicholls's opponent, McEnery. Perhaps fearing that Mealey would drum up enough support for Nicholls in the New Orleans area to sway the election, Claire took the matter into his own hands. In the court of public opinion, Mayor Guillotte seemed to bear the brunt of the culpability for Mealey's demise. One citizen emphatically opined:

> The man who killed Mr. Mealey was a special officer of the police force, and an appointee of the Mayor of this city. He and his associates had assaulted several persons within a few days preceding the murder, and their behavior was a matter of notoriety. The Mayor himself must have been aware of it, yet they were permitted to roam the streets like so many savages running a muck [*sic*] until at last an innocent and peaceable citizen was cruelly done to death by one of their number.[13]

The same citizen concluded, "His [Mealey's] political opponents have assailed him with indiscriminate vituberation," though no evidence existed that Mealey died as a result of any dealings he had throughout his political career.[14] Accusations such as these were commonplace when a person of Mealey's stature and influence was senselessly murdered.

As a result of Claire's actions in the murder of Patrick Mealey, acting police commissioner, Lucien Adams, suspended Louis Claire from the police force and brought him up on charges before the police review board for "conduct unbecoming an officer." As an additional way to help Mealey's family financially, the new police chief, Dennis McCarthy, pledged to pay the dead chief's salary to Mrs. Mealey until McCarthy officially took office as the new chief.[15]

On February 16, 1888, Louis Claire, John Gibson, and William "Billy" Feehan were formally charged with the crime of "willful murder" and said to have, "with malice aforethought," shot, killed, and murdered Patrick Mealey. At their arraignment on February 21, all of the defendants pled not guilty.[16]

Nine months after Mealey's murder, on October 29, 1888, jury selection began in the trial of *State of Louisiana v. Louis Claire, John Gibson, and William Feehan*. The courtroom filled quickly and remained that way throughout the trial, with spectators straining to gain a glimpse of the men who had murdered their beloved police chief. After the jury was selected and the 12 men seated, the court read the indictment and fixed next day for the trial to begin. On the next morning, October 30, Judge R. H. Marr, a no-nonsense jurist who would figure prominently in many cases tried in the Crescent City, called the court to order at 10:30 a.m.

The first witness called by the prosecution, Dr. Stanhope Jones, assistant coroner, testified that he viewed the body of Patrick Mealey (he was acquainted with the deceased) and noticed a bullet wound approximately two inches above the navel. Upon conducting the autopsy, Dr. Jones noted, "The ball passed through the body and lodged in the buttocks. It perforated the intestines two or three times … causing a massive internal hemorrhage resulting in his death."[17]

The prosecution next called Officer John Vigers, the patrolman whose patrol area was located adjacent to the murder scene. Officer Vigers related that after he heard the report of the gunshots, he observed Claire and Gibson hurriedly leave the saloon and stumble into the street. Vigers immediately followed Gibson and later arrested him. Upon cross-examination, Vigers stated that when the shooting occurred, the crowd near the entrance of the saloon had gotten so thick that he could not enter to perform a preliminary inquiry to ascertain what transpired.

W. J. Delaney took the stand after Officer Vigers and testified that he witnessed Patrick Mealey in Johnson's Saloon, where the deceased appeared to be engaged in a conversation with Feehan and then Gibson individually. Captain McCaffrey, Delaney stated, spoke with Gibson and was overheard to say, "I heard you're going to kill Mealey; don't do it." When Claire entered the conversation, he forced Mealey to back up to the lunch counter of the saloon. Delaney then witnessed Claire "jump back a foot or so and shoot Mealey." According to Delaney, Mealey had his hands raised above his head as he hit the floor. The witness testified that he thought it strange that once Claire confronted Mealey, Gibson moved closer to the door as if preparing to escape. After Mealey hit the floor, Delaney claimed to have shouted, "Don't let him [Claire] get out of here alive," and ran after Mealey's assailant, eventually helping Payton in subduing Claire for the police.[18]

George Voorhies, the bartender at Johnson's Saloon on the night of the shooting, took the stand and testified that he waited on the Mealey party when they arrived at the location. Voorhies stated that before the altercation, Mealey purchased a round of drinks for the house, including Claire's party. Claire did not return the favor, which, according to 19th-century bar etiquette, would have been an insult. Nevertheless, Mealey, distinguished and gentlemanly as he was, did not appear to notice the slight.[19] Voorhies noticed that Claire and Mealey were engaged in a conversation at the time the first shot was fired.

The prosecution next called Troisville Sykes to the stand. Sykes testified that on the night of the shooting, he walked into Johnson's Saloon; when Mealey saw him standing at the bar, Mealey invited Sykes to drink with his party. Sykes testified that he heard Captain McCaffrey shout very loudly toward Gibson, "Don't kill Pat Mealey!" Then Sykes witnessed Louis Claire walk up to Mealey. Mealey extended his hand to Claire in the hopes that Claire would accept it in friendship. Instead, Claire stepped back from Mealey, brandished a revolver, and fired into Mealey's midsection. Sykes then witnessed Claire, Gibson, and Feehan fire their pistols randomly around the saloon before the men quickly departed. After Sykes's testimony, the jury requested that they visit the crime scene. Judge Marr recessed the court for an hour until their return.

Several more prosecution witnesses were called to testify, but their stories differed little from what the jury previously heard. The prosecution rested after their testimonies.

The defense began its case by calling W. T. Little to stand. Little's testimony, the defense hoped, would establish that Mealey and Claire were locked in a fistfight at the time of the shooting, which would demonstrate Mealey's death was a justifiable homicide rather than a cold-blooded murder. Little concluded that Claire's face showed signs of blood and he saw Claire shoot Walsh. John Gibson came to the stand next and testified that Mealey walked up to Claire and started an altercation with the defendant.[20]

In a dramatic maneuver, the defense then called Louis Claire to the stand. The defendant testified that on the night of the shooting, he stood outside Johnson's Saloon listening to the bells and the shooting in celebration of the New Year. He remembered that Gibson exited the bar and came outside to wish him a Happy New Year. When Claire returned to his spot at the bar, the witness claimed that Mealey approached him and stated, "Look here, young man, I heard you called me a __________ last week." Claire, who had his arms folded when the two faced each other, unfolded his arms and stated to Mealey, "I did not call you a damned anything. Mr. Mealey, I would not call you a __________." Claire went on to describe how Mealey yelled obscenities at him and began to beat him about the face. Claire stated that when he heard the first shots, he backed away from Mealey. He then shot his way out of the saloon using the weapon that he purchased a few days earlier. When the prosecution cross-examined Claire, he admitted buying a pistol a few days before the shooting, but said that he had lost the gun prior to walking into Johnson's Saloon. Claire claimed that he did not know that Mealey had been shot until he was arrested.[21]

After Claire's testimony, the defense rested. Because of the late hour of the proceedings, all of the opposing attorneys agreed that closing arguments would be brief and to the point so that the trial would not have to continue over another day. Assistant District Attorney John J. Finney presented his summary to the jury first. According to Finney, justice should be dispensed swiftly for the murder of Patrick Mealey, a young man who, "but a beardless boy he answered the call of his country … with undaunted courage he presented a brave front to the enemy … with glory and honor."[22] After his faithful service, Mealey had built a career in business and politics, and was adored by family, friends, colleagues, and the public he served. Mr. Mealey's assailant, however, "had not led an honest or honorable life." According to Finney, Mealey's dying declaration at the hospital sealed the defendant's guilt, in combination with the incontrovertible evidence of Claire's provocation and premeditation in wantonly murdering the well-respected Mealey. District Attorney Lionel Adams then took the floor and reiterated Finney's argument, but dramatically pointed around the crowded courtroom "as an evidence of the public interest in the punishment of the murderers of Patrick Mealey. The assemblage was a testimonial to his memory."[23]

Next, defense attorney Ferdinand H. Earhart stood to address the court on behalf of his clients. Earhart stated that the prosecution did not want a verdict based on justice; rather, he claimed, Finney and Adams sought a decision based upon vengeance. Earhart elaborated, "The assertion of the counsel on the other side that Claire entered the saloon with evil intentions was a creation and a vision not founded on the evidence of this case." The jurist emphasized that the majority of the prosecution witnesses in the case were either overwhelmingly supportive of Mealey throughout his political career or close personal friends. Influenced by grief or a sense of vengeance, he suggested, they acted emotionally in identifying Claire as Mealey's assassin. Earhart stressed that Claire's statement to the court "was the truth told by a man burning up with what he felt and knew. If ever a man told the truth in a court of justice, it was Claire." Earhart closed with an attempt to make a case for justifiable homicide. He passionately urged the jury "to judge of the condition of Claire's mind as it was when he stood in the midst of a mob of enemies firing their pistols at him; Claire believed his life in danger. After the eloquence that Earhart displayed, Claire appeared to show some emotion and remorse, but it appeared contrived to those present on that day.[24]

When the closing arguments for both sides concluded, Judge Marr again took control over the court and began to charge the jury. The jury had to decide, based upon the evidence presented to them, whether Mealey struck Claire, prompting the latter to draw his weapon out of fear of his life. If the jury drew that conclusion, they must find that Claire acted in self-defense and acquit him based on a ruling of justifiable homicide. Alternatively, if they decided that Claire intentionally killed Patrick Mealey, the jury was compelled to find Claire guilty of wanton murder. After Judge Marr gave them their instructions, the jury retired for their deliberations.[25]

At 10:00 a.m. on November 6, 1888, eight days after the trial began, the jury in the *State of Louisiana v. Louis Claire et al.* proceeding informed Judge Marr they had reached a verdict. Judge Marr hurriedly convened the court, which subsequently became filled to over-capacity. The clerk of court, T. A. Marshall, took the verdict form from the jury foreman, C. C. Crawford, and handed it to Judge Marr. The judge read the verdict and returned it to Marshall, who then announced it to the court: Louis Claire and John Gibson were found guilty of murder without capital punishment; William Feehan was found not guilty of all charges. After the verdict had been announced and Judge Marr excused the jury, as they filed past the defense table, John Gibson stated, "You're a nice lot of stiffs."[26]

Judge Marr managed to keep the potential for violence at bay until Claire's sister went after ADA Finney with her umbrella. Deputy sheriffs subdued her and took her away. More drama erupted when the court officers removed Claire and Gibson from the courtroom and took them out into the street, where they awaited the police wagon that would take them back to jail. In the crowd stood "a slender built, genteel-looking youth, beardless and apparently about 18 years old ... [who] advanced and drawing from his pocket a small cheap revolver of an inferior make," put it to Claire's torso and pulled the trigger. Claire shouted, "I'm hit!" and ran back into the court building, followed closely behind by Gibson. The assailant, Ulick Burke, was the nephew of Patrick Mealey. Upset that the two men did not receive the death penalty for murdering his uncle, he decided to take the law into his own hands. Fortunately, for Burke, he merely wounded Claire, who eventually recovered from the shot. Burke was later charged with "lying in wait with intent to murder," but a jury acquitted him of all charges in a trial on March 7, 1889.[27]

On November 17, 1888, acting in the best interests of their client, the defense filed a motion for a new trial. Judge Joshua Baker denied the motion; on November 24, he sentenced Claire and Gibson to life imprisonment at hard labor in the state penitentiary at Angola, Louisiana. Not receiving relief in the lower courts, on December 8, 1888, the defense then went to the Louisiana Supreme Court for a suspensive appeal. In the appeal, they cited as their assignment of error their contention that "the testimony of a material witness had been improperly excluded." The Louisiana Supreme Court granted the defense motion on April 25, 1889, and the new trial started on May 21 of that year.[28]

On May 26, 1889, after a five-day trial, a jury again found Claire and Gibson guilty of murder. Once again, the men were sentenced them to life imprisonment for the murder of Patrick Mealey.

The murder of Patrick Mealey stands out in Louisiana jurisprudence as the quintessential case of good versus evil. A man dedicated to public service who had the ability to gain the trust of both the electorate and his colleagues seems distant from our present public servants. Louis Claire seemed determined to lead a life of debauchery and villainy, whereas Mealey sought to serve his fellow citizens and used his personality, charm, and gentle persuasion to do so. Although Mealey's death did not cause an international incident, unlike the assassination of David C. Hennessy two years later, Mealey is still remembered in Louisiana history for the good works that informed his deserved warm and memorable legacy.

After the second trial, the announcement of a monument erected to Patrick Mealey appeared in the local newspaper. The tomb itself "is surmounted by an obelisk of Italian marble, faces two avenues, and makes quite a display." Captain John Fitzpatrick, a colleague of the late chief, dedicated the monument in memory of his friend and commissioned the work for the family. The spot where his remains rested were blessed by Priest Heslin, and made "sacred the spot where lies the remains of a generous friend, devoted husband, and loving father." To this day, no one can locate the graves of Louis Claire or John Gibson, both of whom died in Angola State Penitentiary.[29]

James W. Reynolds

The year was 1917. The United States had just entered World War I on the side of the Allies, and the nation was preparing for a protracted struggle against the central powers of Europe. Closer to home, Storyville—the small, five-block district of downtown New Orleans where prostitution remained legal—received some bad news from the Secretary of the Navy, Josephus Daniels. Due to a sharp increase in the cases of venereal disease among sailors who spent shore liberty in the city, Daniels ordered the area closed for health concerns. This action ended one of the longest periods of legally sanctioned prostitution in the South.

On August 4, 1917, mourners crowded into the Holy Name of Mary Church in Algiers, Louisiana, just across the river from downtown New Orleans to pay tribute to a family man who gave his life in the service of his community. The Rev. Father Thomas Larkin presented the eulogy: "There is a lesson to be learned from the death of our friend and every member of the force should heed it. A policeman's life is in his hands, and he should always be prepared to appear before his maker."[30]

Following the eulogy, pallbearers, including New Orleans Mayor Martin Behrman, Governor Ruffin G. Pleasant, coroner Dr. Joseph O'Hara, and New Orleans Fire Chief Louis Pujol, grabbed hold of the casket, removed it from its catafalque, and proceeded to carry their departed friend outside the gothic church and into the waiting hearse. The short ride to St. Mary's Cemetery from the church proved more morose owing to the rain and lightning. Even with the inclement weather, however, at the two or three police and fire stations passed along the way, policemen and firemen stood in the rain at attention to honor their fallen leader. Father Larkin recited Psalm 23 at the gravesite and remembered the deceased as a man with principles and honor.[31]

The policeman whom Father Larkins eulogized that rainy August morning was James W. Reynolds, superintendent of the New Orleans Police Department. Born on August 29, 1868, Reynolds's father made his living as a blacksmith. He became one of the first settlers of the area known as Algiers on the west bank of the Mississippi River. In 1892, Reynolds married Rosada Shorey, who later bore him five children.[32]

James Reynolds joined the police force as a clerk and steadily rose through the ranks, first as a plainclothes detective and then, after impressing officials with his skills in investigation, as superintendent in 1911. On the morning of his death, August 2, 1917, the superintendent prayed with his family and left for work with every expectation of returning to his family later that day. After kissing his wife and their young children, he made his way to the Algiers ferry and then to police headquarters. While he was sitting in his office to receive any appointments scheduled for that day, a small, beady-eyed man made his way into the outer office to await an audience with the superintendent. Officer Terence Mullen had joined the force as a supernumerary (probational) patrolman in 1908, then achieved promotion to patrolman in 1909. In January 1916, Captain Gary Mullen (his uncle) and a physician from Charity Hospital attempted to bring Terence Mullen to the hospital for a mental breakdown, but he escaped from the car. Fourteen days later, patrolmen and a police wagon arrived at Mullen's residence; upon finding the escaped man there, they brought him to the "Louisiana Retreat" where, for a whole year, Mullen received treatment for his ailment. Released in late

1916, Mullen again exhibited signs of mental difficulties. On the day of Reynolds's murder, Mullen had been had been recently relieved of duty and placed on leave for what the superintendent deemed a "touch of insanity." His reason for being in the superintendent's office that August morning was to address his reinstatement to the department.

After a substantial wait, the superintendent's secretary, George W. Vandervoort, called Mullen into the main office. Superintendent Reynolds sat behind his desk and Captain Mullen sat at the long table adjacent to the desk in the superintendent's office. Officer Mullen sat down in a chair facing Reynolds and immediately addressed the reason for his visit: "When am I going to work?"

Reynolds replied, "When you are fit."

Mullen quipped, "Ain't I fit now?"

Reynolds responded, "Dr. Bayon [the police surgeon] will have to say when you're fit."[33]

Mullen tried to appeal to Reynolds's charitable side: "I am hungry—I must have money—I tell you—I must have money, do you understand?" Reynolds stated that he would do everything he could to make sure that Mullen had a meal. At this point, Mullen began pounding his fist on the arm of the chair, which alarmed both the superintendent and Captain Mullen. Reynolds ordered that Officer Mullen be arrested. Suddenly, Officer Mullen jumped from his chair, threw his coat open, and yelled, "Now I have the bunch to clear out!" Officer Mullen brandished a pistol and fired a shot point blank into Reynolds's skull, killing him instantly. After the first shot went off, an officer who heard the report rushed to the anteroom of the superintendent's office to investigate the commotion, only to see the door to the main office slammed shut. Officer Mullen fired other shots that did not hit their intended mark, but wounded others nevertheless. Just then, Corporal Edward Smith opened the door and fired two shots. One of Smith's rounds hit Officer Mullen in the right wrist. Secretary Vandervoort received a wound to the head. Detective Theo Obitz and others moved quickly to the superintendent's office and wounded Officer Mullen before other officers disarmed the gunman, throwing him to the floor and putting on handcuffs.

Even though the story related seemed to suggest that Officer Mullen was responsible for the shooting and those wounded attested to the validity of the events as they transpired, Captain Gary Mullen stated that Officer Mullen did not shoot him; Detective Obitz did. This account of the events was corroborated by Detective Walter J. Methe, who averred in his statement that at the time of the shooting of the superintendent, he sat in the detectives' anteroom down the hall with detectives Henry Scheffler, Robert B. Stubbs, and Charles Clifton. The detectives heard some loud conversation emanating from the superintendent's office. When the group of men heard the shots, they rushed to see where the disturbance had occurred. According to Detective Methe, "We started for the screen door leading into the hall when a man in a light suit backed into the screen door. We all grabbed the man. The man had a pistol in his outstretched hand. I think it was Detective Scheffler that took the pistol out of his hand." Later, Detective Methe stated that when the four detectives entered the screen door to the hallway, they saw Secretary Vandervoort sitting in a chair with his head bleeding. Detective Methe then heard someone yell, "Big Mullen is crazy and shooting everybody!" When Detective Methe reached the long hallway to the superintendent's office, he observed Captain Mullen walk out of the office with two pistols in each hand. Detective Methe fired two shots at Captain Mullen—bullets he thought missed his friend and commander. Detective Methe then holstered his weapon and sat in the anteroom to the superintendent's office as Captain Mullen walked out and stated, "Don't shoot me; I been shot."[34]

Captain Mullen and Secretary Vandervoort were taken to the hospital to recover from their wounds. Mayor Behrman vowed to investigate the shooting thoroughly. In the meantime, a police escort took Officer Terence Mullen to Charity Hospital and confined him until such time that a thorough mental examination could be completed. Mullen, however, proved to be a most difficult patient. On Saturday, August 4, 1917, after taking a meal at the hospital, Mullen tried unsuccessfully to escape from the three policemen assigned to make sure he did not abscond from the premises. "There was a wild look in his eyes," one of the policemen noted, "and I immediately suspected that something was wrong with the man. I told the other policemen of what I had noticed and they all agreed with me, and not for a moment did we take our eyes off Mullen." Officer Edward Smith then witnessed the suspect attempting to move his legs and claiming that he needed exercise. Officer Smith warned the suspect that if he continued to move in such a fashion, the bandages used to dress his wound would become loose. Mullen continued to thrash about his bed to the point where the patrolmen guarding him held him down. Finally, "the patrolmen, realizing that they would have to continue holding him down, were compelled to use straps to fasten his arms to the side of the bed." Even with the heavy leather straps, Mullen continued to mutter that the policemen could not hold him down. After a short while, Mullen stopped struggling and went to sleep.[35]

Taking statements from those witnesses in attendance on the day of Reynolds's death, the city's chief executive learned that conflicting statements make for a frustrating inquiry. In an attempt to avoid duplicate proceedings into the death of Superintendent Reynolds, Mayor Behrman met with District Attorney Charles Luzenberg so that the two could focus on a single investigation to discover the truth.[36] The committee met briefly and then scheduled another meeting where the introduction of evidence would take place. After the committee met, Captain Mullen succumbed to his wounds and died earlier that day.

Twelve days after the shooting, on August 14, 1917, the committee investigating the assassination of Superintendent James W. Reynolds met again to hear evidence in the case. The confusion caused by the failure of those present to react appropriately at the time of the incident proved daunting for the investigators. Detective Walter Methe finally admitted under oath that he shot Captain Mullen, but only because he heard someone yell that his commander had gone crazy and shot everyone in sight. However, Officer Martein Scheib stated that immediately after Reynolds's shooting, he witnessed "Captain Mullen and Detective Obitz meet in a doorway, had seen Obitz draw his gun and, holding it against the captain's body, fire; had seen the body 'heave' and surge after each shot." Officer Joseph Conrad then took the stand and stated that after Captain Mullen had been wounded, he staggered to Officer Conrad and expressed flatly that Detective Obitz shot him.

One of the most mysterious accusations made during the probe stemmed from a statement made by one of New Orleans's most incorrigible characters. Dominick O'Malley was a self-styled private detective and entrepreneur; in fact, he was one of the private investigators hired by the defense team at the trial of the 19 Italians accused of murdering Police Chief David C. Hennessy and stood accused of using bribes to influence the jury in that case. O'Malley claimed that the murder of Superintendent Reynolds was a planned operation to make way for other individuals to ascend to the office. The committee dismissed the rumor as gossip, "which has been current since the killing."[37]

Even though Obitz protested that he had not shot Captain Mullen, another patrolman stepped forward to corroborate the story told by Officer Conrad. Officer Scheib stated that as he approached police headquarters, he saw Corporal Edward Smith escorting Terence Mullen out of the building and into the 1st Precinct Police Station. When Officer Scheib entered the building, he saw Captain Mullen standing near the door to the building with two pistols in his hands. He dropped the guns. Detective Obitz then walked up; after hearing Scheib shout that he was going to shoot the wrong man, the detective fired five shots into Captain Mullen's midsection. After the statements had been heard and the evidence collected, Mayor Behrman stated that he would consult with the other members of the committee and make a determination as to their findings.

On the following day, August 15, Frank T. Mooney, the newly appointed superintendent of police, announced that charges would be pursued against certain individuals, but he did not want to mention which witnesses would be pursued. The Police Board investigating the late superintendent's death held that "the evidence reveals the undoubted fact that there was the grossest of laxity of precaution on the part of certain police officials prior to the murder," and "in any and all events there was the grossest inefficiency of protection on certain police officials at the time of the assault."[38]

On August 17, 1917, an Orleans Parish grand jury indicted Terence Mullen for the murder of Superintendent James W. Reynolds. The defendant would later be determined to be mentally incapable of standing trial. Unfortunately, Terence Mullen would be lost to history. Frank T. Mooney, the new police chief, with all the conflicting testimony given to the police board, could not determine exactly what transpired in the police headquarters on that day in August. The shooting of Captain Mullen remained a mystery, and the Police Board charged with investigating the death of Superintendent Reynolds adjourned, never to be reconvened.

Superintendent Mooney would be the police chief during the infamous Axman murders that would start less than a year later. Detective Theo Obitz, the man whom several of his fellow officers named as Captain Mullen's assailant, investigated the first of the Axman murders; while chasing a suspect in an unrelated robbery, he was shot and killed in mid-1918.

This monument stands in front of New Orleans Police Headquarters on S. White Street, behind the Orleans Parish Prison. It contains the names of officers killed in the line of duty (Alan Gauthreaux collection).

James W. Reynolds' name appears on the New Orleans Police Department monument to fallen officers in Sirgo Plaza, in front of police headquarters on S. White Street (Alan Gauthreaux collection).

Overshadowed by the Hennessy assassination in Louisiana history, the deaths of police chiefs Patrick Mealey and James W. Reynolds are often overlooked and their importance to history underestimated. Both of these men had characters that rose far above that of David C. Hennessy. In the case of Patrick Mealey, he confronted evil on terms he may have understood, but could not negotiate. The politics of the 19th and early 20th centuries in Louisiana made for strange theater to observers, but proved deadly to some players. Mealey was a member of good standing in the community, a dedicated family man who was gunned down because he got in the way of an veteran criminal who exhibited animosity at the good-natured public servant because of his political acumen. The murder seems senseless—but when does evil ever make sense?

Despite the fact that Terence Mullen demonstrated bouts of uncontrolled insanity, the evil in his soul dictated his actions. Obviously frustrated with the obstacles he encountered in his quest to rejoin his brethren on the police force, Mullen resorted to violence and murder to achieve his objective. Although his movements may have been controlled by some mental illness, the consequences of his actions were deadly. Both Mealey and Reynolds fell victim to the malevolence of men, but because their deaths did not cause international incidents, they remain largely forgotten in the annals of Louisiana crime.

The Madam's Last Will

"Do not prostitute thy daughter, to cause her to be a whore; lest the land fall to whoredom, and the land become full of wickedness."—Leviticus, 19:29

During the latter part of the 19th century, the scourges of vice and corruption ran rampant throughout New Orleans. Gambling, prostitution, graft, and even murder occurred without much notice, with the laxity in law enforcement attracting the most nefarious criminals from around the world to the city. Prostitution, in particular, produced the types of profits through vice for which the city became known, making millionaires out of enterprising women for whom other vocations presented little or no opportunities for success. Women who were either abandoned or chose to make a life within the "oldest profession" no doubt gained notoriety, but they also accumulated vast amounts of capital and influence through their chosen vocation. This was a far cry from the situation that prevailed when prostitution first made its way to the colony.

With the assistance of the French crown in the late 17th century, thousands of potential colonists had been transported to the New World to stake their claims in Louisiana. As part of that effort, the prisons of France were emptied; Thus, along with the truly dedicated pioneers who looked for a new home elsewhere, the dregs of French society journeyed to Louisiana. Among those who braved the journey were many downtrodden women whose only source of income lay in prostitution; they hoped to found a more welcoming home in Louisiana. In sending these women to the new colony, French officials hoped they would make acceptable wives to the male population already living here. Even the governor of the colony at the time of its founding, Jean Baptiste le Moyne, believed the women who arrived in the colony during his administration to make wives for the male colonists were not morally or physically attractive. Yet, because the men who worked feverishly to make a living in Louisiana had not had the company of women to speak of, most of these females did eventually find mates.[1]

Prostitution continued during the Spanish period of the late 18th-century

Louisiana, but did not gain acceptance; rather, the Spanish administrators abhorred the practice. When Louisiana became a U.S. state in 1812, the newfound freedom that accompanied statehood allowed the practice of prostitution to prosper and expand exponentially. With New Orleans's burgeoning role as a port city, business grew, and so did the profits that could be made from the profession.

Well into the 19th century, in those sections of the city where prostitution flourished, elaborate brothels accommodated "gentlemen" of the city and made fortunes for the madams who managed them. One of the more enterprising madams of this period built a mansion located at 40 South Basin Street, just off the main thoroughfare of Canal Street. The property certainly reflected the grandeur of late 19th-century New Orleans with its French chandeliers, "fireplaces and mantels of white marble ... the furniture of highly polished solid black walnut was upholstered in damask, floors were covered with velvet carpets,"[2] and the finest antique furniture was purchased through merchants in Europe. Walking through the ornate front doors of the establishment, the house opened to a sitting room where the girls would wait to be chosen by the gentlemen entering the brothel while a piano played "ragtime," the music of the day. In fact, the famous "professor" Jelly Roll Morton made many appearances as the entertainment in this and other houses of prostitution. Champagne was served throughout the day and into the evening, making the clientele as comfortable as possible.

The owner of this palace located at 40 South Basin Street demonstrated to her peers and to the city that vice did pay, and paid well. Kate Townsend owned the palatial estate in the heart of what would later be known as Storyville.[3] Kate began her rise as one of the most famous madams in New Orleans as Bridget Cunningham, born in Liverpool, England, in 1839. After abandoning twins born as a result from her liaison with a sailor, Kate sailed first to New York, then continued on to New Orleans in 1857. Often described as a quite voluptuous 19-year-old, Kate worked as a prostitute at various houses of ill repute in the New Orleans area until, in 1863, she decided to rent a house at the corner of Villeré and Customhouse streets. At the tender age of 24, she set out to become one of the most notorious madams in the city.[4] Kate gained influence with local politicians as they returned time and again for the services provided by her "girls," and later accumulated enough money to build the mansion on Basin Street as a testament to her wealth and influence.[5]

Kate enjoyed the riches and the lifestyle from the proceeds of her occupation, taking advantage of all the splendor granted those with wealth. Nevertheless, in addition to her life in the limelight as the city's most famous *Madame de prostituées*, Kate had a reputation for engaging in a violent relationship with a man who became known as her "husband." The liaison between Kate and William Troisville Sykes was volatile, to say the least. Sykes, known as "Bill" to those who knew him, "was of a good family, but has not been recognized by them since he linked his fortunes with that of Kate Townsend."[6] He was described as "a tall, stout man, a sort of biondine, as it were," and the "cherished one of the renowned [sic] town woman Katie Townsend ... [who] sees to all his little wants and will no doubt continue to do so."[7] This description suggests that the couple shared a loving and personable relationship—but history tells a far different story.

Police responded to calls on many occasions to referee disturbances involving the pair. In one of those domestic disputes, while Kate traveled to a city somewhere in the North, Sykes allegedly stole more than $9,000 from Townsend after he discovered her bank deposit book. Upon her return, an aggrieved Townsend described Sykes as her "fancy man," who had "rummaged through her armoire [and] discovered her bank book."[8] After another incident at the Spanish Fort near the lakefront of Lake Pontchartrain, Sykes and Kate appeared before a municipal court in New Orleans to be arraigned for disturbing the peace and fighting. The court assessed a fine against Kate and released her, but found no evidence to jail Sykes.[9] Subsequently, the two reconciled and Sykes returned to the residence he shared with Townsend. The violence between the two culminated in a ghastly incident reflective of their association.

In the mid-morning of November 3, 1883, police arrived at Kate's residence after a patrolman had been summoned after a horrific discovery. According to eyewitnesses at the time, early on that morning, Sykes abided by his daily routine as he went for a morning walk and then drank coffee in the sitting room of the residence at 40 Basin Street. When he finished, Sykes went to Kate's bedroom and no one heard a sound for some time. At approximately 10:00 a.m., a servant heard groaning coming from Kate's room. When asked if anything was wrong, Sykes replied from behind the closed door, "Miss Kate is all right." When the servant threatened Sykes with a call to the police, he hurriedly opened the door and ran up the stairs of the residence to his room on the third floor. As he waited for the police to arrive, Sykes had "changed his clothing, and placed his bloody shirt in a bureau drawer, and thrown the knife with which he committed the murder, a large dirk, out of the window."[10]

When police arrived and entered Kate's bedroom, they found her lying on her bed, lifeless, bloody, and butchered in the most savage way. Over the years, her short demure frame had suffered from the ravages of the "good life"—she had gained a considerable amount of weight, turning her once-attractive figure into that of an obese, slovenly woman. In a cursory examination of the corpse, police noted that she had sustained several deep stab wounds to her torso. In an attempt to conceal the body from others in the house, the officers covered her body with a sheet. This way, the inhabitants who by this time had gathered at the door of the room could not witness what was once their mistress. Police called the coroner, who arrived a short time later and took Kate's corpse to the morgue to perform an autopsy.

A coroner's inquest held later that day revealed that Kate had succumbed to several knife wounds consistent with those made by the blade of a Bowie knife. The inquest documented the cause of her demise as being "by hemorrhage of puncture wounds to the chest." William Troisville Sykes admitted to Kate's killing, but he stressed that her murder took place as a result of her attacking him with the knife, rather than the reverse.[11]

Even though Kate and Sykes had fought incessantly since the very moment they met, tensions between the two had been mounting in recent times. Indeed, the girls in the house as well as the servants working in the home witnessed the two fighting every day. On the day of Kate's death, according to maid Mary Philomene, Sykes left the house for a short walk. When he returned, he asked a servant, Mary, for a cup of coffee. While Sykes sat enjoying the coffee, Kate called down for Philomene to bring her a cup as well. The dutiful maid brought the coffee to Kate, who sat at a table in her room.[12] Finally repulsed by Sykes's actions, Kate determined this would be a good time to inform him she had found solace in the arms of another man and wanted Sykes out of her life and residence.

After finishing his coffee, Sykes went to his room on the third floor. After several minutes, Mary went up the stairs. "Seeing the door slightly open to Kate's bedroom, she pushed it open all the way until she witnessed Kate standing near her armoire, still in her night clothes, and Sykes, in an agitated state, standing next to her bed. Sykes told Mary to "mind her business" and stated that he could handle the situation, dismissing the servant. Mary backed away from the door as Sykes closed and locked it. The maid then went downstairs to the kitchen. Shortly thereafter, she heard screaming and yelling coming from the madam's boudoir.[13]

Mollie Johnson, another one of Kate's servants, stated that at 10:00 a.m., Sykes had passed her door and instructed her not to call the police; he was going to turn himself in to authorities. Mollie then asked Sykes what he had done. Sykes did not respond and continued up the stairs to his room, his shirt stained with blood.[14]

Dr. George W. Lewis, who happened to be nearby, was summoned to Kate's residence and observed her lying on the bed, with one of her girls rubbing whiskey on her feet in hopes of reviving her. Dr. Lewis undertook a desultory examination and then pronounced her dead. In all, Kate received 11 knife wounds from a weapon similar to a Bowie knife. Dr. Lewis also examined Sykes before the police arrived. The madam's paramour had sustained wounds "on the inside of his right leg ... and three perforations of the undershirt a little to the right of the nipple and sternum, were two scratches on the skin deemed to be superficial."[15]

Sykes appeared before a judge on November 11, still nursing his wounded leg, and was formally charged with the murder of Kate Townsend. The judge at the hearing remanded the defendant to the Orleans Parish Prison without bail. While in prison, Sykes received a visit from his brother and informed him of Kate's interment plans.

The citizens of the city witnessed much melodrama in the case, but a red herring soon appeared. Police believed the motive for the murder was merely a lovers' spat after Sykes saw his gravy train ending. However, just like the colorful city where the murder took place, Kate Townsend's murder produced a legend that has withstood time and represents one of the darker episodes in Louisiana history.[16]

Police believed they had their murderer and the motive. After all, Sykes had confessed. Given that the nefarious paramour admitted to the murder and there was a well-documented history of violence between him and the decedent, there was no need to look any further for a motive—or was there? Authorities subsequently discovered that Kate had left a will that had remained unchanged since 1873, naming Sykes as the sole heir of her $200,000 fortune. If he claimed self-defense, then he stood to inherit her entire fortune, including the opulent residence on Basin Street. Conversely, if it was proven that he murdered her for the money, Sykes stood to gain nothing. In the meantime, Sykes could not collect until the will was probated and he was judged not guilty in a trial.

Kate's wake and funeral were not elaborate affairs, but they did demonstrate her love of the finer things in life. Her gown was made of the finest white silk, "embroidered down the front and trimmed with lace, costing $50 a yard."[17] The mourners enjoyed the finest champagne and wines, and one of Kate's last wishes was that no men be allowed to attend. Mollie Johnson, the person left in charge of the arrangements, allowed two reporters and a few of Kate's gentleman callers to come and view her one last time, but frequent male visitors to the mansion waited outside for the cortege to begin. After the wake, a horse-drawn hearse carried her remains to the Metairie Cemetery. The $400 metallic coffin carrying Kate's remains were entombed in a stately resting place.

By the middle of November, Kate's will had become a major topic of discussion around the state. Estate attorneys rushed to sign absent heirs to representation contracts as they predetermined Sykes's guilt for Kate's murder and pressured the court to allow more time for them to contact other persons who might be heirs to Kate's fortune. Sykes's attorneys, meanwhile, sought to expedite the "approval, registry and execution of the will, and for his confirmation as the testamentary executor." The conditions of the will stipulated that if Sykes and Kate died, the money in her estate would revert back to his mother.[18] The judge for Division B, Orleans Parish Civil District Court, Judge W. T. Houston, ordered that the will would be granted approval, without prejudice to the rights of the absent heirs, and Sykes would not be placed in control of the estate "until after a petition and citation be served on the attorney for the absent heirs and Public Administrator," with a hearing on the matter to be heard at a later date. Sykes's attorneys vehemently claimed that no proof of absent heirs existed.[19]

Court resumed the following day, November 13, to deal with the question of the decedent's will. Witnesses called to the stand to testify could not definitively state whether Kate had any relatives with whom she might have corresponded or visited while she lived in New Orleans. With much fanfare and argument, Judge Houston confirmed Sykes as the testamentary executor of Kate's will, despite the fact that he was currently being held on bail in the Orleans Parish Prison for Kate's murder.[20] Notwithstanding the fact that Sykes had won a small victory in succession court, there was still the matter of the trial for his life.

Legal challenges continued regarding Sykes's ability to administer Kate's estate. Nevertheless, his trial for the murder of Kate Townsend began on Tuesday, January 29, 1884.[21] The court set the tone for the trial immediately when the judge declared no tolerance for theatrics, especially when interviewing potential jurors. Judge Roman, the presiding jurist, possessed a reputation of not respecting men who formed their opinions as a result of newspaper articles, and "those who opinions cannot be changed through sworn testimony."[22] One of the men summoned to be questioned for possible jury duty, Louis Lohr, made the mistake of responding to that specific question. Lohr stated, "He had read about the case, did not remember the details, but nevertheless had a fixed opinion which could not be changed if taken as a juror sworn, and sworn testimony introduced." A furious Judge Roman said that the man was "incompetent, that his answer was foolish." The bailiffs escorted Lohr out in handcuffs, having been charged with contempt by Judge Roman. Thereafter, Judge Roman seated a jury acceptable to both sides.[23]

After jury selection was complete and the tone for the trial had been set, Charles Luzenberg, one of Sykes's defense attorneys, stated that his client would like to make a statement before the proceedings commenced. Sykes spoke normally as he addressed the court, calmly describing his version of the events that day as recorded by a spectator in the gallery:

> Kate Townsend met him during the day on Thursday and gave him money to buy an overcoat. She drank heavily after leaving the house and came back into [the house] at night. She was quarreling [with Sykes] and he did not go down to see her. He kept out of her way for two days. On Saturday morning he came down stairs about 9 o'clock and Mollie Johnson met him and told him not to go in, that

> Kate Townsend had a knife and had threatened to kill him. He said that was all right, because he did not imagine that Kate would endeavor to carry her threats into execution. He went in and she did not get up. He went out and waited for breakfast. Coming back into the room he stood at a small table in the room and raised a goblet to take a drink of water. There was another goblet, and Kate Townsend picked it up and struck him over the head with it. He was astonished and asked her if there was something the matter. She made an attack upon him with a knife, and he disarmed her. She got the knife again and he was between the bed and the armoir [*sic*]. She rushed at him and he saw that there was no chance for him to get out of the way. He asked her to stop, but she said: "You French _______, I have you this time and I will kill you." When she rushed at him he knew that he was in danger of his life. He forgot everything and did not know what happened until he found Kate dead. He opened the window, threw out the knife and went out and surrendered himself.[24]

The day before, the court allowed evidence in the defendant's favor where the jury heard how violent and uncompromising Kate could be. In allowing both pieces of evidence, the will and the testimony as to Kate's character, the court determined that both sides would have equal footing in the trial and that the jury would hear everything having to do with the case.[25] Witnesses called by the defense testified that Kate's disposition was one of violence and frivolity, always boisterous and unbridled; in contrast, Sykes displayed attributes completely opposite to those of his madam. The state called more than 20 witnesses whom the defense cross-examined and they would not admit to Sykes's having threatened Kate or causing her undo physical harm.

In testifying to the events surrounding the day of the murder, one of the state's witnesses who arrived on the scene immediately after the murder, an Officer Clarke, stated that he saw that Sykes "had on an undershirt" that day. Noticing Sykes had a wound to the thigh area, "Witness (Off. Clarke) took off and tore it in two and wrapped it around his [Sykes's] leg." When he tended to Sykes, the officer noticed that his chest had several fresh superficial cuts. Officer Clarke proceeded to take Sykes to the local jail, but he did not notice if there were "any bloodmarks on his shirt."[26]

Assistant District Attorney Branch K. Miller listened intently. When Sykes finished his testimony, Miller stepped to the bar to offer the state's theory of the case. Miller maintained that although Sykes averred that Kate's threats to his life were part of their unpredictable relationship and he took them seriously, their importance to the defendant was of little or no consequence. The screeches, Miller claimed, were normal behavior for "women of her class." Miller theorized that if Kate had carried out the numerous threats she made over the length of time that Sykes and she were together, she never would have made a will and left the defendant her entire estate. The orator emphasized, "Communicated threats do not justify killing, unless the party threatening makes some attempt to carry his threats to execution, or the party threatened has reasonable grounds to believe himself in grave danger." Miller also asserted that once Sykes disarmed Kate, as he proclaimed in his statement, this left her open for an attack that resulted in her grisly death. After all, Miller claimed, most of the wounds that Kate received occurred after she lay horizontal on the bed, the way police and the coroner found her when they arrived.[27]

One member of Sykes's defense rose after the state's presentation. Former Judge Arthur Gastinel proclaimed that Sykes acted only in self-defense and noted that if his client had not confessed, the state would have no proof that Sykes had anything to do with the death of Kate Townsend. Additionally, his client never worried about losing money, so the suggestion that Sykes killed Kate to get to her estate was preposterous. Sykes, he said, was a "kept man" who truly loved his mistress, having been in a relationship with her for more than 25 years. "Her money was his money," Gastinel exclaimed. When Kate locked the door to her room with Sykes in it, however, this step ensured that Sykes had no escape: "Even a rat cornered like that would fight, and Sykes, who had no heart to defend himself, fought for his life."[28]

Attorney A. D. Henriques next rose to give his argument for the defense. He simply stated that the law applied to this particular fact pattern in that Sykes, claiming self-defense, had the burden to prove that he acted accordingly in response to an "apparent danger" rather than a "real danger." In applying this jurisprudence, Sykes did not have to wait for Kate to attack him if he believed her actions determined that she planned to move toward him in a threatening manner. Henriques placed the victim on trial in describing the necessity for Sykes's self-defense due to Kate's history of documented violence. Another member of the defense team, Lionel Adams, stated as Sykes entered Kate's room, he carried no weapon; therefore, the defendant did not possess the requisite intent to murder Kate Townsend.

When Adams finished, Judge Romano charged the jury by explaining the differences between the various forms of homicide. The jury then deliberated.[29]

On the very next day, the jury reached a verdict. The court transported Sykes from the Orleans Parish Prison into the Division "A" courtroom in front of Judge Romano to hear his fate. The jury pronounced Sykes not guilty of the murder of Kate Townsend by reason of self-defense.

Immediately, rumors spread that the jury had been bribed. Citizens began to criticize the judicial system, stating that the Sykes case was "another instance of [the] burlesque character of jury trials in criminal cases in this city." Many citizens believed that such cavalier displays of judicial corruption resulted from the political connections of the defendant, or from the money given as bribes to those principals involved with the judicial process. Further allegations focused on the fact that the defendant actually admitted to the crime charged, yet the jury acquitted the admitted murderer. As one newspaper reported of the Sykes trial outcome, "[It is] indeed a sad commentary upon the low and degraded standard of morality that seems to pervade this community, and is so patiently and complacently tolerated."[30]

Sykes and his attorneys left the courthouse immediately, with some observers firmly believing he cheated the executioner. He had indeed paid for the finest defense that money could buy to secure his freedom, having sold the house located at 40 Basin Street to one Leon LaMothe, who in turn leased it to Ms. Mollie Johnson, one of Kate's "girls" and the woman who helped arrange the funeral of the deceased. Sykes also withdrew all the money from Kate's account and appeared to be in possession of some of her most expensive jewelry. At that time, Sykes did not legally possess the right to execute those actions despite being named executor of Kate's will after her death[31]—the issue of the will still awaited adjudication.

In February 1884, the Louisiana Attorney General filed suit in Division "B," Judge Houston's court, asserting that Sykes must provide an accounting of all the money in Kate's account as well as an accounting of any other property or movables that may have been of value. Furthermore, Sykes was ordered to return all property he liquidated, with the exception of one-tenth of the movables, because "he had lived in concubinage with the testatrix."[32] As punishment for his underhandedness with the way Sykes handled his executor duties with regard to Kate's will, Judge Houston ordered Sykes to pay back all the money he withdrew from the account, with interest, and dismissed him as the executor of Kate's will.[33] Although the judge attempted to right the wrongs done by Sykes to Kate's estate, the conclusion of the wrangling over her estate was long from over.

A year passed subsequent to Judge Houston's ruling. In 1885, a young lady stepped forward claiming to be the sister of the late Kate Townsend. Mrs. Ellen Tally, neé Ellen Cunningham, gave a deposition to the effect that she lived in San Francisco, California, and was a party to the suit that had been filed in October where she named Kate's siblings. In a subsequent proceeding, Tally stated that she had not seen Kate Townsend since she left Ireland, but subsequently recognized a similarity between Kate and her given name, Bridget Cunningham, from an issue of the police gazette. Questioned about her sister's background, Tally stated that Kate was not well educated and left Ireland due to a dispute with her father.

Tally arrived in New York in 1858, and then made her way to Galena, Illinois, where she met and married her first husband, Mr. P. McIntyre. Upon his death, he left Tally with a sizable fortune. When the witness moved to San Francisco, she met and later married Hugh Tally. He died several years after their marriage, leaving his possessions to Mrs. Tally as well. Upon hearing her testimony and examining all of the evidence submitted to the court, Judge Houston ruled that the resemblance between Ellen Tully and Kate Townsend extended only as far as nationality and not familial alikeness. Moreover, Judge Houston adjudicated Sykes "to have been guilty of ingratitude toward the deceased, Kate Townsend, and to have forfeited all benefits under the will of the said deceased, dated September 9, 1873, and decreeing that the said will be null and void."[34] Sykes had sold Kate's property, including real estate, and embezzled money from her bank accounts without legal right; as a consequence, he had forfeited any rights to the estate thereafter. The State of Louisiana, therefore, took possession of Kate Townsend's estate, as attorneys for the interveners could not prove that any viable heirs were entitled to the proceeds of that estate. Yet, even this proceeding was not the end of the story of the Madam's Will.

Although Sykes may have walked free for the murder of Kate Townsend, he did not benefit from that murder.[35] In fact, he would face more difficulties as a result of the murder of Kate Townsend and his unsavory actions immediately following her death. On February 18, 1886, Judge W. T. Houston sentenced Sykes to 10 days in the Orleans Parish Prison for his actions as the executor of Kate's will. A subsequent investigation revealed that Sykes absconded with a box belonging to the deceased that contained more than $3,000 in jewelry and various and sundry valuables. Judge Houston received a rule to show contempt why Sykes should not be held responsible for the box and its contents. Sykes ignored the rule to show cause and went to Gulfport, Mississippi, just a short train ride away; therefore, the rule could not be adjudicated. Upon his return to court for further proceedings related to the estate, under questioning, Sykes stated that the box "and its contents had been sold at his instance and for his account" to a broker.[36] Judge Houston ordered that Sykes be placed in the prison for 10 days or until he produced the valuables for the estate.[37] The final ruling on the Townsend affair would be made four months later.

In June 1886, Judge Houston reiterated his findings from an earlier proceeding and determined that the woman known as Mrs. Ellen Tally could not prove, by a preponderance of the evidence presented, that she was, in fact, the sister of Kate Townsend. In regard to Sykes, Houston determined that the petitioner was, indeed, guilty of ingratitude in his actions of selling various parts of the estate. Furthermore, the honorable jurist ruled that the Townsend will, though properly executed before a commissioned notary in September 1873, was null and void. The judgment of the court sided with the State of Louisiana and its representatives against Sykes and Tally, with Judge Houston finding Sykes and Tally responsible for the court costs for bringing the proceedings. The State of Louisiana inherited Kate's estate.[38] However, the interveners, Sykes and Tally, refused to accept Judge Houston's ruling and appealed his decision all the way to the Louisiana Supreme Court. Associate

Justice Felix P. Poché, speaking for the rest of the justices, then upheld Judge Houston's lower court ruling.[39]

Subsequent to the estate proceedings of Kate Townsend, citizens raised questions as to the accounting methods of the state when, a year after the final adjudication in the Louisiana Supreme Court ruled on the behalf of the state administrators, auditors discovered that funds had disappeared from the account.[40] The story would eventually fade from the headlines, however. Only sporadically would the city be reminded of the debacle of the trial and aftermath of the murder of "chief of the courtesans," Kate Townsend.

Even though Kate Townsend and Troisville "Bill" Sykes lived their lives in total debauchery and Sykes walked away scot-free from a murder, he went empty-handed after the murder of his mistress. Instead, the state gained possession of her estate after a lengthy court battle, though the irony of that situation presented itself just a short time later. In November 1888, the State Superintendent of Education announced that the State of Louisiana had made an apportionment from its budget on collection of revenues from the year before. It equaled approximately 18 cents for every citizen of selected parishes between the ages of 6 and 21. The money that boosted this apportionment came from the estate of Kate Townsend. For most people, this meant that the assignment of part of her fortune benefited the citizens of the state even though money represented ill-gotten gains. Even more important, her life, though short and violent, benefited those persons who would not have had the opportunity to receive an education otherwise.[41]

The City of New Orleans continued to struggle with the volatility of its red light district until 1889, when the New Orleans City Council forbade prostitutes from residing on Canal Street. Two years later, in 1891, prostitutes were forbidden from entering cabarets and drinking with the customers. Subsequently, in 1898, to restrict the practice further (and keep the practice from spreading to suburban areas), the City Council forbade prostitutes from meandering on Poydras Street, Claiborne Avenue, St. Louis Street, and the river. Finally, in 1900, City Councilman Sidney Story introduced an ordinance that limited the areas of vice to an even more compact area. Named for the councilman, "Storyville" became one of the most disorderly, unhealthy, and violent areas of the city. Tourists who could afford to visit the city viewed not only the ornate mansions of the like of Lulu White, Josie Arlington, and the "Countess" Piazza in this district, but also the hovels of the less fortunate prostitutes practicing their trade in small one-room "cribs." Eventually, in 1917, the Secretary of the U.S. Navy, Josephus Daniels, along with vice crusaders in the New Orleans area, forced Storyville into extinction.[42]

With Storyville now consigned to memory, New Orleans residents can still cite the most famous of its legacies: prostitution and jazz. Some also remember the story of Kate Townsend. Even though the famous houses of the district are all but gone, the era in which they flourished is a period that is celebrated mostly for the nostalgia, rather than for the vices that thrived there. Kate's place later became an Elks lodge, and then an ear, nose and throat clinic, before eventually being demolished to make way for new urban development projects.[43] Kate Townsend, although she inhabited the environs before Storyville was a legally sanctioned area, is still counted as one of its progenitors. Her murder and the subsequent dispute over her worldly goods have added much to the historical fabric of New Orleans history. Theories abound as to the actual motive underlying her demise, but Kate demonstrated she could thrive in the world's oldest profession and later provide a contribution to society through vice, whether in life or death.

The Case of the Human Five

"It is from the Bible that man has learned cruelty, rapine, and murder; for the belief of a cruel God makes a cruel man."—Thomas Paine, *Common Sense*

With the likes of modern societal experiences such as the Jonestown Massacre in 1978, the burning of the Branch Davidian compound in Waco, Texas, in 1993, and the mass suicide of Heaven's Gate members in 1997, cults have taken on an ominous meaning when dealing with crimes that are committed in the name of a worshipped deity. The mystical power of cult leaders seems to produce tragedy and death in all too many cases. In the annals of Louisiana crime, a series of horrific events in particular interwove the pious with the felonious, culminating in the misinterpretation of the holy word by a homicidal maniac.

On February 11, 1911, in Crowley, Louisiana, just west of Lafayette, police found Walter J. Byers, his wife, and their young child murdered in their home. Investigators surmised that the perpetrator of the crime entered through a rear window of the house located in "a strictly populated part of the colored quarter."[1] Police had grown accustomed to violence occurring in that section of the city, but then they considered the means with which the family had been murdered: "They had been brained with an ax."[2] Authorities responded to murders all the time in the black sections of the city, but never to crimes committed with this much ferocity.

Almost two weeks later, on the morning of February 24, 1911, in Lafayette, Louisiana, Nina Martin sat at the kitchen table in her house, having just been awakened by the morning crow of the rooster. As she sat at the one table in the rundown hovel she called her home, at approximately 7:00 a.m., Lezimie Felix, Nina's son, ran into the abode and told his mother that her sister and brother-in-law had been murdered. When Nina arrived at her sister's house, she opened the door to discover a scene of indescribable gore: Alexander Andrus, his wife Meme, and their two children, Joachim and Agnes, were found dead in their beds with a bloody ax on the floor near the foot of the bed. The coroner of Lafayette Parish determined that the family of four was slaughtered "at the hands of a party or parties unknown."[3]

On March 22, 1911, near Beaumont, Texas, Louis Cassaway, his wife, and their three children suffered the same injuries as the Andrus and Byers families, their bodies battered and the skulls crushed with an ax. The victims in the earlier cases were black, but in the case of the Cassaways, Louis's wife was white. This caused authorities to venture that the murderer(s) hated mixed couples. "It is a commonly accepted theory here," noted one account, "the killing was done by someone who, believing that Mrs. Cassaway was a white woman ... conceived the notion of wiping out the entire family."[4]

Lafayette Parish Sheriff Louis LaCoste investigated the Andrus murders close to his base of operations and believed that a local man of criminal renown, Raymond Barnabet, a middle-aged black man living in the area, might have been responsible for the crimes. He arrested Barnabet on suspicion of committing the Byers and Andrus murders in Lafayette, and possibly having some connection to the Cassaway murders in Beaumont. Although the chief lawman strongly believed Barnabet was involved with the gruesome offenses, Sheriff LaCoste lacked the evidence to hold Barnabet. Ultimately, he released Barnabet from custody.

After Sheriff LaCoste investigated further, he rearrested Raymond Barnabet and placed him in the Lafayette Parish jail. In October, a grand jury indicted Barnabet for the Byers and Andrus murders, setting his trial for the middle of the month.[5]

Raymond Barnabet's trial produced leads that the authorities would not have discovered otherwise. On October 19, Nina Porter, Barnabet's common-law wife, and two of his children, Zepherin and Clementine, testified at the trial for the state. Porter testified that Barnabet had left their home and took a train on the night of the murders around 7:00 p.m., stating that he had to go to Broussard, Louisiana, just a short train ride from Lafayette, and he would "jump" a freight train heading that way. Barnabet, according to Porter, wore "a blue shirt or jumper." When he arrived home at approximately 2:00 a.m. the next morning, he became angry because Porter did not save him any dinner. He was also agitated that he had lost his pipe, which he smoked regularly, on the train ride back to Lafayette. Without food or his favorite pipe, Barnabet went to sleep.

His daughter Clementine, however, offered a different story about what happened on the night of the Andrus murders.[6] The 17-year-old Clementine, who was called as a prosecution witness, testified that her father had returned home much later than Porter stated, somewhere around sunrise on the day after the murders. Upon his return, Barnabet wore the same blue shirt that his wife stated he wore when he left the house at 7:00 p.m. Raymond walked around the house smoking his pipe—the same pipe that he complained he had lost on the train ride back to Lafayette. Clementine added that her father's clothes were covered in blood and brain matter, and she subsequently washed the clothes and hung them out to dry. Clementine stated that Raymond demanded his dinner and claimed that he had just murdered a whole family, and threatened Porter, Clementine, and her brother Zepherin with a similar fate if they breathed a word of what he said.[7]

Son Zepherin testified that his father came into the shack in nothing but an undershirt and some trousers covered with blood and brain matter, as well as blood on his face and hands. His father screamed at him to retrieve his pipe and then proclaimed he had "killed the whole damn Andrus family."[8] Zepherin pleaded with the court to find a way to keep his father behind bars due to his violent and threatening behavior both at the time of the murder and in the past.

The Stevens family, who lived next door to the Barnabet family, also testified in the trial of Raymond Barnabet. The authorities characterized the Stevens family as "representatives [of] the best of their race, [who] were clean, modest direct, and uncontradictory." In contrast, the Barnabets—Clementine and Zepherin in particular—were characterized as having "very bad reputations" and, "were filthy, shifty, degenerate examples of the lowest African type."[9] Sheriff LaCoste felt that Clementine and Zepherin knew more about the murders than they portrayed to the court.

The jury inevitably convicted Raymond Barnabet of the murders of the Andrus family based upon the testimony of his family. Immediately after the trial, defense attorneys filed motions for a new trial on three bases: (1) that the defendant had been drunk during the proceedings, which diminished his ability to testify in his own defense; (2) that the jury failed to follow the judge's instructions in deliberation; and (3) that the prosecution failed to introduce a motive for the murders. On the basis that the prosecution was unable to maintain any consistency with its evidence, the court ruled on October 27, 1911, that Raymond Barnabet be granted a new trial.

While Barnabet waited in the Lafayette Parish jail for the start of his new trial, on the morning of November 27, 1911, again in Lafayette, Louisiana, police discovered the bodies of Norbert Randall, his wife Azema, and their four children, Renee Randall, aged 6, Norbert, Jr., aged 5, Agnes Randall, aged 2, and Albert Sise, aged 8, in their small cabin located on Lafayette Street, "all lying on two beds in the same room, and fearfully mutilated."[10] Sheriff LaCoste, called to the scene upon the discovery of the bodies, observed an ax leaning against a wall near the foot of the bed, apparently washed of all blood. Later information indicated that Norbert Randall, the father, had been shot through the head prior to the murderer attacking him with an ax.

Based on the evidence at the Byers, Andrus, and Randall crime scenes, along with the multitude of victims, authorities investigating the murders believed that more than one killer had committed the crimes—not separately at different locations, but in collusion. The day after the Randall murders, Sheriff LaCoste arrested Clementine Barnabet at the residence of a friend when deputies uncovered "a complete suit of woman's clothes in her room, saturated with blood and covered with human brains."[11] Thinking it impossible for this small, demure black woman to have been able to lift the children by herself, police also arrested her brother Zepherin (also known as "Tatit"), along with two other men, Edwin Charles and Gregory Porter. Sheriff LaCoste then sought (with the assistance of the Acadia Parish Sheriff's Office and the Crowley police) to link all of the suspects to the rash of murders that had plagued Lafayette and Crowley for the last year and a half.

Investigators at the Lafayette Parish sheriff's office, under the supervision of Sheriff LaCoste, interrogated Clementine about the bloody clothes discovered in her closet. Strangely, during this confrontation, the young girl laughed and stated she had nothing to do with the crime. This behavior, though odd, did not deter the police from holding her until more evidence could be gathered. Zepherin had established an alibi for the night of the murders, but until that information was confirmed, he stayed in the local jail along with Charles and Porter.[12]

Using a more scientific approach to connect the bloodstained clothing to Clementine, investigators brought the clothing to New Orleans for a chemical analysis. Clementine continued to proclaim her innocence while offering no reasonable explanation for the bloody clothes. During her lengthy interrogation by investigators, Clementine "maintained a sphinxlike attitude."[13] In her defense, several people did come forward and say that Clementine ran the streets that night and could not have been responsible for the Randall murders. The suspect offered no explanation as to how the blood and brain matter came to stain her clothing.

Police theorized that Clementine went to the Randall residence and grabbed an ax on her way into the house. Norbert Randall, the father, was the first to die, followed by his wife. When Clementine went into the children's room, she removed the covers and began to slaughter the children, one by one. The coroner indicated that Norbert Randall's head wound occurred postmortem, and police failed to find the pistol that the killer used on some of the victims.[14] Moreover, authorities still maintained that Clementine could not have committed the Randall murders, or any of the previous murders, without the assistance of one or more accomplices. Further investigation into her character and habits revealed interesting information that would contribute to a better understanding of the motive for the murders and explain Clementine's odd demeanor during the course of that investigation. Specifically, the investigators' inquiries revealed that the murders had a spiritual purpose and established that a group of people were responsible for the brutality. With Clementine and her father safely incarcerated, albeit in different locations to prevent any communication between, Zepherin, Edwin Charles, and Gregory Porter walked away from jail as free men—the authorities had found no evidence of their complicity in the crimes.[15] Clementine and Raymond would sit in jail until their trial, even as interesting developments continued to surface.

Sheriff LaCoste's investigation revealed that a cult did, indeed, exist within his parish. This revelation came about when investigation into some of the victims verified they were members of the "Church of Sacrifice." Under the guidance of the Rev. King Harris, church members were "[so] intensely moved and impressed by the teaching of the testament sacrificial ideas and ceremonies that they [were] incited to commit heinous crimes."[16]

Sheriff LaCoste believed the two persons responsible for the carnage sat incarcerated in his jail. However, at approximately noon on January 18, 1912, in Crowley, a small town located approximately 50 miles east of Lake Charles, in a district known as the "Promised Land," Harriet Crane looked across the street at the small house occupied by her daughter, Marie Warner, and her three children: Pearl, aged nine years; Garey, aged seven; and Harriet, aged two. Warner's husband had recently moved to Beaumont, leaving the young mother to fend for herself and her three offspring. Crane noticed that the place looked empty and asked a neighbor, Dorney Birdsong, if he had seen Marie or the children. Birdsong responded that he had not. Crane and Birdsong then walked across the street to see if there were any signs that the inhabitants were awake in the small hut. The pair walked around to the back of the structure and noticed the back door ajar. Too frightened to go into the house, Crane and Birdsong summoned a young black man, Ben Robinson, to go inside to see if the family had awakened. Robinson "entered the hut and found the mangled remains of the four occupants on a bed in the front room."[17] When officers from the Acadia Parish sheriff's office arrived at the scene, in addition to observing the corpses, they found a bloodstained ax in the same room with the victims. As authorities examined the crime scene, they noticed two sets of foot tracks in the moist mud outside the back door. At first, bloodhounds were gathered to start a search for the killers, but local police soon called off the search when the dogs lost the scent.

Just three days later, at 10:00 a.m. on January 21, 1912, at 331 Rock Street, in Lake Charles, Louisiana, in the southwestern part of the state close to the border with Texas, police discovered the bodies of Felix Broussard, an "industrious man who is without enemies," his wife, and their three children, Margaret, Alberta, and Louis; all of the children were younger than the age of eight. The children, once again, were found lying on the bed with their skulls crushed and mangled by the blows of an ax, which was found underneath the adults' bed. The perpetrator(s) gained entrance to the house through a kitchen window. The crime scene, however, contained clues as to who the perpetrators may have been. A Bible inscription, written in blood, appeared on the front door: "When he maketh the inquisition for blood, He forgetteth not the cry of the humble." On the side of this inscription the perpetrator(s) wrote, "Human Five." Adding an even more ghastly touch to the acts of the killer(s), police discovered a bucket that had been placed underneath the murdered children's heads as they lay on the bed to collect the blood that dripped from their wounds.

Sheriff LaCoste believed that more investigation into the Reverend Harris was the key to catching the murderers. He arrested the holy man immediately after the Broussard murders, not only for the Reverend Harris's own protection, but also to delve into the alleged teachings of the Church of Sacrifice in an effort to find the person(s) responsible for the carnage that had occurred over the area between 1911 and 1912.[18]

When police interrogated the Reverend Harris, he stated that the Church of Sacrifice was an unofficial sect of the Christ Sanctified Holy Church located in Lake Charles, Louisiana. To the best of his knowledge, the Reverend Harris claimed, the religion did not advocate the wanton killing of men, women, and children, and rather sought to persuade "people to follow in the footsteps of Christ, believing in the Holy Ghost and [in] fire and not immersion, pouring, or sprinkling." The reverend added that nothing in the teachings of his church excused the crimes that had occurred to the black families in the area. Another minister in the area also endured the questioning of Sheriff LaCoste and his detectives; finding no evidence to hold him as an accessory, they released the visibly shaken preacher.

The black populace of the areas affected—Crowley, Rayne, Lafayette, and Lake Charles—sought answers from law enforcement as to whether they were any closer to identifying the mysterious murderers. Although two people were already incarcerated for their involvement in two sets of the murders, the fact that more killings continued to occur frightened the local residents. In the meantime, a well-to-do black businessman named Deshotel received what he called a "black hand" letter. A type of missive also well known with the Italian community, the black hand letter demanded money in exchange for protection, or as a ransom demand for the kidnapping of a loved one. The note allegedly composed in blood to Deshotel stated that he should "eat well and drink well in preparation for the death which will overtake him."[19] Subsequently, the threat failed to materialize, but it did not quell the concerns of the black populations in the area.

The citizens of Breaux Bridge, Louisiana, a small farming community located just east of Lafayette, feared that the ax murderer might visit them in the middle of the night, and their fears created a frightened agitation within the city itself. The entire black citizenry took to sleeping with weapons, taking shifts staying awake to watch over family members, and suspecting everyone, even those who were once close.[20] Collectively, they shuddered in fear of one another. No one knew who would be next.

Despite these personal precautions, something else had to be done on a larger scale to ease the trepidations of blacks in the vicinity. On Sunday, February 11, 1912, 150 blacks from the areas affected by the murders met at the Good Hope Baptist Church in Lafayette. At that meeting, the black citizens of Lafayette swore that they would "render all assistance in our possession to authorities and officers of our city in bringing to justice the perpetrators of these crimes." The group further resolved to supply information that would lead to the apprehension of the murderer(s) as well as act as agents of law enforcement to bring the reign of terror to an end. As an added affirmation of their support, the members of the group gave grateful acknowledgment to the white citizens of Lafayette "for their instruction and advice."[21]

The extra measures taken to ensure the safety of all concerned seemed to have a calming effect on the residents. The increased patrols, citizen involvement, assistance with locating witnesses, and participation of law enforcement agencies in the area seemed to deter any further murders in the Lafayette area. Southwest Louisiana remained quiet, with authorities assuring the people that the two murderers were in custody (though both were suspected to be leaders of the brutal cult) and hoping that no followers of the two would continue the pattern of savage sacrifices.

All of the extra policing and community involvement forced the killer(s) to return to an old hunting ground. On Tuesday, February 20, 1912, nine days after the community meeting, at a residence located at 1428 Cable Street in the north end of Beaumont, Texas, the rampage continued. This time, the victims of the ax murders were Hatie Dove, aged 26, Ernest Dove, 14, Ethel Dove, 16, and Jamie Quirk, 13. An ax found at the scene had been stolen from a house yard some two blocks away and wiped of all blood, as evidenced by the stained towel discovered nearby.[22] Police believed the murders to be the work of the same person or persons responsible for the deaths of the Byers, Andrus, and Randall families, as well as the deaths of the unpublicized victims, Marie Warner and her three children. With Clementine and her father incarcerated in Lafayette and nearby Crowley, authorities were certain that Clementine alone, or in collusion with her father, must be providing guidance to followers regarding further commission of ritual murders.

Sheriff LaCoste raised the hopes of the citizenry that the murderers would be caught when he received a letter in the mail postmarked from New Orleans. LaCoste thought the letter had very little credibility, but the author made an interesting statement that lingered in the minds of law enforcement throughout the investigation. According to the badly written note, "There is a leader who goes from town to town selecting victims." This declaration established part of what law enforcement believed: that there was a cult at work and perhaps the two people police held in the city and parish jail were the leaders of the band that had run amok for the last year and a half, killing blacks in southwest Louisiana and east Texas.

At first, Clementine had protested her innocence to authorities with regard to the ax murders in and around Lafayette, and then remained silent and apathetic throughout her stay in the Lafayette jail. Two weeks after the Dove murders, however, she surprised all those paying close attention to the case by giving a wholesale confession as to her involvement with the wave of bloodshed, and shared insights with authorities regarding how she came to participate in such a murderous lifestyle.

Clementine stated she was born and lived near St. Martinville, Louisiana, and moved to the Lafayette area in 1909, settling into a life she called "degradation." On a visit to the New Iberia area, just southeast of Lafayette, she and four companions—two men and three women altogether—met an old black woman who showed them the way of "hoodoo," and bought some "candja" bags from a "conjurer." These bags, the old woman assured them, would protect Clementine and her accomplices from detection by the police should they desire to commit a crime.[23]

Clementine then set about to prove the power of the candja and hoodoo and went to Rayne, Louisiana. In the dead of night, she dressed as a man and prowled the streets. She stole an ax from an unknown person and proceeded to commit her first murder. Clementine's confession continued:

> I saw the mother sleeping on the bed, then I decided I would enter the house [cabin] and there begin the work which we had planned. On entering the house, I struck the woman on the right temple and killed her instantly. One of the children was awakened by the noise, and before he could raise his head from the pillow I struck a blow somewhere near the left ear, then I struck the other two. I left the man's clothes which I wore in the house and left in women's clothes, returned to my sister's house and later during the same night I boarded a night train for Lafayette, arriving here about midnight.[24]

Clementine insisted that she had used a gun only once, to shoot Norbert Randall. She recalled every grisly detail of the murders she allegedly committed and even stated that she had a penchant for fondling people after death, where "the sex of the dead object of her caresses did not matter."[25] Authorities reasoned that even though others may have assisted in the execution of the crimes, Clementine, Raymond, and Zepherin (whom police later arrested and held for the same charges) vicariously led the killers to their prey. The murderess stated she killed the children because she did not want them to be orphans. To continue her "work," Clementine stated she testified against her father at his original trial at the insistence of her brother,

Zepherin.[26] Clementine maintained that she, and she alone, committed the murders in Lafayette.

After her confession, the district attorney for Lafayette Parish, Howard E. Bruner, formulated a theory based upon the suspect's demeanor and the words she used in her confession. He did not think that the Texas crimes had anything to do with the Louisiana murders, but rather were "copycat" crimes (as they would be described in modern-day psychopathy). Bruner believed Clementine to be "a moral pervert and [gave] her little credit for her attempts to involve [an]other and probably mythical person."[27] Soon thereafter, alternative theories of what occurred during her rampage would be introduced—some interesting, others outlandish. Nevertheless, the focus remained on finding other murderers out there who remained fanatical in continuing to do Clementine's bidding.

As the case progressed, confusion added to the barbarity of the crimes committed. The public, after reading Clementine Barnabet's confession in local newspapers, could not accept that this teenaged girl could have wielded an ax and had the wherewithal to commit the murders. Other perpetrators, just as fanatical and zealous, had to be responsible along with Clementine. In their search for the truth, authorities followed every clue that she gave within her confession, especially those statements where she mentioned her association with others. Sheriff LaCoste and others investigating the case deemed the religious fanaticism angle to be implausible and placed "no credence in Clementine's hoodoo version and many other of her illusory flights of imagination in giving her confession."[28]

Despite the need to investigate further, District Attorney Bruner filed charges against Clementine on April 4, 1912, with the Lafayette Parish Criminal Court, stating that "on the 27th day of November A.D. 1911, [Clementine Barnabet] did unlawfully, willfully, feloniously and of her malice aforethought kill and murder" Norbert Randall, Jr., Norbert Randall, Sr., Renais Randall, Mrs. Norbert Randall, Sr., Albert Scythe, and Agnes Randall.[29] For her part, Clementine continued telling her story to whoever would listen as she sat in the jail. Newspapers attributed more than 35 killings to Clementine and her accomplices. Police confirmed Clementine's claims about her whereabouts on the nights of the murders in Rayne and Crowley, and her meeting with the Rev. King Harrison on the night of the Randall murder.

Sheriff LaCoste then traveled to New Iberia and arrested Joseph Thibodaux, the alleged "conjurer" who gave Clementine and her party the candja bags to protect them from detection. When the jailer took Thibodaux to Clementine's cell, she identified him as the man who sold her and the others the candja bags. Sheriff Fontenot, from nearby Crowley, Louisiana, remained a skeptic, however. He stated that most of Clementine's confession contained too many inconsistencies; he doubted that Clementine was responsible for any of the murders and waited for a plausible explanation of the crimes that pointed to viable suspects.[30]

While authorities worked in Louisiana to solidify their case against Clementine Barnabet and her so-called accomplices in Louisiana, police in San Antonio, Texas, investigated another ax murder. On April 12, 1912, authorities there found the mutilated bodies of William Barton, his wife, their two children, and his brother-in-law, Leon Avers. Authorities surmised that the same killer(s) responsible for the murders of black families in southwestern Louisiana had committed the most recent Texas attack, dispelling the copycat theory. The killers provided no clues as to their identity, but the crime scene was reminiscent of the murders that had taken place in Lafayette, Rayne, and Crowley.

Investigators continued searching for further leads in the case. On April 21, 1912, Zepherin Barnabet confessed that he and his father, Raymond, killed the Andrus family. Zepherin clarified that Clementine, a man named Ute Thomas, his son Darman, and another black woman acted as accessories to the crime. Thomas and his son were immediately arrested. Despite Zepherin's testimony, Clementine would be tried only for the Randall murder until more concrete proof could be obtained that she was responsible for the death of more than five people.[31] Police rearrested Raymond Barnabet and believed that, over time, the mystery as to the actual culprits in the massacres would be solved and the criminals brought to justice.

As the Barnabets and their co-conspirators waited in various jails around Lafayette Parish, remaining separated so that they could not lie in unison, another ax attack occurred in San Antonio, Texas. On August 20, 1912, the ax attacks continued with a second attempt on the lives of James Dashleil and his family. An unknown attacker had previously attempted to kill Dashleil and his family three months earlier. Returning to finish his work in August, the assailant entered the house through an open kitchen window and made his way to the parents' bedroom. He attacked Mrs. Dashleil first with an axe blow to what the assailant thought was her head. Fortunately for the woman, her arm laid across her head where the ax blows came down, protecting her head. She screamed and when the assailant attempted a second blow, Mrs. Dashleil started kicking desperately at her attacker, so that the ax landed a blow only on her right foot. The screams aroused Mr. Dashleil, who fired a shot at the attacker but missed, forcing the attacker to flee from the Dashleil residence.[32]

The attack on the Dashleils shared similarities with the previous attacks in Rayne, Crowley, and Lafayette, leading authorities to believe that indeed a band of murderers continued to perpetrate these ghastly crimes. Blacks in both Texas and Louisiana continued to tremble in fear and struggle to protect themselves from the threat of entire families being annihilated in a single night. Sales of pistols increased as the black populations of multiple cities prepared themselves to become the next target of the ax killer(s).

Although blacks took safeguards to protect their families in Louisiana and Texas, they could find little solace with the commencement of the proceedings against Clementine, knowing that her homicidal followers still lingered in the shadows. When authorities had first arrested Clementine, her behavior seemed uncharacteristic of someone who stood accused of more than 20 vicious murders, unless another cause for her stoic behavior explained her solemnness while awaiting the results of the investigation. On or about October 16, 1912, attorneys for Clementine filed motions to have her examined by a series of psychiatrists to determine her sanity. George P. Lessley, J. J. Fournet, and John L. Kennedy filed a motion with the 18th Judicial District Court of Lafayette Parish, Louisiana, suggesting to the court that:

> they have reason to believe that said defendant [Clementine] is insane, and she should not be brought to trial herein until the question of her mental condition and her consequent moral and legal accountability or non-accountability for her acts and her statements is inquired into by a commission of experts in the diagnosis of mental diseases.[33]

The court summoned three psychiatrists to determine Clementine's sanity. Drs. E. M. Hummel, John Tolson, and R. D. Voorhies, after careful examination of the defendant, testified about their findings at a hearing on October 21, 1912: "We found the subject to be morally depraved, unusually ignorant, and of a low grade mentality, but not deficient in such a manner to constitute her imbecile or idiotic." The doctors concluded that Clementine did not possess any "acquired insanity."[34] Now judged to be sane, and even though she confessed to the crime, Clementine's trial began that same day.

On October 24, 1912, the prosecution rested with all evidence presented, including the defendant's confession. On the following day, the jury returned a verdict of guilty and sentenced Clementine to "be incarcerated in the State Penitentiary at Baton Rouge, La., for the term of her natural life."[35] Those watching the events at the time felt sure that she would receive the death penalty for not only the crimes themselves, but also her ability to convince others to perform the most heinous acts on their fellow human beings.

With the alleged leader of the Church of Sacrifice sentenced to prison for the rest of her natural life, authorities hoped that her "followers" would cease their grisly work. Law enforcement expectations proved too optimistic: On November 22, 1912, the killers added another state to their hunting grounds. Police in Philadelphia, Mississippi—a small town just 100 miles northeast of Jackson—discovered the bodies of William Walmsley, his wife, and their four-year-old child: "All had been murdered with an axe." Police deduced that the Walmsley family were once members and now victims of the "sacrifice sect" once led by Clementine Barnabet. The crime scene revealed no clues, and the suppositions of authorities would need further, more intense investigation to prove. Again, police had no clues and wondered if Clementine's influence would ever wane.[36]

As the year 1913 approached, the murders ceased. The trail for the perpetrators went cold. With Clementine behind bars in the Angola State Penitentiary, it appeared that her influence had, indeed, diminished with the passage of time. Historical sources give no indication of what happened to many of the alleged accomplices arrested at the same time as Clementine. Zepherin Barnabet, after being released from jail, was arrested in a separate incident on or about November 5. After that there is no record of him, or his father, Raymond Barnabet, for that matter.

Authorities brought Clementine to Angola State Penitentiary on October 29, 1912. She tried to escape on July 31, 1913, but prison officials captured her that same day. In 1918, she was assigned as a cane cutter. Suddenly, on August 28, 1923, Clementine walked out of the gates of Angola, with only hints of her whereabouts whispered as part of an urban legend.[37]

How did someone who allegedly committed so many brutal murders walk out of prison after serving only 10 years? In 1902, the Louisiana legislature passed an act that allowed for commutation or diminution of life sentences if the individual requesting that particular relief could demonstrate he or she had abided by the rules of the prison system and deserved clemency.[38] With the exception of the escape attempt soon after her arrival at Angola, Clementine became a model prisoner.

The legend of Clementine Barnabet hides behind a veil of disbelief as far as history is concerned. Official historical records do not reveal what became of Clementine after her prison stay or what happened to her family. The mystery persisted for nearly 90 years until a story appeared on the World Wide Web—and then the legend took on a life if its own.

One individual, who identified herself only as "voodoogal11," told the tale of visiting her great-grandmother in 1985. Her great-grandmother was celebrating her 103rd birthday in the August heat of that year. During voodoogal11's visit with the centenarian, her great-grandmother related stories of a maddened killer who went on a killing rampage in 1911, in southeast Louisiana. In describing the killer, the great-grandmother stated that Clementine "was a black woman so beautiful with alabaster skin and eyes so piercing she would look at you and turn you to stone"; her gaze was so wanton and enticing that no man could refuse her.[39] Clementine would then turn a whip on her suitors to demonstrate her brutality and loathing for human life. Voodoogal11 asked her great-grandmother if the story she told held any truth, or whether she had just invented it to entertain her great-granddaughter. "She just sipped her iced tea and continued rocking in her chair."[40] Later that year, voodoogal11 related, her great-grandmother died. As the young woman never knew what her great-grandmother looked like as a young woman, she visited her ancestral home again for the funeral and requested that her grandmother show her a photo of the old woman when the latter was just 20 years old. In the words of the storyteller, when she gazed upon the portrait of a young mulatto woman, "She had alabaster skin, long Black curly hair and very light eyes and then I started trembling."[41] Her great-grandmother turned out to be Clementine herself.

A Respectable Poisoner

"Murder is like potato chips: you can't stop with just one."—Stephen King, author

The individual with a cold, calculating, and methodical personality and sociopathic traits has proved throughout history to have a specialized cunning in the execution of a crime. Control over others brings contentment to an otherwise chaotic environment for such a person. When that control is contested or defied, the family annihilator seeks to redeem that control through intimidation, abuse, or even murder. At the beginning of the 20th century in New Orleans, the most unexpected suspect began a campaign of death in carrying out a devious plan of murder that shocked southern society and made for sensationalism of the highest order in the media.

On September 19, 1911, Elise Crawford returned home from working as a stenographer to the residence she shared with her uncle and aunt, Mr. and Mrs. Robert Crawford, and her two sisters, Annie, the oldest, and Gertrude, the youngest. Once inside the home, she complained of stomach pains and general malaise that rendered her tired and nauseous. Annie took the young woman upstairs and put her to bed. Others in the house also assisted in taking care of Elise as she tried to recover from her most recent malady. The worry surrounding the sickness of the young woman preyed heavily on the minds of those who were present, taking into account the tragedies that occurred within the last year: The three daughters had lost their father, Walter Crawford, their mother, and a younger sister, Mary Agnes Crawford, due to mysterious causes.

Prior to this episode, Elise had been treated for extreme nervousness by Dr. Marion McGuire. Annie Crawford summoned Dr. McGuire to examine her younger sister to determine her malady. He prescribed capsules filled with calomel and soda to relieve the stomach distress that she seemed to suffer. Annie then went to the drugstore to retrieve the prescription; when she returned, she administered the medication to her sister.

On Tuesday, September 20, Elise rested as much as she could, in an insensible condition, but on the next day, her condition worsened. Dr. McGuire prescribed a course of electrical treatment for the young woman, and Annie took her sister to receive the treatments. On Thursday, Elise remained in bed. On Friday, she awoke and went downstairs, where she had a cup of broth. She laid down on the couch in the sitting room and fell asleep. Later in the day, Annie woke her sister and brought her to her room to rest, giving her another capsule to ease her discomfort.

In the early morning hours of September 22, Elise's Aunt Mary went into her room to check on her. When Mary made her way into the room, Elise sat in a rocking chair, motionless. As Mary investigated further, she raised the young girl's arm and let it drop. The arm was limp. Mary then called out to Annie and said they needed to summon a doctor. "Does she always snore when she sleeps?" Mary asked Annie. Annie replied, "Sometimes." In a panicked accusatory tone, Mary asked, "Annie, what did you do?" implying that the eldest Crawford daughter had something to do with her sister's condition. Annie remained quiet and ran next door to use the telephone to summon Dr. McGuire to the residence, as Elise still would not respond. When she returned to the Crawford household, thinking her aunt had lost her senses for accusing Annie of causing Elise's condition, Annie rushed into the upstairs bathroom and returned with something for her aunt to take to calm her down. When she returned to the room where her aunt tried to revive Elise, Annie handed Mary the concoction, which the aunt summarily batted out of her niece's hands. Elise appeared to be breathing in a very shallow manner. An ambulance arrived at the residence to take her to Charity Hospital. When Elise arrived at Charity Hospital, Dr. McGuire met the family there. At 6:30 a.m. that day, Elise Crawford died, never regaining consciousness. The Crawford family buried their beloved Elise on Sunday, September 24, 1911, in the same plot with Walter, his wife, and Mary Agnes in St. Patrick Cemetery.

After her death and prior to her embalming, Dr. McGuire acquired several containers of Elise's bodily fluids to examine them for anything extraordinary. Called in to consult, Dr. Abraham L. Metz, the chemist for the city of New Orleans, lent his expertise to the examination. Dr. Metz discovered, after several chemical tests, that the fluids extracted from Elise's corpse contained several grains of morphine—enough to kill five grown men. Dr. McGuire and Dr. Metz immediately summoned the police to investigate.

On Tuesday, September 26, 1911, investigators arrived at the Crawford residence on Peters Avenue, where boxes lined the floors and furniture had already been moved from the residence. The girls' aunt, Mary Crawford, stood in the house when the investigators arrived and informed them that the family was separating. Before they all went their separate ways, police quickly escorted the whole family to headquarters, where they would be questioned regarding the death of young Elise. Police evacuated a passing streetcar so that all the family members could be transported to police headquarters simultaneously.

Once there, the family endured intensive questioning by Police Inspector James J. Reynolds, Assistant Chief of Detectives Dan Mouney, and celebrated District Attorney St. Clair Adams. The three seasoned investigators interrogated the family one by one, starting with Robert Crawford. The uncle stated that he did not pay much attention to the women of the household with the exception of his wife, and really had no information concerning Elise's demise. The interrogators excused Mr. Crawford to wait outside of the office for the rest of the family. One by one, the rest of the Crawfords faced the questioning of the detectives and the district attorney. Mary Crawford, the aunt, stated that Annie seemed reticent to call for Dr. McGuire until Mary forced her to do so. This drew the investigators' attention toward Annie, who exhibited a controlling personality in her influence over the other sisters.

Gertrude, the youngest, told investigators that Elise summoned her to the latter's room the night before she died, where Elise handed her two rings and a necklace. This jewelry never left her sister's possession and Gertrude wondered why Elise wanted her to have these keepsakes. According to Gertrude, Elise believed she would not be alive much longer to wear them. When pressed as to why she thought Elise shared this information, Gertrude did not answer. Perhaps Gertrude feared that she would be implicated in the death of her sister.

The investigators questioned Annie Crawford last. At first, Annie was hesitant to tell anything different from what the rest of the family proclaimed to be the facts surrounding Elise's death. The way she conducted herself in the initial questioning made the investigators suspicious, however, and they held Annie over for the night at police headquarters, hoping she would reveal more of what she knew. DA Adams and Inspector Reynolds made arrangements for a juvenile court matron, Mrs. O. C. Kennell, to sit with Annie in one of the offices of the headquarters and perhaps coax more information from her. The ploy worked. After a brief nap on the couch in one of the offices, and a long conversation with the prison matron, Annie Crawford made a full statement to DA Adams.

Adams could not expect the surprising developments from his second questioning of Annie Crawford. Adams learned that Annie had worked at the New Orleans Sanitarium for six and half years and was discharged because of "incompetence."[1] As a staff member at the sanitarium, Annie became addicted to morphine and frequently took capsules containing the narcotic. The habit consumed her for the previous four and a half years prior to Elise's death. When asked if she gave Elise morphine, Annie responded, "Yes, I gave her three of them [capsules]."[2] Annie thought she had given her sister capsules from the prescription dictated by Dr. McGuire, but she became confused and gave Elise the morphine instead. When Annie noticed the effects of the drug on her sister, she did not call the police or a doctor because she believed Elise would just "get over it."[3]

Adams grilled Annie about the insurance policies, not only for her sister Elise, but also for her parents and her younger sister, Agnes, who had died the year before. Immediately after Elise's funeral, Annie visited the Metropolitan Life Insurance offices to demand the payment of the policy on Elise's life, but the company refused payment due to the absence of a death certificate. A year before, when Agnes died, the insurance policy paid out $300; her mother had a life insurance policy that also paid $300 in a death benefit; and Annie's father, Walter Crawford, had various life insurance policies, including, but not limited to, a policy through the Druids Social Club for $500. His total succession amounted to more than $1,000. To ensure that Gertrude, the youngest, would benefit from the succession, Walter Crawford emancipated his youngest daughter. In all of the insurance policies, Annie was the beneficiary. In each case when the decedents became sick, Annie was the one who called the doctor and set up treatment.[4]

DA Adams saw a case for murder and held Annie over for arrest. Later that day, police escorted the young spinster to the Saratoga Street station, where she was booked for the murder of her sister, Elise. Because of his suspicions about the deaths of Walter Crawford, his wife, and Agnes, Adams moved to have those bodies exhumed for examination.

On September 28, 1911, in the chambers of Judge John B. Fisher of the 1st City Criminal Court, Annie Crawford appeared for her arraignment. When asked if she would plead guilty or not guilty, the defendant did not respond. In a second attempt to enter her plea, Judge Fisher ordered a plea of not guilty be entered into the record on behalf of the defendant since she would not state so on her own. DA Adams would try Annie only for the death of her sister Elise, as there was no evidence that she murdered her parents and her other sister—unless she confessed, that is. Dr. Metz, the New Orleans city chemist, stated that exhuming the other bodies would prove useless: "After death, vegetable poison would be in a state of decomposition and the result of the analysis would be nil."[5] Judge Fisher asked Adams if there existed a clear motive for the murder and he replied, rather ambiguously, that because Annie was the beneficiary of the life insurance policy, her motive appeared to be collection of the death benefit.[6] The pattern that DA Adams attempted to establish with the earlier deaths of Walter Crawford, his wife, and Agnes would prove to be circumstantial. Upon being charged with the murder of her sister, Annie requested that she be appointed an attorney. "I want the best sort of lawyer," she stated. DA Adams replied, "I will impress upon the court to appoint one of the best lawyers here to act as your counsel."[7]

While the prosecution began preparing for trial, stories began to appear in the local media about the Crawford family. Robert Crawford "has always borne an excellent reputation ... for many years he was a motorman on the Henry Clay Line, and by his politeness and attention to passengers earned for himself an excellent reputation."[8] Later, Robert Crawford gained employment at a local saloon, "where the work was not so heavy and the weather not so inclement." Within those same pages, the media also speculated as to the guilt or innocence of the young lady. "Is Annie Crawford a Lucretia Borgia of the twentieth century, or is it that the self-confession made by her emanated from a brain rendered not responsible by the use of drugs?" As she was unable to raise bail, Annie was consigned to sit in her prison cell, shadowed by a prison matron, until her fate was decided by a jury.[9]

On October 10, 1911, a special session of the grand jury heard arguments for an indictment against Annie Crawford for the murder of Elise Crawford. Dr. Metz testified regarding the poisoning Annie allegedly perpetuated against her sister during the week of September 18 to 23, and even heard whispers of the strange deaths of her parents and her other sister, Agnes. In a careful review of the evidence, the grand jury returned a true bill against Annie, formally charging her with the death of Elise. Even with an indictment for the murder, however, DA Adams still speculated about Annie's motive. Was it money? Did Annie's loss of control prove too unbearable? Or did she possess a fascination with the machinations of poison on humans and death? Did she experience mental illness due to prolonged use of a strong, addictive painkiller? The anxious district attorney would have to wait until the trial to discern the motivation behind the murder of Annie's family member(s).[10]

Annie still needed counsel, and out of the New Orleans upper crust came Lionel Adams (no relation to the district attorney), one of the South's finest legal minds. (Adams had acted as the defense counsel for the 19 Italians accused of the murder of New Orleans police chief David C. Hennessy in 1891.) Adams stepped forward with one of his associates, Joseph Generelly, to represent Annie Crawford. Ordinarily high-priced counsel, Adams and Generelly announced they would defend the accused *pro bono* as they expressed deep interest in the legal issues that might be presented at trial. Annie Crawford, meanwhile, sat in the women's section of the new prison waiting for her trial.

The trial of the *State v. Annie Crawford* began on March 13, 1912, with the selection of the jury. The defendant walked into the courtroom in Division "B" on that day dressed all in black with a veil to cover her facial features from onlookers. "The form advanced in a slow, labored step, placing its frail weight on the heavier form of a deputy sheriff," one account stated, "and as the two entered the courtroom all eyes were turned in their direction."[11]

DA Adams and his assistant, Warren Doyle, questioned potential jurors on three main points: (1) whether they possessed any objections to a sentence of capital punishment should the defendant be convicted; (2) whether the gender of the defendant would have any bearing on finding her guilty of the crime charged; and (3) whether they could reach a verdict of guilty based on the mostly circumstantial evidence that the prosecution planned to present at trial. One of the jurors questioned during *voir dire* stated simply that he "would not find a verdict of guilty against a woman because it would be violative of his ideas of chivalry towards women." Others questioned would not serve if the defendant received a sentence of death.[12] The jury pool for that first day was eventually winnowed down to the point that both sides agreed on only three jurors. It would take another two days before the full jury of 12 men would be seated to hear the evidence.[13]

Finally, on March 15, 1911, the court began to hear testimony in the trial of Annie Crawford, with Judge Frank D. Chretien presiding. Mary Crawford, Annie's aunt, gave testimony indicating that she suspected Annie's culpability in the death of her sister. Mary also testified, most importantly, that "Annie displayed not the slightest trace of emotion when Elise died." Gertrude, the 19-year-old youngest sister, took the stand after her aunt. While "biting her lips to control her emotion, she told of Annie's strange actions preceding and just after Elise Crawford's death." More interestingly, Gertrude added that "she had seen Annie give Elise 'something in a glass' the night before she died."[14]

The next day, Dr. McGuire appeared on the stand for a brief time and stated that Elise died as a result of opium poisoning. "The pupils of her eyes were contracted to mere pinpoints.... Her respiration was very slow at the rate of one or two a minute. I considered her condition grave and ordered that she be sent to the Charity Hospital," the physician testified.[15] During the course of the doctor's testimony, his assistants carried glass jars containing the victim's stomach and kidneys into the courtroom.

With that witness excused, Dr. Metz took the stand. He stated that "never before had he found such a large quantity of crystallized morphine in the human body." After careful examination of the organs, Dr. Metz found four and half grains of the poison in Elise's body. Anyone witnessing Annie Crawford during the course of the doctor's testimony noticed that the defendant exhibited no emotion and demonstrated scant interest in the testimony. Annie sat stoically, occasionally opening her black fan in front of her already-veiled face.

On the weekend following the testimony of Dr. McGuire, DA Adams clandestinely ordered the exhumation of Elise Crawford's corpse. During the last trial session, Adams had sought to prove that Annie intentionally poisoned Elise, and the prosecution wanted to "clinch things by establishing the true and correct ante mortem condition." After the exhumation, Dr. C. William Groetsch, the assistant coroner for Orleans Parish, removed the brain, the heart, and the spinal column for analysis. Dr. Charles W. Duval of Tulane University in New Orleans examined the organs and determined that "the only thing to mar them was the lesions on the spleen, indicating that death had been caused by opium poisoning."[16]

On the morning of March 19, 1912, defense attorneys Lionel Adams and Joseph Generelly recalled Dr. Metz to the stand where he explained the stomach contents he found in the deceased. Even though Elise's body contained enough morphine to induce death, according to Dr. Metz, this did not preclude death occurring from another cause. However, common medical knowledge at the time indicated that two to four grains of morphine "was a fatal dose."[17] Dr. Metz further testified as to his experience with addicts: "Morphine fiends should not be believed unless corroborated by reliable persons. My [Dr. Metz's] experience with them was that they are inveterate liars, and no dependence was to be placed on what they said. They always tried to hide their fault."[18] Dr. Metz then related that recovery from morphine addiction could not occur without the afflicted person vomiting. Elise vomited the day she came home from work feeling poorly. Even as Dr. Metz described the dimensions of morphine addiction and his findings in front of the court, defense attorney Adams insisted that the doctor's conclusions contained not a scintilla of truth. DA Adams then rose and argued incessantly with the defense about the witness's impeccable credentials in this field.[19]

After a brief recess, the prosecution called Dr. C. William Groetsch, the assistant coroner, to the stand. After he answered a few questions concerning his qualifications, DA Adams submitted the doctor for cross-examination by the defense. Dr. Groetsch admitted under oath to the defense that DA Adams did not produce an order for the exhumation and that the extraction of the deceased's organs took place in a shed near the graveyard. The defense then excused the witness.

The next witness, Dr. Duval, then took the stand. He stated that he performed the autopsy on the deceased at the cemetery where she was buried. During the course of his questioning, Dr. Duval ordered his assistant to bring a series of boxes into the courtroom and place them before the prosecution table. Each box contained a jar with the individual organs of the deceased, which were different from the organs previously produced during Dr. Metz's testimony. When the jars were placed in front of the witness, the doctor explained his findings as they related to each of the organs. The spleen was particularly interesting. According to Dr. Duval, "These lesions in the spleen were the direct result of the opium.... There was no evidence of arteriosclerosis, no diabetes, no apoplexy, not even malaria and as I said before, it all summed up to opium poisoning." The defense attorneys rose in objection, protesting that they were never allowed to examine the evidence presented, nor were any of their experts present at the autopsy. Judge Chretien realized that this point of contention might escalate and removed the jury from the courtroom. The defense reiterated its objection to the evidence and strongly suggested that a defense expert be allowed to examine the organs. The learned jurist granted the defense request and recessed the trial until the following day.

Because of the severity of the offense at stake and the zealousness displayed by the opposing counsels in the case, tempers had begun to flare from the first day of the trial. The opposing sides took swipes at each other to the point that Judge Chretien had to remind the distinguished gentlemen that their decorum did not suit his courtroom and warn them that they should restrain themselves, extending every courtesy to each other in alignment with their profession. Following the court's admonishment, each side abided by the judge's order, but over time the tension between the two sides intensified.

The trial resumed on March 20 with some excitement. When DA Adams continued his examination of Dr. Duval, defense attorney Adams rose quickly and prodded the prosecutor, lecturing him about the finer points of the law. DA Adams protested that he would not be lectured in open court and became enraged at the defense's manner of elaboration. The defense then moved to have DA Adams barred from the courtroom for the duration of the trial. Judge Chretien called the court to order and sternly cautioned the two attorneys against repeating that type of behavior in his courtroom. For a time, the verbal grenades halted. The animosity between the two men had built to a point of perilous mass when DA Adams rose from the prosecution table and approached defense attorney Adams. When the elder jurist saw the young district attorney rise, he rose in response and met his opponent halfway between the two tables. They stood there when defense attorney Adams stated, "If you're looking for trouble, I'll send my friends to you." DA Adams did not cower and replied, "I couldn't fight a duel with a man of your character." Attorney Adams struck his opponent across the face with an open left hand. At that point, Judge Chretien lost all control and the courtroom broke into a brawl. During the commotion, Dr. Duval's samples of Elise's organs crashed to the floor and his glass slides were crushed underneath the feet of the parties as they continued their fistfight. Sturgis Adams, DA Adams's brother, also a member of the bar, jumped into the fray when he witnessed two men grab his brother from behind. During the fracas, the defendant Annie sought the security closest to the bench, where she cowered away from the violence.

Judge Chretien quickly ended the altercation by summoning the police officers in the corridor adjacent to the court to help restore order. DA Adams and his allies exited the courtroom and went to his office located down the hall, while Lionel Adams and the rest of the defense team remained in the courtroom. Inspector James J. Reynolds gave Corporal Casey instructions to arrest the combatants. The corporal complied and arrested both of the Adamses, but informed them that Inspector Reynolds would parole them provided they gave their "word of honor" that they would not fight again. The two men relented and were immediately released.[20] This did not end the accusations flying between the two parties, however: The prosecution contended that the defense started the fight to purposely destroy Dr. Duval's evidence—a claim the defense vehemently denied, taking offense at the implication.

With order restored, on March 22, the trial began again in earnest. The prosecution sought to discover and then reveal the motive behind Annie's crimes. Gertrude Crawford took the stand as a matter of redirect and stated that Annie forged checks to obtain family money that she did not earn. Under oath, Gertrude insisted that she did not discover Annie had forged checks in her name until she officially stood accused of murder. These statements, combined the fact that Annie was the beneficiary for the insurance policies for her sister, mother, and father, supported the prosecution's theory that greed was Annie's motive in committing the poisoning.[21]

DA Adams also paid particular attention to the testimony of several nurses at the sanitarium where Annie had worked prior to the death of her sister. Helena Parker, one of the nurses at the former sanitarium, stated that she saw Annie at the hospital in the medicine dispensary two weeks prior to Elise's death. "The drug [morphine] was kept in bottles and it was the custom at the hospital to leave the cupboards open," Parker testified. "Annie was standing directly in front of the cupboard." At the time, Parker could not tell how long Annie had been standing near the shelves containing drugs without any supervision.[22]

At this point in the proceedings, DA Adams offered two exhibits into evidence: the first statement Annie Crawford made where she denied the use of narcotics, and the second statement where she admitted to the use of morphine. Judge Chretien accepted the statements the prosecution entered, especially the second statement, as a confession.

In the last day of the trial testimony, DA Adams called Mr. C. F. Laws, a bookkeeper at the Hibernia National Bank. Laws testified about the accounts held by various members of the family, including Annie and Gertrude. In an account Annie opened in July 1911, the balance at the time of the death of her sister was $1.27. The prosecution sought to show that because of her dwindling funds, along with the paranoia she experienced as a morphine addict, Annie panicked and searched for ways to acquire more money to bolster her account. Through this testimony, coupled with Annie's effort to defraud her younger sister, Gertrude, of the funds she had in her checking account, DA Adams tried to establish Annie's motive as greed.

DA Adams then recalled Gertrude to the stand, where he presented a check allegedly written by the witness on June 13, 1911, in the amount of $20.00. When asked about the check, Gertrude stated that she did not authorize her sister to sign the document in her stead. Another check DA Adams presented to the witness had $7.52 written in the blank showing the amount of the check. The witness stated that she wrote the original check in the amount of $7.00 and her sister Annie filled in the $0.52 at a later date. She recognized the handwriting of the added number and averred that was not her handwriting. "When I gave her the check for $7.00," Gertrude testified, "I did not know that she had exhausted my account entirely.... Annie had charge of my banking account. I had originally $131 to my credit in the bank.... Annie was my agent and I had perfect confidence in her."[23]

To attest to Annie's character and lessen the effect of the damning evidence presented by the prosecution, the defense sought the testimony of a man of the cloth who would defend Annie in the darkest of circumstances. The right Rev. J. L. Sutton, chaplain to the state penitentiary in Baton Rouge, frequently visited Annie in her cell in the Orleans Parish Prison. In his visits with Annie, the Reverend Sutton made many observations concerning the defendant that defense attorneys Adams and Generelly wanted placed into the record. The Reverend Sutton testified:

> I have seen many criminals in the time that I have been chaplain of the state penitentiary in Baton Rouge.... A criminal is always bitter or sarcastic when approached by anyone, even though he is a friend. Annie Crawford is not such a person ... she is always just as polite as though she is entertaining someone in her own home, and her manners are polished.... The Annie Crawford I knew is a tender-hearted girl who ... who is prayerful and fears God.[24]

When asked if Annie discussed the case with him, the Reverend Sutton stated that he had mentioned her sister Elise on several occasions; when he did Annie, she would sob uncontrollably. Her demeanor during the trial, the Reverend Sutton concluded, did not properly represent the character within her that the Reverend Sutton observed.[25]

After the presentation of evidence that Annie Crawford had a morphine addiction, embezzled family money, acted as if she were in control of the Crawford clan, and eventually murdered her sister to conceal her shortcomings, the defense stepped forward. Near the conclusion of the trial, Annie's legal team attempted to show that Elise Crawford wanted to kill herself. Defense attorney Adams based this theory on the fact that six years prior to her death, Elise had given birth to a child that she gave up for adoption. Adams suggested, "Elise was morose and despondent because of this dark chapter in her life and took poison."[26]

In a final attempt to vindicate their client, the defense called Annie Crawford to the stand to testify on her own behalf. The defendant slowly made her way to the stand from the defense table in her usual black dress and waist coat, with her face covered with a thin black veil. Annie moved the veil from her face, swore before the court, and sat down gingerly. She stated that she had "mixed morphine tablets, which she intended taking herself, with calomel and soda tablets she had been mixing for her sister during her illness." The defendant continued: "Although she knew Elsie was a morphine fiend, it was the first time she had told any of it since the trial began."[27] Annie also testified that after giving her sister the lethal dose, she flushed the rest of the morphine tablets down the toilet. With her brief testimony on the record, the prosecution had no questions for Annie, and Judge Chretien adjourned the court until the following Monday.

Closing arguments repeated the differing theories of the crime offered by the two sides. The prosecution and the defense closed their cases on the late evening of March 25. Judge Chretien then charged the jury and stated that he would stay in his office for a reasonable amount of time until the jury reached its verdict. In the early morning hours of March 26, the jury reached a decision. Due to the late hour, however, the respected jurist stated they could announce their decision when the court convened later that day.

On March 26, 1912, court in Division "B" reconvened at 10:40 a.m. to hear the much-anticipated jury verdict in *State v. Annie Crawford:* "The jury stood nine to three for acquittal, the minority holding out for a verdict of murder with capital punishment." Given the forgery accusations that had arisen during the trial, the prosecution debated whether to charge the now-vindicated spinster, but decided another trial would be too expensive. DA Adams declared on March 30 that the prosecution would not retry Annie for the murder of Elise.[28]

Released on bail, Annie Crawford left New Orleans and moved to Port Arthur, Texas, with her other sister, Mrs. Edward Lee. After she left the city, history lost track of the once-accused murderer.

The case of Annie Crawford tested all the assumptions of a civilized society. Annie came from a respectable family, but that respect declined as the circumstances surrounding her alleged sins were made known in the media. The charges that she remained cold and aloof during the course of her trial seemed to have merit. Her predilection to control both the finances and the lives of her family, combined with her addiction to a dangerous narcotic, suggested the makings of a treacherous personage. But would she be willing to go as far as murdering members of her family to collect the death benefits associated with each member's demise? The answer to that question remains a mystery. An all-male jury determined Annie Crawford to be a woman of her time, even with the burdens that she carried, and found her incapable of murdering Elise, her sister, much less her whole family. The case of Annie Crawford warrants mention as one of the most bizarre and tragic cases in the annals of Louisiana crime.

The Mysterious Case of Dr. Weiss

> *"I am not gifted with second sight. Nor did I see a spot of blood on the moon last night. But I can see blood on the polished marble floor of this Capitol. For if you ride this thing through, you will travel with the white horse of death..."*—Representative Mason Spencer, Louisiana Legislature, September 8, 1935

A respectable Baton Rouge, Louisiana, physician received a letter from a nun living in Cork, Ireland, where she expressed heartfelt emotions at the recent loss of the physician's son:

> I cannot refrain from coming to you this morning with my whole sympathy.... I have talked of nothing else during the last day or two but of the awful catastrophe which has befallen you. Our hearts ache for you as the artful death of your gentle, intellectual wonderful son.... If only he had been somebody else who had delivered the state of this man! You may be sure that God had regard for the motives and intentions more than the acts, and your boys' intentions were noble and patriotic. May he rest in peace.[1]

In another message of sympathy and strength, signed only as "Seven Friends," a telegram arrived for a young widow who had lost her husband at the same home. The writing conveyed a martyr-like sentiment. The spokesman for the Seven Friends lamented, "We hope it will somewhat assuage your grief and enable you to bear your sorrow to know that the heroism and self-sacrifice which prompted your husbands [*sic*] act have excited the admiration of a group of Americans ... we believe this expression to you expresses the opinion of millions of our fellow citizens."[2]

In perusing these documents, a reader would think that the individual being praised for his valor had single-handedly defeated an enemy of the United States, giving his last full measure in achieving that objective. In actuality, the sympathy that poured from these historical artifacts belongs to a man who for more than 80 years has been made a fiend—the assassin of a godsend. The young man, history tells us, was Dr. Carl Austin Weiss, Jr., who has forever been demonized as the man who shot and killed Senator Huey "Kingfish" Long; Dr. Weiss died immediately after killing Long, in a torrent of more than 61 bullets fired from the weapons brandished by Long's body-guards.

For as long as historians have been investigating this case, controversy after controversy has confronted those who researched the circumstances leading to this seminal event, ultimately raising more questions than answers. Many investigators have endeavored to prove that Dr. Weiss conceived and executed the assassination plan on his own, with his motive stemming from the auspices of the "Long Machine" in operation in Louisiana. Other investigators have hatched various theories of conspiracy to add more myths than facts about the events. To understand the events as they transpired, one must examine both Long and Weiss to definitively comprehend the clashing of their destinies. Then, and only then, can we understand the machinations at work that seek to keep any conspiracy theories alive and cast Dr. Weiss as a malevolent villain.

Huey Pierce Long was born on August 30, 1893, in Winnfield, Louisiana, the eighth child to Huey P. Long, Sr., and Caledonia Tyson. One of the children died while still in infancy, but the rest lived to take a lively part in Louisiana politics for the next 60 years. Long's mother had a photographic memory, which Long inherited and demonstrated throughout his life with pinpoint accuracy. The young man educated himself even when not in school, though he was not a good student, nor did he like the hard-scrabble life his father consigned to the children. In fact, while enrolled at Winnfield High School, Long was expelled from the institution just before his 17th birthday, in 1910, when he masterminded and oversaw the actions of a cliquish group with behaviors that would later define his political career.

While in high school, Long formed a secret brotherhood whose members would not obey the rules prescribed by the school's administrators. Long led a group of young people who wore red ribbons on their lapels that distinguished them from the rest of the student body. If students refused to wear the red ribbon, they were ostracized and forbidden from participating in certain school activities, such as the baseball team and the debating team. Teachers warned him that his behavior warranted suspension, but Long continued his brazen antics and even published a newsletter where he condemned teachers. School officials quickly grew tired of Long's actions and expelled him from the school. But Long did not stop there: He circulated a petition around Winnfield and got the principal fired.[3]

Leaving high school without a diploma, Long felt deterred from leaving the small town of his birth and striking out on his own. Nevertheless, at 17 years old, Long took a traveling salesman job selling Cottolene, a lard substitute. In that role, he went from town to town in the South, hosting baking competitions to prove his product was better than the competitors'. According to one biographer, Long "became a persistent and skillful salesman who combined his wit and outgoing personality with iron-willed determination to make a sale."[4] Although he did not believe in organized religion, because of his eidetic memory, Long was able to quote Scripture at will—a tactic he used to influence the same clients into buying the product. Despite his best efforts, the company fired him due to slumping sales.

Long then took a job with a company selling cured meats and canned goods, but the young salesman drained his expense account so quickly that the company had no choice but to fire Long. At that point, in 1911, Long's mother, Caledonia, convinced Long to move to Shawnee, Oklahoma, where Huey's brother, George, operated a dental practice. Caledonia hoped that Long would be a preacher. Although he enrolled at Oklahoma Baptist University, Long lasted only one semester, later telling George he was not cut out to be a preacher. At that time, Long decided he wanted to be a lawyer and enrolled at the law school at the University of Oklahoma in Norman. On the way there, however, he lost his money at a roulette wheel. While wandering the streets, he eventually convinced a produce company to hire him as a salesman while he went to law school part-time. Subsequently he attended the law school, but his grades were less than stellar: three Cs and an Incomplete for the four classes in which he enrolled. It appeared that the Norman nightlife was too much of a distraction for Long.[5]

Looking for employment again, Long found a position with the Faultless Starch Company, where he became a regional sales manager in 1912. During this time, Long developed his skill for oratory—he could convince nearly anyone to buy the product that he sold at the time. It was also during this time that Long took a Christmas vacation in which he asked for the hand of a woman he had met while hosting a baking contest in Shreveport two years earlier. Rose McConnell rejected Long's proposals several times before she finally relented. The two were married on April 12, 1913, and the union subsequently produced four children. In the following year, the Faultless Starch Company laid Long off, but he soon gained employment with the Chattanooga Medicine Company, though this sojourn would also prove to be short-lived.[6]

In the summer of 1914, after being convinced by his brother Julius, Long decided to attend Tulane Law School. Julius Long would finance his brother's studies. Huey P. Long studied law for a year and then asked the Louisiana Supreme Court for special dispensation to test before the bar. Long passed the exam easily and then returned to Winnfield to practice law as a member of the Louisiana bar.[7] Even when he became a lawyer, Long knew that this profession would not be the end of his rise; he had more ambitious goals in life—governor, senator, perhaps president.

In 1918, Long won the election to become Railroad Commissioner of Louisiana. In this role, he introduced a theme that would dominate his speeches and his actions throughout his political campaigns in the future. Long aimed his sights at the "Wall Street money devils" and large corporations that fed upon the weak and downtrodden to produce outrageous profits, not sharing their wealth with anyone. With the death of his superior, John T. Michel, in 1921, and the succession of Francis Williams, Long became the lone commissioner. When the state legislature rewrote the Louisiana Constitution in 1921, the Railroad Commission became the Public Service Commissions and Long its head commissioner.

As Public Service Commissioner, Long embarked on a campaign of lambasting political opponents. The new commissioner slandered then-governor John M. Parker by stating that the state's chief executive was a pawn of Standard Oil Company. Authorities arrested Long on charges of criminal libel and later released him on a $5,000 bond. The court, under Judge H. R. Brunot, found Long guilty of two counts of libel; it gave him a $1 fine for the first count and a 30-day suspended sentence for the second. When Long refused to pay the penalty, a collection was taken up in the courtroom where the trial occurred to pay Long's fine. Voters remembered Long's chutzpah when it came to dealing with Louisiana's political power elite, and the ever-ambitious Long decided to run for governor in 1924.[8]

Canvassing the state with circulars and stumping speeches, Long's campaign for the 1924 gubernatorial race hinged upon the issue of race and religion. One candidate, Hewlett Bouanchaud, campaigned as an anti–Klan candidate; Henry L. Fuqua advocated ending the racial and religious discord; and Long was acknowledged as the "champion" of the Klan. Long placed a distant third in the primary, but would not be deterred by his poor finish. Immediately after the 1924 loss, Long set about to campaign for the next election to be held in 1928.

Setting his sights on the governor's office, Long promised free textbooks so that children would be able to attend school, highways and roads improvements, lower utility rates, free bridges, and construction of more charity hospitals and insane asylums. He also promised the poor people of Louisiana that the rich men of the nation—more particularly, Standard Oil Company—would be held accountable for their fabulous wealth and inaction to assist the poor people of the country. Long won the 1928 gubernatorial election and then set his sights on punishing his political enemies, garnering power to control every facet of local government, and filling his coffers with riches in exactly the way that he so publicly condemned. Even though he won with a plurality in the northern part of the state, the votes of the electorate in New Orleans always eluded Long—and it was there that he first sought to show the city that now he was in charge.

Upon assuming the governorship in 1928, Long quickly sought to keep his campaign promises while at the same time launching an all-out frontal assault on the Standard Oil Company. The new chief executive believed that if he could get Standard Oil to pay for the improvements and reforms that he promised, the poor people of Louisiana would be eternally grateful and continue to allow his bidding to take place within the state. Of course, Long would have to deal with the members of the Louisiana legislature for his program to receive approval. With a stealth that reflected the sort of shrewd politician he became, Long went to the legislature and bribed its members into action. When that tactic did not work, lawmakers were apt to find themselves the targets of his wrath. In one instance, when Long stated what he wanted to accomplish by going after Standard Oil Company, a legislator who vehemently resented Long's tactics put a hardbound volume of the Louisiana State Constitution in front of him and asked, "Maybe you've heard of this book? It's the Constitution of the state of Louisiana." Long arrogantly replied, "I'm the Constitution around here now!"[9]

On March 18, 1929, Long called a special six-day session of the Louisiana legislature to consider a bill that would have placed an occupational tax of five cents on every barrel of refined crude oil. The leaders of Standard Oil, learning of the proposal, stated that if the bill passed, they would have to lay off thousands of their workers in Louisiana. Moreover, the legislators from the small oil-producing parishes would have to face angry, out-of-work voters in their next election, as the tax that Long proposed would devastate employment in their respective districts. Additionally, on March 25, 1929, Representative Harvey Bogan of Shreveport introduced legislation that would reassert and define the powers between the three branches of government, thereby hamstringing Long's efforts to effect despotic control over the state. Fearing that the resolution would pass, Long panicked and tried to have a key supporter, Speaker of the State House John Fournet, adjourn the House *sine die* without any date assigned for resumption of the proceedings. After several loud protests from the House floor, a fistfight began between pro– and anti–Long forces in the chamber. Several of Long's most outspoken critics in the House lashed out in fisticuffs to gain control of the free-for-all. On the following Monday, Speaker Fournet returned and apologized, but the damage had been done. Not seeing any other alternative, the House of Representatives decided that Long had to be removed from office, and impeachment proceedings began immediately.[10]

On April 8, 1929, impeachment proceedings began in the State House. Long's opposition filed charges on 19 counts of abuse of power including, but not limited to, taking bribes and offering bribes to other members of the legislature. They even went as far as charging the new governor with plotting to have a member of the legislature murdered (although this charge may have been a little far-fetched for the state's new chief executive).[11] The witnesses called included state representatives who accused Governor Long of bribing them with state jobs to vote for the occupational tax on refined crude. Representative Adolphe Gueymard, of Iberville Parish, testified that "Governor Long tried to win him over to the support of his proposed occupational tax on oil refineries by offering him a job with the Highway Commission," and sought to influence a bank into forgiving a loan that Gueymard had made with a local bank. Gueymard's testimony was corroborated by a senator from Iberville Parish, C. K. Schwing. Representative Dave Richarcce of St. James Parish testified that he saw and overheard Governor Long offer Representative Felix Delaune of St. Charles Parish employment with the Highway Commission if he would change his vote to support Long's proposed tax on crude oil.[12] In all, 10 witnesses testified in the impeachment hearings. When the final vote was taken, on April 7, 1929, the Louisiana House voted for Long's impeachment.[13]

Facing the loss of the most coveted political office in Louisiana, a crafty politician such as Long still had one last gasp of political breath. The Louisiana Senate needed only a two-thirds majority to convict Long. However, at the midnight hour, several senators who owed Long political favors signed what became known as the "Round Robin," where they questioned the procedural aspects of the indictment and denied the necessary two-thirds of the Senate votes needed to convict the governor. Without support from the Senate to oust Long, the incident died, but Long became even more determined to hold all power within the state and make sure his enemies never crossed him again. When he asked for supporters to grant him the power he desired before the impeachment proceedings, he would sat "please." After the impeachment proceedings, he became what he termed a "dynamiter": If people would not agree to his demands, "I dynamite 'em out of my path."[14]

In the first few months following the impeachment, Long politicized every state office he could think of at the time. In every parish in Louisiana, "Longites" held an office so that if local authorities refused to support Long's designs, the governor would make sure that local funds would not be received or a new badly needed road would bypass a particular municipality. Julius Long, Huey Long's older brother, once said of his sibling, "There has never been such an administration of ego and pomposity since the days of Nero."[15]

With control of the state firmly in his grasp, Long next set his sights on national office. When he became governor, Long founded a newspaper entitled the *Louisiana Progress*. In it, he advocated his dream of sharing the wealth of the nation's richest corporations with poor people all over the United States. Strictly populist in scope, Long hoped to exert the same influence he had in Louisiana over the rest of the nation. With that goal in mind, in 1930, Long announced he would run in the 1932 election for the U.S. Senate seat occupied by J. E. Ransdale. In his campaign, Long played on the anger of the common people by going after the conservative Ransdale, who had been serving his constituents faithfully since 1913. In an audacious move, Long also announced that he would not resign from the governor's office unless his lieutenant governor, Paul Cyr, who was a fervent anti–Longite, failed to carry through Long's programs. Essentially, when Long eventually won the election for Ransdale's seat, he served as both governor and U.S. senator—an illegal and unethical practice. Publicly, very few people opposed Long, but secretly, a base of dissension grew as he went to Washington, D.C., and attempted to use the same tactics there as he had in Louisiana. Unfortunately for Long, his behavior, demeanor, and lack of respect for his colleagues proved detrimental to anyone taking him seriously. The old adage of "a big fish in a little pond" certainly applied to Long, but he was a U.S. senator and even began to make his way into the national government spotlight. In turn, the powers that be in the nation's capital started keeping an eye on the junior senator from Louisiana.

When Long arrived in Washington, D.C., he displayed the attributes that made him popular with the poor of Louisiana and disgusted the polite society with which he had contact. Scratching his backside while making speeches and waving his hands incessantly gave the new senator an air of buffoonery, while at the same time hiding an intelligence that could sway even the most stubborn opponent. However, immediately after arriving in the capital and taking his senatorial oath of office, Long rushed back to Baton Rouge, the state's capital, to deal with a power grab by the ousted lieutenant governor. A few days later, Long returned to Washington, but this would become a pattern with the new senator: He spent more days away from the senate than the number of times he actually voted in his first year in office.

Whenever Long rose to give speeches and introduce new legislation, he always targeted the rich. His accusations repeatedly claimed that the failure of rich corporations to share any profits with the common people was one of the causes for the Great Depression. He even introduced a tax bill under which people with personal incomes exceeding $2 million would be forced to relinquish 65 percent of those earnings back to the government as a surtax. No bill that Long introduced in the Senate ever received the votes needed to pass, and his colleagues began to ignore the senator from Louisiana.[16] President Franklin Delano Roosevelt, however, would later realize that Long's popular and seemingly backwoods rhetoric masked an evil and dangerous political genius.

Even while maintaining his rather unsavory reputation with the other senators in Washington, Long still kept his eye on elections within Louisiana. In September 1932, Long backed his friend and longtime supporter, John Overton, against his former-ally-turned-bitter-enemy, Edward Broussard, in the upcoming state senate race. Long also campaigned heavily for two New Orleans representatives to ensure he maintained control over Louisiana politics.

When the campaigning started for the upcoming senatorial election, rumors circulated regarding corruption throughout Louisiana. These rumors reverberated back to Washington. Overton won the election, but accusations of voter fraud proved true. In one New Orleans precinct, for example, voting commissioners tabulated the votes before the polls officially closed. After the election, Broussard alleged that Long used dummy candidates and enlisted the help of Texas Senator Tom Connally to support his nefarious aims. Connally held hearings, questioned witnesses, and then reported his findings to the U.S. Senate. That august body would wait until 1933 to investigate the elections any further.[17] Later, a full-fledged Internal Revenue Service investigation would lead to more telling reports of corruption.

By mid–1932, Long controlled Louisiana through his hand-picked successor (and puppet), Oscar K. Allen, and set his sights on the highest office in the land. Long took his local politics to the national stage. When Roosevelt won the Democratic nomination for president of the United States and then the general election, Long felt that the new chief executive owed him favors because of all the hard work that Long had put into the campaign. Soon after the election, Long perceived that Roosevelt had no intention of keeping his campaign promises and set about to denigrate the administration, much as he had done to so many political enemies back in Louisiana. However, detractors at home now began to complain to the federal government about the political conditions in the state.

In a pamphlet sent to the Louisiana legislature on May 9, 1932, a concerned citizen named Harry Gamble from New Orleans spoke for the common-sense faction of Louisiana, when he so eloquently articulated his complaints:

> A virulent political pestilence seized Louisiana four years ago. Bombastic promises, bombastic modes of campaign, bombastic exaggeration of every evil, bombastic cures for everything.... Bombast was enthroned, and Bombast was sworn in as governor. There followed the most dazzling era of high pressure selling, colossal waste and stealage, impudent misrepresentation, and scandalous self-praise.[18]

Gamble played on the emotions of those who had either figured out the dastardly motives of the state's chief executive or benefited from the corruption and honestly believed Long to be their Messiah. "Communities prostrated themselves at the feet of a political bully," Gamble lamented, "courageous and honest men dropped to their knees, and for civic benefit suffered insults and endured crack-brained mastership, that otherwise would have met with a horse whip."[19]

Citizens in Louisiana, in addition to Gamble, felt the need to express their concerns over Long's behavior and blatant corruption, along with the way that the senator's administration ran roughshod over the people of his home state. The people did not want the corruption to spread to their nation's capital in the same way that it had in Louisiana. An attorney from New Orleans, Mr. Shirley G. Wimberly, thought the exposure of Long's evil empire important enough to travel all the way to Washington, D.C., to deliver a radio address to the nation, "with a view of acquainting them [Americans] with the facts concerning Long and his evil reputation." Wimberly's original idea failed when the local radio stations refused to allow his access to the airwaves to slander a sitting U.S. senator. Not to be deterred, Wimberly mimeographed the address he intended to read on the air and sent copies of the scathing Long indictment to every sitting senator in Washington, D.C. Wimberly generalized his allegations in such a way that he sounded knowledgeable, yet frustrated at the lack of attention to the ruin that "Longism" had brought to Louisiana and the threat it posed to democracy.

In his address, Wimberly rambled on to describe several instances of Long's petulant temper tantrums and narcissistic behavior, his consistent and heavy-handed attempts at controlling every aspect of Louisiana politics, his vile and vitriolic remarks directed toward his enemies or anyone he considered an enemy, and his practice of "rewarding his faithful henchmen with a pitiful part of the enormous spoils, and dealing out punishments and reprisals with a ruthless and pitiless hand to all who dare to oppose or defy him." Wimberly pleaded with the senators to reopen the Broussard-Overton investigation, seeing it as a meaningful gesture "that the United States Senate is still a place where Evil and Wrong are not countenanced and where justice and Right prevail."[20] The Overton investigation, Long's political foes hoped, would finally bring the "Kingfish" and his minions to justice for the pillaging of Louisiana. (Long adopted the nickname "Kingfish" after the humorous leader of the Mystic Knights of the Sea lodge in the popular radio comedy show, "Amos-n-Andy.")

Answering Wimberly's plea, on February 3, 1933, the Senate Committee on Elections reopened its investigation into the senate election of John Overton. Even Long's brothers, Julius and Earl, testified as to the acceptance of bribes from various road contractors and utility companies. In typical Kingfish fashion, after the hearings adjourned on February 17, 1933, and as soon as Long returned to Washington, the senator began making speeches on the floor of the Senate berating the committee investigating the Overton election. Long resorted to calling the lead counsel of the committee, Samuel Ansell, a "liar, crook, scoundrel, forger, dog-faced son of the wolf," compelling Ansell to file a lawsuit against Long for libel wherein Ansell sought $500,000 in damages. Ansell later resigned from the committee. When the hearing reconvened in October 1933, the committee members found that even if Louisiana had held an honest election, Overton would still have been the victor. The committee also found that Louisiana elections were characterized by "fraud" and "abhorrent practices," no doubt due to the actions of the Long machine.[21]

In June 1933, in an attempt to sway Long into returning to Roosevelt's fold, the president summoned the Louisiana senator to the White House for a meeting. The one issue that Long could not be dissuaded from promoting was state control over local patronage. Long hoped that he could convince the president into returning control over federal patronage back to him. At this meeting, Roosevelt ignored Long's homey behavior for a few short moments. When Long left the meeting, he became more frustrated and vowed he would not work with President Roosevelt.

In August 1933, a songwriter by the name of Gene Buck invited Long to spend an evening at the Sands Point Club on Long Island, New York. Long was known to be a heavy whiskey drinker, and his excesses when presented with the finest alcoholic drinks became evident that evening. Eventually, he made his way to the men's room to relieve himself. While in the restroom, the Kingfish stumbled to a urinal and began to urinate. He then turned toward the gentleman standing at the next urinal to his right and began urinating on the man's shoes. The outraged man promptly slugged Long in the face, opening up a severe cut over his left eye. Those who despised Long offered medals to the man who assaulted him and celebrated the embarrassment with great fanfare. Gentlemen all over the nation expressed regret that they were not the ones who taught Long a lesson in manners. In a vain attempt to lessen his chagrin, Long claimed that bankers planned the attack and that, instead of one man using a fist, three or four men with knives had assaulted him. The senator even suggested that Al Capone orchestrated the whole incident at Sands Point at the behest of Long's banker enemies. The assault on Long Island signified the beginning of an assault on the Kingfish's empire, both in Louisiana and the nation's capital.[22]

The Kingfish usually threw himself headlong into the elections in the New Orleans, but with his most recent troubles, his advisors strongly suggested that he stay away from Crescent City politics. As usual, Long felt he knew better and chose to get involved again. Mayor T. Semmes Walmsley, once Long's close ally, had distanced himself from the senator after Walmsley expressed his support for the Roosevelt administration and the New Deal. Walmsley also led a faction of the Democratic Party in New Orleans known as the "Old Regulars," who had controlled the political machinations in the city since Reconstruction. When Long controlled the federal patronage, he blocked any member of the Old Regulars from gaining any employment under federal auspices. When Walmsley ran for reelection in 1933, Long sought to punish the Old Regular's disloyalty by running his own candidate; the resulting election can only be described as the beginning of a second Civil War.

On December 3, 1933, prior to the congressional and mayoral elections, Long announced that National Guardsmen or state troopers would be sent to the 6th Congressional District where the Long candidate, Mrs. Bolivar Kemp, was running for the seat once occupied by her late husband. The citizens of the district Kemp represented resented the fact that no other candidates had entered the race. In turn, large groups of men traveled to Amite, Louisiana, where Mrs. Kemp lived and "raided two courthouses to seize and burn ballots, and [halt] State Highway Department trucks loaded with campaign circulars and burned the literature." The First Assistant Attorney General for the State of Louisiana, Long supporter George M. Wallace, invoked federal election law, which threatened to punish anyone interfering with a federal election with a $5,000 fine and 10-year stint in federal prison. From his headquarters in New Orleans, Long and his cronies met to discuss strategy. His aides heard the Kingfish state, "We are going to have that election." Election officials later discovered that candidates other than Mrs. Kemp never appeared on the ballots for that election.[23] Long, it seemed, feared leaving Louisiana meant that he would lose the omnipotent control over the state he once enjoyed.

When he returned to Washington, Long skirted his committee assignments. That abandonment of his duties, combined with his Sherman tank approach to diplomacy, the alienation of his senate colleagues, and his open disdain for President Roosevelt, signaled his demise as a U.S. senator. One observer noted:

> His Louisiana empire tottering, the Roosevelt administration treating him like a smallpox epidemic, and his senatorial "bloc" in complete desertion, Kingfish Huey's ears are ringing with a horrid but unmistakable murmuring: "It won't be Long now" ... But equally true is the fact that the Senate, sharply out of patience with the Senator from Louisiana, his demeanor, and his methods, is cocked and primed to dump him unceremoniously down the Capitol steps at the first opportunity—not waiting until 1936.[24]

Although his national colleagues wanted him gone, even their ostracism was not enough to restrain Long. It seemed as though the more exposure his corruption received, the more paranoid he became and the more he blamed the financially affluent members of American society for his own lack of character and moral direction. Long's subsequent actions tested the loyalty of even his most trusted subjects, and his political power waned.

In 1934, to counter President Roosevelt's New Deal legislation, Long introduced his "Share the Wealth" plan in the Senate. In it, he proposed everyone would have a home, a car, a radio, and "ordinary conveniences." Senate support for Long's proposal was dismal at best, but the poor around the nation who had been suffering from the ravages of the Depression flocked to Long's standard, joining chapters of the Share the Wealth Society as fast as they could be organized around the nation. Building upon the idea that he started in Louisiana with the newsletter *Louisiana Progress,* Long and his assistants adapted the state publication for national consumption in the form of *American Progress.* The problem with Long's utopian plan rested on the numbers themselves and the means by which the program would work. Long responded with ambiguity whenever questioned about the particulars. With his societies and his theme song, "Every Man a King," drawing public notice, Long hoped this crusade would draw attention away from his actions against what he termed the disloyal political machine in New Orleans.

Mayor Walmsley had emerged victorious from the mayoral election of 1934 despite Long's meddling. But the Kingfish embarked on a short and vindictive campaign to punish Walmsley and the Old Regulars for their betrayal. Because of his Share the Wealth Plan, Long's popularity on the national stage grew substantially. Most of the poor who joined the societies saw Long as their champion against the rich and the wealthy bankers who seemed to rule the country, according to the senator. Meanwhile, the anti–Long forces in Louisiana planned a *coup d'état* against the Long political machine.

In mid–May 1934, before a scheduled legislative session, approximately 500 anti–Long armed men made their way to the state capitol building with the goal of forcefully dismantling Long's government. Long, through his vast network of informants, learned of the plot ahead of time and cajoled, bribed, and threatened legislators. Long's opponents capitulated and the small army disbanded. Long became even more incensed with Walmsley and the Old Regulars who, Long surmised, were behind the plot to unseat him.[25]

While in Baton Rouge, Long "proposed" a series of bills that would cede control of New Orleans to him on both the political and economic fronts. Long even took control of the New Orleans Police Department, raised taxes on the Cotton Exchange, and allowed a $2,000 tax exemption everywhere except the large cities, including New Orleans. Long also strengthened his hold over the election processes in the state when he had a law passed wherein security for ballot boxes would rest with Long-appointed election supervisors instead of with the respective parish sheriffs. Moreover, he proposed a law making it illegal for local jurisdictions to interfere with state election commissioners who removed voter registration rolls from respective registrars' offices from around Louisiana. As usual, the Louisiana legislature rubber-stamped Long's proposals.[26]

On July 20, 1934, Long sealed the fate of New Orleans, which he felt need to be punished for the Old Regulars' disloyalty. He ordered the state police and the National Guard, now under his direct control, to move into the city and close all of the illegal gambling houses and brothels. Although this was a half-hearted effort on Long's part, the administration of New Orleans saw it as a direct threat to their sovereignty and took up arms to ensure Long went no further. City policemen stood guard over the district attorney's office, daring the soldiers and the troopers to encroach on it. The superintendent of police, George Beyer, stated "he would ignore any orders of Governor O. K. Allen to surrender his office." Just a few days later, in an effort to demonstrate more force, army trucks carrying Louisiana National Guardsmen rolled into New Orleans on July 30. When they dismounted from their trucks, the soldiers marched through Lafayette Square and into the registrar's office located in the Soulé Office Building just off the square. A few hours later, after being alerted to the military presence, Mayor Walmsley approached Gallier Hall, the location of his office. Seeing the Guardsmen across the square, he ordered the police to form a defensive perimeter around the building. A standoff began between the Long and anti–Long forces, as Mayor Walmsley openly defied Long and ordered the police to arm themselves with machine guns from their arsenal. Mayor Walmsley exclaimed, "I hear Huey Long is planning some new kind of *coup d'état* with his troops today. If he tries it, there's going to be plenty of trouble."[27] Even though Mayor Walmsley sought redress and proved successful in gaining an order for the Guardsmen to vacate the registrar's office, Long arrogantly ignored the adjudication of the courts when it came to his exercise of power.

As a result of Long's despotic actions, several New Orleans citizens, through an attorney, made an impassioned plea to the U.S. Justice Department to launch an investigation into Long's actions. Seth Guion, an attorney representing some voters who discovered that their names had been stricken from the voting rolls, wrote a lengthy memorandum to Warren J. Coleman, Assistant District Attorney for New Orleans, where Guion not only outlined his clients' grievances, but also alluded to the graft and corruption that emanated from the highest political offices in the state of Louisiana. Guion elaborated:

> Huey P. Long is neither a peace nor a law officer of the City of New Orleans, State of Louisiana; that he has, with the servile consent and approval of O. K. Allen, governor of Louisiana, taken over all powers and functions confided and trusted by the Constitution ... [and he is] himself exercising and performing the same unlawfully, tyrannically, high-handedly ... with the purpose of endeavoring to break down a Republican form of government in the State of Louisiana and the City of New Orleans.[28]

In an effort to further humiliate Mayor Walmsley, Long rushed through the state legislature a law that made him the virtual dictator of Louisiana. With state statutes in hand, Long announced that he would personally conduct investigations into the corruption in New Orleans city government. Most considered this ironic since Long's administration was the actual source of the corruption in government within the state of Louisiana.[29]

In any event, Long held his hearings in a suite at the Roosevelt Hotel in downtown New Orleans, calling witnesses he wanted to humiliate in front of a broadcast radio audience. Long accomplished his main objective, but the hearings largely served as great theater for citizens of the city and those who witnessed Long make every attempt to consolidate his power. Not content with merely embarrassing his enemies, Long sought to crush, debilitate, and even eliminate their very existence from political life. The poor people of Louisiana viewed Long as their savior and champion; more informed constituents knew that a megalomaniac ruled over their state. By the end of 1934, state forces under Long's control had relaxed their grip on New Orleans, but Long was being compared at the time to other dictators like Mussolini and Hitler who threatened peace. This assertion was not too far-fetched when one considers that while in Washington, Long would rush back to Louisiana at the slightest inkling that a threat to his rule might become manifest. Even with the meteoric increase in membership in the Share the Wealth chapters around the United States, in his home state, anti–Long operatives worked diligently to topple the Kingfish. With the conclusion of the elections of 1934, the National Guardsmen mounted trains and left New Orleans at the end of September. Still, the anti–Long forces looked toward a solution to the problem known as Huey Long.[30]

Near the end of 1934, Long called several special sessions of the state legislature to pass more legislation that he had authored. In that same time period, the mayor of New York City, Fiorello LaGuardia, clamped down on illegal gambling in his city, particularly slot machines. While the Louisiana senator was in Long Island, New York, mob boss Frank Costello approached Long with a lucrative proposition: allow members of Costello's organization to operate slot machines around Jefferson Parish where Carlos Marcello, reputed local mob boss in that area, owned the Jefferson Music Company. The machines would be shipped to Marcello's company and then distributed to bars, restaurants, pharmacies, and gas stations. Long expressed no concern over the transaction because he knew it would be profitable: One of the close members of his circle, state senator Jules Fisher, ran Jefferson Parish as his own fiefdom. Within a short period of time after the installation of the slot machines, Long's organization collected 10 percent of the profits for protecting Costello's operation.[31]

Some of the not so clandestine details of Long's political career surfaced publicly when, after the repeal of Prohibition in 1933, President Roosevelt requested the Treasury Department, under Secretary Henry Morganthau, bring more investigators to bear on the Long case. Even though Long enjoyed ever-increasing national popularity, beneath the brazen buffoon exterior the senator from Louisiana could not help but think that Morganthau and his agents were getting close to exposing his corruption and sending him to a federal penitentiary for a long stay. One might think that Long would have tempered his behavior in the face of this threat; instead, his verbal attacks on the Roosevelt administration became more vitriolic and outlandish. Long voted against every law President Roosevelt proposed aimed at easing the suffering of a weary nation. It appeared that despite his critical rhetoric regarding the rich of the nation and his claim to be the champion of the "little man," Long really strove to be a king in his own right and used the backs of the little man to reach his throne. His ultimate goal, it seemed, was to use those same backs to walk into the White House.

Throughout 1935, Long set the stage for a presidential run against Roosevelt in the 1936 election. Long even went so far as to write a book entitled *My First Days in the White House*. It was purely fantasy, as far as his opponents were concerned, but Long laid the foundation for his run nevertheless. The hatred his enemies exhibited did not seem to faze Long at all, but whispers of assassination, whether real or contrived, preyed on his mind. The Kingfish displayed the paranoia of a dictator, as was duly noted in his 1935 speeches, but Long continued to fight for his Share the Wealth program, taking verbal jabs at whoever felt the necessity to banter with the "distinguished" gentleman from Louisiana. Additionally, Long continued to call special sessions of the Louisiana legislature to do his bidding. One special session in September 1935, in particular, would prove especially significant in the annals of Louisiana history.

The life of Huey P. Long as documented here seemed tailor-made to create conflict and attention; in fact, Long craved both. The boisterous, ill-mannered, and obnoxious man from Winnfield, Louisiana, certainly made his mark on the people of the state and by September 1935 had impressed—or more appropriately, embossed—his brand of politics on the American fabric. Carl Austin Weiss, in contrast, led a tamer, more controlled, and more reputable existence than the man he allegedly murdered. Examination of Weiss's background has left history with many questions about his alleged motive for being remembered as an assassin.

Born in December 1906 (historians cannot exactly target whether it was December 6 or December 18), Carl Austin Weiss was the eldest son of Carl Adam Weiss and Viola Maine of Baton Rouge.[32] The elder Weiss practiced medicine in the Baton Rouge area as an ear, nose, and throat specialist—a rarity in Louisiana. A diligent and dedicated man, the elder Dr. Weiss hardly took time away from his busy practice for relaxation. Described as rather tough on the outside, the elder Dr. Weiss was a very gentle and pious man who had been raised by a strict father who really wanted his son to become a doctor. Carl Adam did not want to enter the medical profession, but abided by his father's wishes.

Dr. Carl Adam Weiss first studied at Jesuit College in New Orleans, apprenticed with a druggist, became a pharmacist, and then studied medicine at Tulane University, where he graduated in 1900. Subsequently, Dr. Weiss returned to medical school to learn a specialty and returned to Baton Rouge to open an ear, nose, and throat clinic. The clinic became a success, and Dr. Weiss became well known to his colleagues as both hard-working and innovative. It was in these footsteps that his son would follow, ultimately becoming more successful than his father.[33]

From all historical indications, Carl Austin Weiss exhibited a quiet personality and a gift of genius. In his early life, he very seldom lost his temper, but his family remembered one time in particular where his temper got the better of him. One Sunday morning, while attending mass at his local Catholic church, Carl noticed that during the sermon one of the regular attendees at the church walked in late. The priest delivering the sermon growled in a low tone, but just enough for the congregation to hear him. Carl went to the priest after the service and made it known that the priest should not have growled at the tardy parishioner. Carl was known throughout his life to stand up to bullies, though he would grow to be a lanky 5 feet 10 inches and weigh no more than 160 pounds. Throughout most of his formative years, young Carl expressed a more than avid interest in a variety of pursuits, including photography and fencing. But guns held a special fascination for him. He loved to hunt, and his first firearm was a .22-caliber Remington rifle. Carl later acquired pistols and became quite the marksman.[34]

At 15 years of age, Carl graduated from St. Vincent's Academy. He immediately enrolled at Louisiana State University, where he majored in engineering, but found he wanted to study medicine. The elder Weiss tried to dissuade his eldest son from becoming a doctor, but Carl would not be deterred and enrolled at Tulane University for his medical studies. Graduating in 1925, Carl then attended the university for two more years of graduate studies. In his last year, he received an internship in pathology from Touro Infirmary. He graduated in 1927 with an M.D. degree.[35]

Following his graduation from Tulane, Carl began a journey of discovery, as he sailed to Europe to study medicine at the American Hospital in Paris. Carl also studied in Vienna, where he learned the latest surgical techniques. Upon his return to the United States in 1930, he served another internship at the world-renowned Bellevue Hospital in New York City. When Carl returned to Baton Rouge, he joined his father in an ear, nose, and throat practice and built quite a patient base on his own.[36]

While working in the clinic, the elder Dr. Weiss remembered a patient who came to visit him with some minor eye discomfort. As he treated the attractive young lady, she mentioned that she studied abroad at the Sorbonne in Paris. The elder Dr. Weiss told the young lady that his son recently returned from studying in Europe and introduced Carl to Miss Yvonne Pavy. When the two met, it was love at first sight. The two courted and on December 27, 1933, Carl and Yvonne were married at the St. Landry Catholic Church in Opelousas, Louisiana.[37]

Carl Weiss had married into one of the most political families in Louisiana. Although Carl's interest in politics was cursory at best, he soon learned of the bitterness of his wife's family toward Huey P. Long. Yvonne's father, Benjamin Pavy, had presided as a district court judge over St. Landry and Evangeline Parishes since first being elected to that position in 1910. Judge Pavy earned the respect of his colleagues and he exhibited the wisdom of Solomon on the bench; very few, if any of his decisions were overturned on appeal. Strong-willed and determined politically, Judge Pavy formed an early opinion of Long when Long approached the judge in open court and offered him a bribe. The judge favored the pretentious politician with some choice expletives and had Long forcefully removed from the court. St. Landry Parish was never a Long stronghold, anyway, so the senator also resented Judge Pavy for his lack of support there.[38] Judge Pavy held a position of great influence within the state and Long could ill afford to have such an enemy. After the confrontation in Judge Pavy's court, Long and Pavy became sworn enemies. Long even had Pavy's brother, a local high school principal, removed from that position and the judge's other daughter removed from her position as a teacher because of his feud with the judge.[39]

Judge Pavy's opinion summed up perfectly what the brazen politician represented: "He [Pavy] considered Huey a false prophet, a shallow politician riding on the backs of lower orders, a pied piper duping the masses with illusions of grandeur—behind it all, a dangerous man, a menace, the nearest thing to Hitler in America." Even though the judge swore his disdain for Long, he did not go out of his way to provoke any unwarranted conflicts with the politician. However, being a principled man and not one to back down from a fight, in 1932, Judge Pavy had five pro–Long election commissioners arrested for violating an injunction and sentenced the Long men to 10 days in jail. Senator Long then called on his stooge, Governor O. K. Allen, to pardon the five commissioners.[40]

Despite the loathing that Judge Pavy had for Long, Carl respected his father-in-law a great deal, and the elder statesman of the Pavy family accepted his new son-in-law with pride and satisfaction. He was even prouder when Carl and Yvonne announced in the summer of 1934 that they expected their first child in the early part of the following year. Yvonne worked at Louisiana State University, and she worried about telling her supervisor that she was pregnant; she was afraid she would not be able to finish the fall semester. Moreover, she and Carl would have to find another place to live because their present residence had stairs that she would not be able to climb as her pregnancy progressed. Carl had planned to build a new house with an office so he would not be far from his family, but the house was far from completion and Yvonne would give birth sooner than they first thought.

Carl's mother, Viola, came up with a solution to their dilemma: Her father had left several houses to her in his estate, and one of them was close to Carl's parents. The house was located at 527 Lakeland Drive in Baton Rouge, not more than a few blocks from the newly completed capitol building. On June 7, 1935, Yvonne gave birth to a baby boy whom the couple named Carl Austin Weiss, Jr.[41]

From all indications, the Weiss and Pavy families enjoyed life to its fullest even as the rest of the world around them struggled with the effects of the Great Depression. Carl enjoyed success in his chosen profession. As the political shenanigans of the Long machine continued unabated, however, the Weisses and Pavys would soon become embroiled in a spectacular controversy that would contribute to a dark Louisiana legacy.

Even though Long faced legal troubles over his control of the election process in Louisiana and questions regarding his business dealings, his unconstitutional actions as both a U.S. senator and governor of Louisiana (for a time he illegally held both offices), and his unquestioning hatred and public loathing of the Roosevelt administration, Long knew he could still exert his influence in his home state. In an attempt to further punish his enemies, Long pushed Governor O. K. Allen to call a special session of the state legislature in early September 1935 to meet and pass some laws he wanted enacted immediately.

On September 7, 1935, Allen contacted legislators around the state for a special session to consider 39 bills later that evening. The bills would take longer than just that night to consider, as discussions lasted until the early hours of Sunday morning. The most telling legislation had to do with House Bill No. 1, which Long clearly aimed at Judge Pavy and the St. Landry district attorney, Lee Garland, who had held that office for more than 44 years. Like Judge Pavy, DA Garland did not think highly of Long. House Bill No. 1 would gerrymander St. Landry Parish to merge it into two adjoining districts allied with Long. This bill easily sailed through committee and was distributed to the House members when they convened later that Sunday morning. Furthermore, Long intended to start a rumor that the Pavy family line contained "negro" blood. In fact, Long prepared a New Orleans printer to print circulars proclaiming that rumor, which were ready to be distributed on the day he was shot. In the racially charged times of 1930s Louisiana, such a claim could prove devastating to the Pavy family, and especially to young Carl, Jr.[42]

The House session began at approximately 10:00 a.m. on February 8, 1935, and extended into the early afternoon hours. At Long's direction, Speaker of the House Allen J. Ellender called for an evening session to commence at

8:00 p.m., to complete voting on the bills. When the legislators broke for a meal and a little relaxation before the evening session, Long retired to his suite on the 24th floor of the capitol building for a light dinner of cheese, crackers, and fruit. At approximately 8:45 p.m., Long, with his entourage of bodyguards, made his way down to the House floor, where he meandered over next to Speaker Ellender and watched the legislators he controlled very carefully to make sure they voted the "right way."[43]

Just before 9:30 p.m., Speaker Ellender adjourned the House for the day. Long walked out of the north door of the House and headed down the hallway to Governor Allen's office. Long wanted to make sure that all of "his" people would be in attendance at the House morning session so that all business could be concluded that day. Long walked into Governor Allen's office but then quickly dashed out, prancing too fast for his bodyguards to keep pace with him. Eyewitness accounts of what occurred next are slightly skewed. Louisiana Supreme Court Associate Justice John Fournet, an avid Longite, stated that he wanted to speak with Long at the time when he saw the senator in the House. Fournet witnessed Long leaving the chamber and tried to catch him before he disappeared from the justice's sight. Once Fournet got to the House floor, he inquired as to where Long was going in such a hurry; the men there responded Long was going to the governor's office.[44]

Fournet then walked leisurely toward the governor's office and happened upon one of Long's bodyguards, Joe Messina. Messina and Fournet were walking together toward Governor Allen's office when they noticed Long rushing out past them. Long walked very briskly with his entourage trying to keep pace. Fournet elaborated:

> Huey made some statement about getting everybody on hand early the next morning, and somebody told him that had been attended to. At that time, a small man in a white, or almost white, suit flashed among us and flashed a gun and shot almost immediately. I immediately put my hand on the man's arm, my left hand, trying to deflect the bullet. There was quite a bit of confusion. One of the boys grabbed him. I shoved him and whoever was holding him, and he fell to the floor—they both went down.[45]

The first shot, according to Fournet, hit Long in the stomach. The senator then ran from the scene, claiming to have been wounded. The man whom Fournet claimed had fired the shot did not lie flat on the floor, but rather crouched and attempted to fire again.

Murphy Roden, another Long bodyguard, attempted to disarm the assailant and suffered a wound to his thumb as it got in the way of the ejector slide of the assailant's weapon, but to no avail. While Roden attempted to subdue the assailant, bodyguards Eliot Coleman, Joe Bates, and Joe Messina raced toward what they believed was gunfire. Just then, shots rang out in the marble hallway, and the assailant's body writhed with every round that struck

The "Assassination Wall" located inside the Louisiana State Capitol Building in Baton Rouge, Louisiana. It is still maintained in remembrance of Long's assassination (Alan Gauthreaux collection).

his head and torso from the weapons of Roden, Messina, Bates, and Coleman.[46] The assailant fell to the hard marble floor again, face down with his face in the crease of his left elbow. By all accounts, the bodyguards emptied the clips of their automatic .38s, culminating in 61 rounds being fired into the body of the assailant. Authorities later identified the man who fired the first shot into Long as a Baton Rouge physician, Dr. Carl Austin Weiss.

The wounded Long staggered down the steps of the capitol. Jimmy O'Connor, a Long supporter, heard the commotion and witnessed Long coming down the stairs holding his right side and bleeding from his mouth. The blood from his stomach wound trickled through his fingers and dripped on the marble floor. "I've been shot," Long murmured to O'Connor, and the young man helped Long to a car outside and shouted to the driver to take them to the Lady of the Lake Hospital.[47]

When O'Connor arrived at the hospital with Long, Fournet was not too far behind them. Fournet removed a pocket knife from his coat and began cutting Long's clothing away so the doctors could examine his wounds. The physicians noticed the senator had a small cut on the inside of his mouth and some slight bruising. Melinda Delage, one of the nurses present at Long's admittance to Our Lady of Lake, also noticed the split lip. When one of the doctors asked Long how the wound occurred, he stated, "Oh, that's where he hit me!" Dr. Arthur Vidrine, superintendent of the Charity Hospital in New Orleans (and a Long appointee to that position), happened to be in Baton Rouge on business and made his way to the hospital in all haste. Long remained conscious as Dr. Vidrine examined the senator. His pulse was weak, but faint and rapid. Dr. Vidrine located what he determined to be an entrance wound just below the right rib cage and an exit wound located on his back just below his ribs on the right side. Another surgeon, Dr. William H. Cook, received a telephone call and immediately made his way to the hospital.[48]

Dr. Vidrine cleaned Long's wounds, typed his blood for a transfusion, and moved him to a room usually reserved for Catholic dignitaries. Drs. Vidrine and Cook noted that Long was going into shock and exhibited symptoms of internal bleeding. The surgeons consulted and pronounced that Long needed emergency surgery if he was to survive his wounds. A small gathering of the senator's advisors and aides met with the surgeons and determined that surgery was the necessary course of action.[49] In the late evening of September 8, Drs. Vidrine and Cook summoned other surgeons to the hospital. The procedure began at approximately 11:00 p.m. After anesthesia had been administered, the operation began. The operating theater became populated with Long's advisors and other unsterilized individuals, still in the suits they wore the whole day, as the surgeons worked to repair the damage caused by a gunshot.[50]

Once the surgery began, surgeons noted that Long had a hematoma in his small bowel and a perforation in his colon. The surgeons sutured the colon and his abdomen. Dr. Vidrine commented after the surgery, "It was nothing. Just a perforation of the intestines."[51]

However nonchalant Dr. Vidrine's statement appeared, Long's condition worsened after the surgery. State police guarded the capitol building and the hospital where Long languished, moving in and out of consciousness. Well-wishers poured in from all over Louisiana and the nation hoping for Long's speedy recovery. Even President Roosevelt stated on the morning after the attack, "I deeply regret the attempt made upon the life of Senator Long of Louisiana. The spirit of violence is un–American and has no place in a consideration of public affairs."[52] All throughout the day of September 9, notes of regrets and sympathy arrived at the hospital, along with wishes for the Kingfish's recovery.

But the hopes of a rapid recovery proved for naught. On September 10, 1935, at 4:10 a.m., Huey P. Long slipped into a coma and died. Mrs. Long requested that no autopsy be performed on her deceased husband.[53]

After Long's death, theories began to surface as to whether a conspiracy existed to kill the senator. Certainly during the course of his political career Long had thrived on the conflict he provoked. One citizen opined that Long made so many enemies in Louisiana that "his career was dotted with predictions that at last he had gone too far and would be overthrown." Calls to investigate Long's death went all the way to Washington, D.C. Clare G. Fenerty, a member of the House of Representatives from Pennsylvania (who also received an appointment in late 1934 to investigate the Long machine in Louisiana), insinuated that a group of men had hatched a plot to murder Long; instead of investigating "the political activities of Senator Long in Louisiana," he said, the commission "should investigate the men who were responsible for instigating the attempted assassination."[54] Fenerty believed the killing of Senator Long registered more strongly in the hearts of the people than any political shenanigans that may have occurred in Louisiana. Fenerty also made the point that Long represented the outspoken opposition to the New Deal legislation; had he formed a new political party, he conjectured, Long was "fully determined to oppose the re-election of President Roosevelt in 1936."[55]

On September 12, 1935, Huey Pierce Long, Jr., was buried on the capitol grounds beneath a sunken garden in front of the building that Long constructed as governor of Louisiana. It has been estimated that more than 200,000 people flowed past the bier while his body lay in state in the capitol rotunda. Just two days before, on September 10, funeral services for Dr. Carl Austin Weiss had been held at St. Joseph's Catholic Church in Baton Rouge, Louisiana. Drawing criticism for attending the funeral and acting as pallbearers were two former governors of Louisiana—John M. Parker and J. Y. Sanders, both diehard Long political enemies. Whether the two stood with the Weisses and participated in the requiem for an accused assassin as a political statement or as a genuine showing of grief and compassion for the slain man has never been revealed. Even though the Weiss funeral did not garner the same number of mourners reported for the Long cortege, Carl Austin Weiss was nonetheless respected and the people in attendance served as a testament to his dedication to his profession, his patients, and his character.[56]

After the burials took place, East Baton Rouge Parish district attorney Fred M. Odom conducted an inquest into the deaths of Long and Weiss on September 15, 1935. DA Odom called a number of witnesses that day in an attempt to discern what motive Carl Weiss could have possibly had in going to the capitol building that night. When the elder Dr. Weiss was called to the inquest stand, he testified that he had been with his son and daughter-in-law all day on September 9, 1935. According to the elder Weiss, that morning his son and daughter-in-law brought their three-month-old son over to his house so that Carl and Yvonne could attend church services. After services, Yvonne returned to the grandparents' residence while Carl made a stop at a flower shop to pick up a bouquet that someone left for their newborn baby boy. After retrieving the bouquet, Carl returned to his parents' home to pick up

The bullet-riddled body of Carl Austin Weiss following his alleged assassination of Huey P. Long on September 8, 1935 (courtesy Louisiana State Archives, Huey P. Long Assassination Collection, Dr. Florent Hardy, Archivist).

Yvonne and the baby and return to their Lakeland Drive home. At approximately 1:00 p.m., Carl, Yvonne, and Carl, Jr., returned to his parents' home for dinner. According to the elder Weiss, "My son ate heartily and joked during dinner." After finishing their meal, the whole Weiss family retreated to the family camp on the Amite River. Yvonne and Carl left their baby son with

Carl's parents on the banks of the river while they indulged in some swimming. Viola, Carl's mother, commented to her husband that Carl looked a little skinny and tired and must find some time to rest.[57]

After the family sojourn at the camp, Carl, Yvonne, and Carl Jr., returned to their home at approximately 7:30 p.m. At approximately 10:00 p.m., Yvonne called her father-in-law looking for Carl. Yvonne sounded worried and informed the elder Weiss that Carl had left the house earlier to attend to a call. At no time during DA Odom's questioning did the investigator ask Dr. Weiss about Carl's state of mind.[58]

DA Odom next called to the stand a witness credited with firing the first shots that hit Weiss—bodyguard Murphy Roden. In recalling the events of the night of September 8, Roden stated that he followed Long out of the House chambers after the session adjourned at approximately 11:00 p.m. Long walked briskly down the corridor leading to Governor Allen's office. Long walked into the governor's office for a brief moment to make sure that all the representatives would be there the next morning to finish the voting for his proposed bills and then walked out again, almost knocking Roden over. As Long walked past him, Roden testified, "At this moment somebody brushed by me, pulled a gun, and thrust it at the senator's stomach and fired." Roden added that after the first shot he grabbed the assailant and they both fell to the floor. "I jerked loose, got up, pulled my gun and began firing." Roden stated that one of his shots hit the assailant in the chin.[59]

Joe Messina, another of Long's bodyguards, testified that he had heard of a plot to kill the senator. In a very emotional manner, he stated that a friend, Sidney Songy, wanted to meet with Long to confer about the plot he overheard. Messina never got the chance to approach Long about the alleged plot on the senator's life. Further into Messina's testimony, he became incoherent, struggling between crying and speaking clearly. Gaining his composure temporarily, Messina averred, "When Dr. Weiss shot, I saw Senator Long jump back and I knew that he had been killed." Messina recalled two men wrestling on the marble floor when he happened upon the scuffle; in response, he "pulled my gun and emptied it at the man who shot Senator Long." DA Odom never contradicted Messina's testimony and it appeared that the official account of what happened that night would rest with those who were closest to Long, both in proximity and in relationship. Even though Roden claimed to have witnessed Weiss pull the gun and force it into Long's stomach, no one actually saw the flash of the muzzle.[60]

DA Odom conducted an inquest into the whole shooting incident, yet never asked any probing questions that would prove more exculpatory for Weiss. With his inquiry concluded, Odom announced that he would conduct no further proceedings into the investigation of the Long and Weiss murders."[61]

After the inquest, the elder Dr. Weiss stated emphatically that his son did not shoot Long, but rather that "in all probability he [Long] was not shot by my son but by one of his bodyguards." Dr. Weiss let it be known that members of the Long political machine steadfastly maintained that young Carl Weiss plotted with anti–Long forces to kill the senator. The elder Dr. Weiss even wrote to Governor Allen and requested an official investigation into the shooting of his son and Senator Long, but the governor never responded to the request. The grieving father told the chief state executive:

> We [the Weiss family] hoped that the whole truth would come to light in the vindication of the memory of our dead son, and if not, then at least the dead would not be slandered and the tragedy exploited for political purposes.... Feeling impelled by that duty which every father owes to protect and guard the memory of their child who has been silenced by death, and can no longer defend himself against slander and calumny.[62]

The elder Dr. Weiss's concerns were not unwarranted. The propaganda generated by the surviving Long machine included unsubstantiated rumors and innuendo regarding Carl Weiss that ranged from the ridiculous to conspiracies of assassination that seemed plausible. For example, Rose Long, Huey Long's bereaved widow, received an anonymous letter from a source identified only as "X We." The author of the letter claimed to know both the Weiss and Pavy families and stipulated that "poor Carl was paid three thousand dollars and the promise if he died his wife and baby would be cared for." The author related that Weiss tried to return the money, but the conspirators who attempted to engage the young doctor as an assassin refused to take the money back. Weiss worried about his family and Benjamin Pavy, Carl's father-in-law, tried to stop Carl from carrying out the plan, but Pavy failed. The author concluded the letter by insinuating that Carl Weiss's loyalty to both families drove him to shoot Long.[63]

One of the more credible stories surfaced during a somewhat clandestine investigation by General Louis Guerre, commander of the Louisiana Bureau of Identification and Investigation. General Guerre sent operatives all over the state to investigate any hints of a conspiracy to murder Senator Long. In one report, the investigator stated that two to three months before the assassination, a meeting took place at the De Soto Hotel in New Orleans in July 1935. At the meeting, anti–Long members of a group calling itself the "Minute Men" gathered to discuss Long's latest abuses of power. Long learned of the meeting and, prior to the gathering taking place, rented a dummy room on the floor above where his aides had microphones on fishing poles hanging in front of the windows to record whatever transpired. The senator expressed particular concern about the activities of the men who met there because of his paranoia. During this meeting, Carl Weiss was allegedly in attendance. The meeting was just a smaller part of a conference organized to plan a march

Monument to Huey P. Long, Capitol Grounds, Baton Rouge, Louisiana. Beneath the statue lies the remains of the former governor and senator (Alan Gauthreaux collection).

on Baton Rouge to oust Long's machine from office, killing the senator if necessary.[64]

After Long's men prepared the transcript from the De Soto Hotel bugging, the senator made a speech on the Senate floor where he became more animated than usual, waving the transcript in the air with theatrical emphasis. Long quoted from the transcript and made an even wider accusation when he proclaimed in front of his Senate colleagues, "Does anyone doubt that President Roosevelt would pardon the man who rids the country of Huey P. Long?"[65] General Guerre's investigation, however, never provided enough tangible evidence to prove that a conspiracy of the anti–Long faction in Louisiana plotted to assassinate the senator and used Dr. Carl Weiss as their instrument of death.[66]

Despite allegations that Dr. Carl Weiss was the scapegoat for a statewide conspiracy fostered by anti–Long forces, Long's bodyguards had to fend off accusations that they murdered the senator. In one response to these accusations, the bodyguards bought an advertisement in a local newspaper in which they vehemently denied any wrongdoing whatsoever. A Democratic candidate for governor in 1936, Cleveland Dear, claimed in a radio interview that one of Long's bodyguards who mistakenly shot the senator had been committed to a mental asylum in Louisiana, where he kept repeating, "I killed my best friend." The accusations against the bodyguards would not be an accepted part of the assassination lore—but years later, their culpability in Long's death would face closer scrutiny due to advances in forensic technology.[67]

Immediately after Long's death, his supporters pleaded with the U.S. Department of Justice to conduct its own investigation into the Long assassination. The jurisdictional questions were clear because of the office that Long held at the time of his death. However, the Department of Justice decided it would not exert its jurisdiction to investigate the circumstances leading to Long's death unless those requesting the investigation could provide irrefutable proof that a plot to kill Long existed, or that any federal laws were violated. The Rev. Gerald L. K. Smith, a Long associate, sent a telegram to President Roosevelt asking why such an investigation had not already commenced. (Long appointed Smith to run the Share the Wealth societies across the United States in early 1935.) In his message to the president, Smith implied that three men who conspired to assassinate the senator had received federal jobs as their reward for murdering Long. Because Smith would not name the men, a federal investigation would not be forthcoming. The decision to refrain from any investigation was reinforced through the directives issued by the acting attorney general of the United States at the time, Stanley Reed.[68]

The federal government might not intervene in the Long murder case, but since 1934 the U.S. Treasury Department had been investigating Long

State Capitol in Baton Rouge, built with the money appropriated under the auspices of the Huey P. Long administration (Alan Gauthreaux collection).

and his associates. By 1936, many associates of the deceased senator found themselves facing either stiff fines or jail time for income tax evasion, graft, and corruption. Although Long's machine appeared to be crumbling, it would take another 20 years for all semblances of Long's influence to disappear. The one thing that failed to dissipate surrounding Huey P. Long was the mystery surrounding his death. Speculation piled upon hypotheses were the ultimate legacy of the assassination, including questions about whether Carl Weiss acted under a conspiracy, acted alone, or may not have been responsible for Long's murder at all.

In the early 1990s, historians discovered that Mrs. Mabel G. Binnings, the daughter of General Louis Guerre, the head of the Louisiana Bureau of Identification and Investigation in the Long administration, inherited some items from her father after his death in 1966 and then placed the items in a safety deposit box in New Orleans. Among the items were a series of documents, photographs, some torn clothing, and a small .32-caliber automatic handgun along with six rounds, one of which was spent. The gun was allegedly the weapon owned by Carl Weiss and for years suggested to be the weapon he fired into Long's midsection on the night of September 9, 1935. The documents turned out to be the Louisiana State Police investigative file of the Huey P. Long assassination. Typical protocol called for the file to revert back to the State Police; once the case appeared closed, the documents would be catalogued by the state archivist. In this case, however, the file and assorted photos were made part of an inventory list for the estate of the deceased law enforcement chief. With the release of the documents and the other artifacts, historians and researchers hoped that long-unanswered questions would finally be resolved. In 1991, in an effort to ensure thoroughness in the process and dispel any myths about the newly discovered material, the Louisiana State Police launched a reinvestigation into the Long assassination.

Lieutenant Don Moreau headed the reinvestigation into Long's assassination based upon the materials found in Mrs. Binning's safety deposit box. He issued his final report on the investigation on April 20, 1992. Lt. Moreau noted that the documents he received for investigation were incomplete; the documents attested to more of a conspiracy than to anything forensically tangible. One of the more useful items to Lt. Moreau was the .32 automatic weapon and the cartridges contained within the safety deposit box reputed to have been owned by Dr. Carl Weiss. After the Louisiana State Police Crime Laboratory performed ballistic tests on the weapon, Lt. Moreau reported:

> All projectiles, both the fired and the six unfired, were tin-plated, copper jacketed .32 auto calibre. The fired projectile had visible rifling impressions on its surface and on the nose of the projectile was deformed. Scientific analysis of the fired projectile by the Louisiana State Police Crime Laboratory proved that the fired projectile could not have been fired from the .32 calibre pistol identified as the weapon

> used to shoot Senator Long. Due to the complete lack of any chain of custody of the weapon, or its possible use since the assassination, it was not possible to draw any conclusions regarding the origins of the fired projectile.

Given that ballistics tests demonstrated that the spent cartridge could not have come from the weapon found with the other artifacts, where did the spent cartridge originate? There are no historical records pertaining to whether Long's bodyguards carried any weapons other than the .38-caliber automatic on a .45-caliber frame. The comparison of the spent round would also have been more helpful if any slugs had been preserved from Long's body. Perhaps this was too much for historians and investigators to hope for.

In another examination, Lt. Moreau viewed the clothing worn by Long on the night of the shooting that had been cut away at the hospital by Justice Fournet. Lt. Moreau observed the holes in the front and back of Long's coat and stated that these were contact appearances that a weapon was held close to Long's body when fired. Again, Lt. Moreau relied on this evidence to proclaim that the official version of the assassinated must have been correct. However, taking into account the "chain of custody" that Lt. Moreau relied on with other evidence he examined, could the holes have been made later, or might some other form of decay have caused the holes, leading to a false conclusion?[69]

Lt. Moreau also discounted a story from one of the morticians who embalmed Huey Long. Merle Walsh stated in 1983 that a close friend of Long who assisted with his surgery, Dr. Clarence Lorio, appeared at the funeral home after normal hours to view Long's body. According to Merle, Dr. Lorio put on a pair of rubber gloves, undid the abdominal sutures, and reached into the cavity created by the incision. After a few minutes, Dr. Lorio removed his hand. Between his fingers was a slug from a large-caliber handgun—much larger than the .32-caliber gun that Weiss allegedly used to shoot Long. Lt. Moreau's reasoning in questioning the credibility of Merle's account is that when a pathologist looks for a bullet, most of the time there need to be more incisions made. Just undoing the sutures and searching may not produce the desired result. Additionally, Dr. Lorio was a close associate of Long's and his actions clearly discredited the one-bullet theory being forwarded as the "official" version of the shooting. Therefore, if Dr. Lorio performed this action it is highly mysterious.[70]

At the conclusion of his analysis, Lt. Moreau noted, rather contradictorily, that no evidence existed to change the official story and that if Dr. Weiss were put on trial with the evidence that the State Police had most recently reviewed, the alleged assassin would be convicted. Nevertheless, Lt. Moreau commented, "The State Police cannot absolutely prove that Weiss was the assassin."[71]

Simultaneously with the discovery of the Guerre file and the weapon

LOUISIANA STATE BOARD OF HEALTH
Bureau of Vital Statistics
CERTIFICATE OF DEATH

1—PLACE OF DEATH
Parish E.Baton Rouge
District No. 17-5760
3
File No. 5773
Baton Rouge
Registered No. 10587
No. Lady of the Lake San
2—FULL NAME Huey Pierce Long Jr
(a) Residence. New Orleans Ward. Orleans Par

PERSONAL AND STATISTICAL PARTICULARS

3. SEX male
4. COLOR OR RACE white
5. SINGLE, MARRIED, WIDOWED, OR DIVORCED married
5a. If married, widowed, or divorced HUSBAND of (or) WIFE of Rose Connell
6. DATE OF BIRTH August 30, 1893
7. AGE 42 Years 0 Months 11 Days
8. Trade, profession, or particular kind of work done U.SSenator
12. BIRTHPLACE Winnfield La.
13. NAME Huey Pierce Long Sr.
15. MAIDEN NAME Caledonia Tyson
17. INFORMANT Rabenhorst Funeral Home Records (Address) Baton Rouge, La.
18. BURIAL State Capitol Ground Sept 12.1935
19. UNDERTAKER Rabenhorst & Co (Address) Baton Rouge, La
20. FILED 9/12 1935

MEDICAL CERTIFICATE OF DEATH

21. DATE OF DEATH Sept 10.1935
22. I HEREBY CERTIFY ... to have occurred on the date stated above, at 4.10 A M
Accident, suicide, or homicide? Homicide
Where did injury occur? In La State Capital BR
In public place, (State Capital)
Pistol shot wound of abdomen (Homicidal)

Death certificate, Huey P. Long. Against protocol, and even legal statute, coroners did not perform an autopsy on the dead senator subsequent to his death (courtesy Louisiana State Archives, Huey P. Long Assassination Collection, P1993-193.).

that Carl Weiss allegedly used to assassinate Senator Long, Dr. James E. Starrs, a forensic pathologist and law professor from George Washington University, received permission from Dr. Carl Austin Weiss, Jr., Carl Weiss's son, to exhume his father's body to perform an autopsy that should have been conducted at the time of Weiss's death in 1935. Dr. Starrs stated, "There's an endless sea of fabulous fictions about this case. I hope that science can put some of them to rest." What Dr. Starrs actually discovered fell short of his expectations. However, in examining what little remains there were for Dr. Weiss, Dr. Starrs noted that Weiss's chin did not contain a bullet wound where bodyguard Murphy Roden stated his first shot struck the assailant in his testimony. Additionally, Dr. Starrs questioned the State Police's rejection of the ballistics test performed on the basis "that no 'chain of custody' existed for either the gun or the spent bullet."[72] Dr. Starrs argued that the spent round "could well have been the one that hit Long." The pathologist reasoned, "At the very least, its disappearance soon after the shooting added to a pattern of silence and concealment of evidence." Dr. Starrs believed that Dr. Weiss did not kill Huey P. Long, but that his reputation, legacy, and family name had greatly suffered as a result of either a botched investigation or the desperate concealment of valuable evidence to hide the ruthless incompetence of Long's bodyguards.

The murders of Huey P. Long and Dr. Carl Austin Weiss, in their official telling, remain the accepted rendition of what may have occurred on the night of September 8, 1935. Examination of Long's movements that night have been well documented, but historians continue to search for the meaning of Weiss's presence at the capitol building on that balmy fall night. The authors do not claim to know what exactly occurred, but we suggest the following general scenario for the events that transpired based on an examination of the available evidence.

After spending the day with family and returning to his home at 7:30 p.m., Dr. Weiss received a telephone call later that night and told his wife he had to answer a call. His route to Our Lady of the Lake Hospital took the doctor past the capitol building, and Weiss knew Long would be there. Examination of Weiss's personality denotes a calm, cool, and balanced man who could not be excited easily; he was not an individual who would resort to anger to settle an issue.

The capitol was located only two blocks from Weiss's residence. At approximately 9:00 p.m., Weiss parked in front of the capitol building and walked up the 48 steps to the entrance of the "House that Long Built." Weiss decided to walk inside and confront Long about the treatment the senator had doled out to members of his wife's family. He did not intend to harm Long, just confront him. Weiss walked through the front doors of the capitol building and past the governor's office because he believed Long might be there. After waiting a few minutes, at approximately 9:40 p.m., Weiss heard Long's voice from down the hallway and decided to hide his presence behind one of the marble columns in the hallway. As Long walked past him, Weiss stepped out and tried to stop Long and speak with him. Long became belligerent with the young doctor and rudely nudged past him. Weiss did not retreat that far and approached Long again. The senator pushed Weiss, a little more forcefully this second time, and Weiss reared back and struck the Kingfish in the mouth. Murphy Roden then grabbed hold of Weiss and threw him to the marble floor. Roden got up and Weiss tried to regain his footing. Just at that moment, Joe Messina rounded the corner and attempted to draw his weapon, a .38 component on a .45 chassis. The weapon discharged before Messina could fully extend his arm, striking Long in the back and exiting the front of his torso underneath the rib cage. Long staggered to the far stairwell and then down through the basement into the waiting arms of Jimmy

O'Connor; the blood flowed from his mouth from the hit he sustained from Weiss's fist.

When Roden and the other bodyguards heard Messina's misfire, they aimed at Weiss. Roden's first shot did not hit Weiss in the chin as he first testified. Rather, the bodyguards' weapons were unloaded into the hapless doctor as he lay on his stomach. Sixty-one needless rounds caused Weiss's body to stir from this position.

Not knowing where Long had gone, the bodyguards searched Weiss's body in a desperate quest to identify the man and perhaps locate some sort of weapon to justify their overreaction. Weiss did not carry a weapon with him. The bodyguards searched the bullet-riddled body and found some identification—Carl Austin Weiss. Now that they knew the man's name, the bodyguards set out to blame Weiss for the assault on Senator Long. Since members of the bodyguard detail were also members of the Louisiana Bureau of Identification and Investigation, once they discovered Weiss's identity, they used their connections at the bureau to find out whether he owned a vehicle and whether he took that vehicle to the capitol. They discovered the sedan in front of the building. The bodyguards then searched the vehicle and discovered a Browning .32-caliber automatic wrapped in a sock in the car's glove box—a weapon that Weiss brought back from Europe and stored in his car to ensure his safety during late-night doctor's calls. The bodyguards brought the weapon back into the hallway where Weiss's body lay in a pool of blood and placed it in his right hand. Now together in the hallway, Roden, Messina, Supreme Court Justice Fournet, and the rest of the security detail concocted a justification for the 61 rounds the guards had pumped into the dead man's body. It was at this point that the conspiracy began.

At the inquest, Roden, Messina, and Fournet basically told the same story. One must remember, of course, that all of these men worked for the senator and owed their livelihoods to his good graces. Although Messina became emotional during his testimony, his tearfulness was most assuredly genuine, as he fired the shot that eventually killed Huey Long. The conspirators relied on the gullibility of the true believers to digest anything put forth through the Long machine.

The poor population of Louisiana felt the death of their champion deeply, while others who viewed the Kingfish with a discerning and astute eye recognized Huey P. Long as a brilliant megalomaniac with eyes toward the nation's highest office, with his ascension there to be followed by more corruption and power. At that time, Long would not have been a proper and savvy representative for the United States on the world stage. It is doubtful whether other world leaders would have viewed the senator as anything but an ill-mannered, uncultured buffoon. To think that "President" Huey P. Long would have been the chief executive to deal with the likes of Adolf Hitler,

Benito Mussolini, and Hideki Tojo during one of the most trying times in human history causes consternation. The same type of backwoods mannerisms that gained him special notoriety and endeared him to the common people of Louisiana would not have fared well in the volatile diplomatic world of 1930s politics.

Throughout *Dark Bayou*, the authors have portrayed evil in all its forms. In this chapter, the line between good and evil has been inadvertently blurred. On the one hand, a ruthless politician bulldozed his way to the most powerful office in Louisiana and then went on to display his corrupt and overbearing style to the rest of America, capitalizing on the misery that plagued most of the nation during the Great Depression to gain notoriety. On the other hand, an altruistic, respectable, highly intelligent individual who sought to help others, Carl Austin Weiss, has been slandered and castigated for more than 80 years. As his family was the target of the evil scourge that ruled Louisiana, Weiss might even be seen as justified in his actions if he were, in fact, Long's assassin.

Huey P. Long did not deserve to die. However, those who exhibited hatred for the Kingfish certainly believed that his tyranny had to be stopped and considered assassination the only solution. Whether Weiss was the instrument of that assassination will probably never be known, but those who were closest to him believed him incapable of performing such a deed. Therein lies the mystery.

Louisiana Burning

"It has been said, 'time heals all wounds.' I do not agree. The wounds remain. In time, the mind, protecting its sanity, covers them with scar tissue and the pain lessens. But it is never gone."—Rose Kennedy

No other period of American history proved more volatile and combative than that of the Jim Crow era and the subsequent civil rights movement. In Louisiana, especially, blacks felt determined to change the mindset of whites who still longed for a return to the antebellum subjugation of the black population of the state. It can be said with all historical affirmation that whites in the South never became acclimated to black protest of southern racial mores. The more belligerent and steadfast whites who maintained the dogma of racial supremacy sought extra-legal means to make their argument. The utilization of lynching (and blatant murder) to instill fear in the black population of the state proved a time-honored, macabre, and effective method of perceived behavioral control; perpetrators of these crimes remained unknown or were not held accountable.

Before the battle for civil rights became prevalent in U.S. society, Jim Crow laws made discrimination and racial prejudice *de jure* protection against prosecution for any acts against blacks in the name of racial superiority. In Louisiana alone, 389 lynchings took place between the years 1880 and 1970, with 333 of the victims being blacks who were executed using extra-legal means by "person or persons unknown." Some of the murders occurred with the cooperation of law enforcement, as these authorities, in most cases, participated as part of the bloodthirsty mob. In all of the cases, the perpetrators were never identified out of fear of retribution from the white community. In Washington Parish, the racial animus boiled over at different times during the course of Louisiana history and proved detrimental to race relations well into the 20th century.

On October 28, 1901, what eyewitnesses described as a "race war" broke out in Balltown, Louisiana, in Washington Parish on the Mississippi border. A week before, a young black man named Morris had been burned alive for allegedly assaulting a white woman. Since then, tempers had been on edge.

Another, more brutal altercation began when local authorities took action against a local preacher who was believed to operate a restaurant without a license out of a local church (a misdemeanor under the statutes of the time). A posse of white deputies surrounded the local store owned by preacher Crea Lott. Before the shooting began, Lott reportedly yelled, "One negro has been burned but a damn white man will be next."[1] When Lott stood at the window, he opened fire, killing two of the deputies with his first volley. Deputies returning fire killed Lott instantly. Other blacks barricaded themselves inside Lott's store. Then, "a negro preacher, Connally by name, rushed out of the building with a double-barreled shotgun, which he had leveled at the whites. Before he could pull the trigger, he was killed."[2] Connally's daughter was also a victim of the gunfire, having perished within the first few seconds in the exchange.

Authorities believed that what had occurred at the Lott property "had no direct connection with the burning of the negro Morris in that section last week, but it is undoubtedly the sequel to that tragic event."[3] Even though the violence felt into a lull for a few hours later in the evening of October 29, authorities received reports that blacks in Washington Parish had planned meetings to discuss other attacks to take place that evening or early the next morning.[4]

In response to reports that the violence would escalate, Louisiana governor William Wright Heard telegraphed the governor of Mississippi, Andrew H. Longino, for permission to allow Louisiana National Guardsmen to pass through the neighboring territory to quell any disturbances that might arise. Additionally, the fear of a black uprising prompted white farmers in Washington Parish to gather near Balltown, where they planned to resist any further efforts of the supposedly rampaging, armed blacks.[5]

With posses armed, tempers on edge, and National Guard troops patrolling parish-wide, the violence calmed down. Black families thereafter packed all their belongings and left Washington Parish at an alarming rate for destinations unknown. In early December 1901, subsequent to the riots, Judge James M. Thompson, acting in the Washington Parish District Court, called the attention of a grand jury to the events that culminated in the deaths of more than black citizens within his jurisdiction. The grand jury received a mandate from Judge Thompson "to take action to maintain the good name of the community, which had been much injured." Instead, the grand jury condoned the actions of the men who served as the catalysts for the riots when they proclaimed, "The men who participated in the burning [of the black man Morris] were among the best citizens of the country, and nothing but a desire to protect those who are nearest and dearest to them would move them to undertake such measures."[6]

In response to the holding of the Washington Parish grand jury, the

African Baptist Association, located in Amite City, Louisiana, issued the following statement: "A special committee on Southern barbarity and lawlessness declares that acts of lawlessness and barbarism are permitted by both races, and that the tendency toward lawless is growing among both races, especially among the younger element." This black benevolent association attempted to provide protection for Louisiana blacks where none existed. The African Baptist Association resolutely maintained that *any* criminal assault "should be punished to the fullest penalty prescribed by law, that is by death, and at once, but by a lawfully constituted tribunal."[7] Despite the protestations against extra-legal violence, lynchings, burnings, and whatever other means of intimidation that whites chose to use on the local blacks in Louisiana (and in the rest of the South as well) continued unabated as a means to effect societal control and racial compliance. In fact, the struggles became even more brutal as time went on.

In the summer of 1934, in Franklinton, Louisiana, some 20 miles north by east of Bogalusa, lived John Wilson, a black landholder in the parish. Wilson, who was considered "one of the pioneers in that section of the parish," had five sons and three daughters, all of whom lived with him. He raised corn, cotton, and sugar cane and developed a knack for spotting a deal when it pertained to livestock. Wilson had amassed an estate worth more than $10,000 and had "a good reputation among better-thinking people of the parish." On July 21, 1934, the Wilson farm had a visitor: a local livestock inspector named Joe Magee, who was "said to be notorious and a bad character,"[8] Magee came to the farm and stated to one of Wilson's sons, Jerome, that he had to impound one of the family's mules because it had not been dipped for ticks as required by the government. Magee and Wilson began arguing. When John Wilson left the farm to get the required permit to dip the mule for ticks, Jerome requested that Magee leave the property immediately.[9]

A short time later, Magee, Deputy Sheriff Delos C. Wood, Deputy McCanley McCain, and another law enforcement officer returned to the Wilson farm. Jerome believed that in the face of these reinforcements, despite his father not being present, he should turn the mule over to the sheriff and the inspector. Jerome walked to the porch, where the rest of the Wilson family had congregated. When Deputy Sheriff Wood made his way to the porch, Jerome "told him to go get the mule out of the lot."[10] In fact, the deputies accompanying Magee and not just come for the mule; they wanted to arrest Jerome as well. Magee, it seems, had portrayed the incident to law enforcement as being more serious than the case actually warranted.

When confronted with his possible arrest, Jerome stood still, not moving while his brother, Moise, asked the sheriff to see the warrant for his brother's arrest. The request for the warrant made Deputy Sheriff Wood visibly agitated, and he drew his pistol from its holster. Wood and the deputies then moved to grab Jerome. A struggle ensued between the lawman and Jerome's brother Moise. The weapon discharged, striking Moise in the abdomen. Witnessing the wounding of his brother, Jerome Wilson ran through the door of the porch and grabbed a loaded shotgun kept near the door. When he exited the porch door with shotgun leveled, Deputy McMain, Wood, and the other deputy had their weapons drawn. Wood fired his weapon, striking Jerome in the right thigh, with the round exiting his leg. Jerome fired both barrels of the shotgun, striking Wood in the head and killing the chief deputy instantly. One of the remaining lawmen fired his pistol; the bullet hit Jerome in the thigh, exited his body, and lodged in the leg of his younger brother, Felton, who had run to escape the gunfire. Jerome's other brother, Luther, received a gunshot wound to the hand, but he ran into the woods surrounding the farm.[11]

After recovering from the shock of seeing Wood murdered, the other deputies overwhelmed Jerome Wilson and wrestled the shotgun from his grasp. The deputies immediately arrested the whole family: along with Jerome and the mortally wounded Moise, their mother, Tempie Wilson, two sisters, and an uncle. When John Wilson returned to the farm, authorities took him and two other sons, Sammy and Bruce, holding the three as material witnesses even though they were not present at the time of Wood's death. A manhunt would later find Luther Wilson and bring him to the Franklinton jail with the rest of his family.

Memorial plaque commemorating Chief Deputy Delos Wood from the Washington Parish "Fallen Heroes" memorial located at the Washington Parish Sheriff's Office Headquarters (Alan Gauthreaux collection).

On the night of their arrest, members of the Wilson family sat in their jail cells listening to the more 500 white citizens of Franklinton clamoring for the prisoners' heads. Moise Wilson, who received a bullet wound in the stomach from Wood's pistol, went to sleep after receiving rudimentary medical treatment. On the morning of July 22, Moise Wilson "was found dead in a jail cell," having succumbed to his wounds sometime around midnight.[12] Sheriff H. L.

Brock stated that he was totally oblivious to the dead prisoner until the next morning after he managed, with the assistance of State Representative R. D. Jones, to successfully disperse the crowd that gathered outside the jail the night before.

A coroner's jury, composed of the Rev. J. H. Smith, Rufus Breland, Archie Magee, W. J. Carpenter, and Frank Shilling, assembled the day after Deputy Sheriff Wood's death. After testimony from the principals involved (including statements from some of the jailed Wilson family), they determined that "Deputy Wood came to his death at the hands of Jerome Wilson by gunshot wounds in the back of the head and neck."[13] The jury also found that Moise Wilson's death was caused by Deputy Wood's actions in self-defense. "The eight negroes in jail will be held for grand jury investigation."[14]

On July 24, 1934, Chief Deputy Wood was laid to rest after a Masonic ceremony at the Magee Cemetery in Franklinton, Louisiana. On that same morning as the citizens paid their respects, Judge C. Ellis Ott "called for a special session of the grand jury" to consider the charges against the Wilson family regarding the death of Dalos Wood. In an expeditious manner that was characteristic of the court's actions throughout the trial, Judge Ott also summoned a jury to sit for a trial and appointed attorneys for the defense. From a historical and procedural standpoint, the judge's actions appear less than impartial and his rulings premature, rushing judgment in a particularly delicate case.[15]

The grand jury met throughout the course of the day. Based upon the testimony heard, they returned indictments against Tempie Wilson and two of her sons, Jerome and Luther Wilson, for the murder of Delos Wood. Sammy Wilson, an uncle of the two Wilson boys, "was charged with attempting to destroy evidence after the killing and therefore as an accessory after the fact." Judge Ott ordered the other five Wilson family members held as material witnesses.[16]

Even as the grand jury handed down their indictments of the Wilson family, local media were praising Sheriff Brock for his ability to defuse the volatile situations he encountered as a result of the Wilson occupancy of the Franklinton jail. In one instance, he dispersed a crowd on the night of the Wilsons' arrests. Later, on several occasions throughout the course of the prisoners' incarceration, he contended with a mob's intent to exact "justice." Moreover, members of a large crowd who had just attended Wood's funeral arrived at the jail bent on getting revenge for the lawman's death. In all of these confrontations, Sheriff Brock maintained control—for the time being, that is.

The St. Tammany/Washington Parish District Attorney, Sidney Frederick of Covington, motioned the court to schedule the Wilson trial for the following Monday, July 30, 1934. This meant that any defense counsel would have only six days from the court's ruling to prepare a proper defense for the accused—an obvious advantage for the prosecution.

The trial began on the appointed date. Each day Jerome Wilson endured the agony of being brought into the courtroom strapped to a chair; he was still recovering from the bullet wound to his leg that he received from Deputy Sheriff Wood. The trial lasted three days. On August 1, the all-white jury found Jerome Wilson guilty of the murder of Dalos Wood. With the verdict announced, Judge Ott sentenced the defendant to death by hanging. "Upon hearing the sentence," one account documented, "men, women, and children, who had crowded into the small courtroom, immediately let go a tremendous burst of applause," with the noise summarily being quelled under the judge's banging gavel.[17]

On August 7, defense attorneys Ellis Ittoby, M. I. Varnado, and B. M. Miller appeared before Judge Ott to request a new trial for Jerome Wilson. The defense argued that several jurors "were unwilling to agree to a verdict of guilty as charged." The reason for their rushed verdict, it seems, was that they learned a lynch mob gathered outside was determined to execute the defendant. In turn, they voted quickly to avoid any violence that might occur.[18]

Ittoby, Varnado, and Miller also argued that Judge Ott erred in refusing to allow the defense more time to prepare for trial. The defense also contended that Wilson's condition made it difficult for him to endure a highly charged, emotional trial. Judge Ott summarily denied the motion, prompting the defense to accept an invitation from the National Association for the Advancement of Colored People (NAACP) to become involved in the case. One citizen opined that Jerome Wilson's predicament:

> Threatens to be a case very much similar to the now famous Scottsboro case.... To save the necks of four Negroes, one of them a mother, and to prevent the remaining fourteen from being incarcerated in prison, every Negro must contribute at once to this mammoth drive.... There must be immediate response so that the proper counsel may be secured and this counsel be given enough time to work out a case that will free the innocent persons who violated no law, but attempted to protect their own flesh and blood from the willful attack of a deputy sheriff who attempted to make an illegal arrest.[19]

As a result of the intervention of the NAACP and the money raised from black citizens around Louisiana, the organization hired a white attorney named G. Wray Gill to lead the Wilsons' defense team. In one of his first acts as lead counsel, Gill introduced the fact that failure to dip mules for ticks was classified as a misdemeanor and did not warrant police intercession. Furthermore, Gill cast impunity upon Joe Magee's reputation, noting that he "precipitated the trouble" and had "considerable trouble with both white and race members."[20]

Attorney Gill sought to further discredit Magee when he interviewed a local grocer who had a brief but telling conversation with the animal inspector. According to the grocer, Magee complained after the initial incident at the Wilson farm that "there were a bunch of Negroes up there that needed training."[21] Although the grocer insisted that Magee had the power to settle the dispute peacefully, the inspector persisted in summoning the authorities to the Wilson farm. Gill felt confident that he could prove beyond a reasonable doubt not only that Magee escalated the encounter, but also that his client and the rest of the Wilson family acted in self-defense in the death of Delos Wood.

Despite these new revelations, Jerome Wilson and his family remained in the Franklinton jail. They would continue to languish there, as Judge Ott refused to grant a new trial based upon the evidence that attorney Gill introduced. The defense, realizing that Judge Ott would not grant a new trial, sought relief at the highest court in Louisiana.

On January 8, 1935, the Louisiana Supreme Court, in a ruling that stunned whites all over the state, set aside Jerome Wilson's conviction, holding that "Wilson had not received a fair and impartial trial and [remanding] the case for a new trial."[22] This turn of events only exacerbated white animosity toward the Wilson family; whites in Washington Parish believed that justice had been served through the verdict reached in the original trial. Because of the inadequately conducted trial and many procedural and evidentiary mistakes, Judge Ott's lack of impartiality proved a critical factor in the high court's ruling. Although the granting of a new trial was cause for some celebration, the Supreme Court decision would subsequently prove tragic for the Wilson family.

At approximately 3:00 a.m. on January 11, 1935, a mob of six to eight men with handkerchiefs over their faces to avoid detection broke into the Franklinton jail and searched the cells for their intended victim. The angry and determined men finally located their quarry, Jerome Wilson, who "begged for mercy and then began to scream."[23] In an effort to quiet Wilson so that anyone outside would not hear his cries, the mob leveled their weapons at the caged prisoner and opened fire, killing him instantly. One of the men from the murdering horde then sawed the lock from the cell door. When they entered the cell, one of the murderers, who had a hammer, beat Jerome Wilson about the skull until he remained motionless. "The mob then dragged the negro's body out of the cell, placed it in an automobile, drove about three miles north of Franklin[ton] and there dumped the body out on the side of the road." The coroner, A.W. Martin, determined that Wilson died as a result of gunshot wounds and massive head trauma inflicted "by person or persons unknown."[24]

Sheriff Brock, who had previously remained vigilant in the protection of his prisoners, demonstrated a matter-of-fact attitude toward Jerome Wilson's murder. Reports documented Brock's comments when describing the perpetrators of Wilson's death as "a group of seven or eight men who were minding their own business" and decided to kill Wilson as a matter of alleviating boredom. Sheriff Brock had displayed a willingness to protect his prisoners before this incident, yet acted with malfeasance on January 11 in allowing the death of one of his prisoners at the hands of "unknown" assailants.[25]

A local black newspaper provided a summation of the struggle against Jim Crow laws in Louisiana by citing Wilson's murder as an example:

> No greater argument than is expressed by the quoted statements of the Franklinton sheriff can ever be presented to hasten the day for federal legislation against the evil of lynching. When the dictates of the Supreme Courts of any state are so scorned and belittled as were those of Louisiana in this most recent outrage, surely even those most prejudiced toward the sovereign right of states will see that something stronger than state laws are necessary if the whole country is to be kept from knowing similar moronic, sadistic and brutal crimes.[26]

In the age of Jim Crow, even established jurisprudence did not make a difference to the whites in Louisiana who found blacks inferior and never quite adjusted to post–Civil War racial relations. The only positive outcome gleaned from the tragic events in Washington Parish in 1934–1935 was a firmer resolve on the part of blacks around the state to achieve what had eluded them throughout the late 19th and earlier 20th centuries—equality. This struggle continued, but sadly, more degradation and deaths would occur before any semblance of civil rights could be declared.

A generation after the Jerome Wilson murder, as the civil rights movement became more prominent in the late 1950s and early 1960s, black leaders looked for areas of the United States where the fight could receive more attention. The key to presenting the case for civil rights was to strongly advocate for the right to vote as a result of the Voting Rights Act of 1964, which had been signed into law by President Lyndon B. Johnson in that year. This act guaranteed the right to vote to persons despite their race, color, or creed, and allowed the Justice Department to seek relief based upon violations of the act. Despite this federal mandate, whites in Louisiana—and in the rest of the Deep South, for that matter—remained defiant and equally determined to disregard the human rights status of blacks.

President Harry S Truman had given new force to the civil rights struggle in 1948, when he issued Executive Order 9981, which effectively ended segregation in the armed forces.[27] In 1952, blacks saw an opportunity to achieve equal status with whites before the law when the NAACP petitioned the Orleans Parish School Board to integrate schools and eliminate the inequalities that had been plaguing black youths since the institution of this discriminatory practice. At that time, schools in New Orleans were segregated in each neighborhood, with two separate school facilities being provided that white and black children attended based upon their race. The school board members ignored the court orders calling for desegregation and effectively maintained distinct black and white schools throughout the New Orleans area.

With the landmark U.S. Supreme Court decision in *Brown v. Board of Education of Topeka, Kansas* (1954), southern whites firmly believed that the federal government had intruded into what they considered to be a time-honored system. Whites were determined not to tolerate the federal interference.[28] For the rest of the 1950s, the New Orleans schools remained segregated, and it appeared that the highest court's order had been ignored.

According to whites, in ending the inequality, as was required by the highest court in the land, their schools would suffer from an infestation of "Negroes." Civil rights leaders, seeking redress through the court, sought to force the Orleans Parish School Board to abide by the court's previous order in 1960, which had demanded that the school board of that parish desegregate its schools. Instead, the school board set into motion a plan to slowly implement certain "test" schools. This plan proved too incremental for those who sought immediate integration; thus, in the *Bush et al. v. Orleans Parish School Board* lawsuit, the plaintiffs asked that all previous attempts instituted by the Orleans Parish School Board be invalidated in favor of immediate integration.[29]

While civil rights advocates pursued the integration of New Orleans schools, other events around the area also demonstrated the determination of minorities that equality should prevail in Louisiana. Various sit-ins and protests occurred, with civil disobedience being the order of the day. At one Woolworth's store on Canal Street, protesters sat at the counter and refused to move until they were served. Although New Orleans proved one of the premier battlefields for the civil rights movement in the 1960s, other, less populated, yet still impassioned areas in the state demonstrated that the clash of ideologies and justice provided the foundation for racial disharmony.

Located just north of New Orleans, Washington Parish became a hotbed of racial conflict in the 20th century. Populated with numerous farms and dotted with small hamlets throughout the parish, in the early to mid–20th century this area was permeated with the undertones of virulent racial tensions and even darker connotations of death. Underneath the friendly country exterior sat a time bomb of sorts—an explosion waiting to happen that would shift focus away from the big city and to this picturesque model of rustic living.

Bogalusa, Louisiana, grew from a small country hamlet into a thriving lumber town in the early 20th century. Despite this growth, blacks and whites kept their lives separate, never mingling as per the Jim Crow laws that both officially condoned and encouraged prejudice. Throughout the 20th century, this area of Louisiana saw its share of violence, but never to the extent seen when the civil rights movement reached its fever pitch there in the 1960s. Indeed, once whites realized that Bogalusa would become the battleground for the civil rights movement in Louisiana, white supremacists left the confines of the shadows to aggressively pursue a course against those in the area who did not support the Klan's militancy regarding segregation and racial supremacy—and it did not matter whether those opponents were black or white.

When the focus of the civil rights movement shifted from New Orleans to the more rural area of Washington Parish, racial tensions in the latter became more prominent. In 1964, the Ku Klux Klan clandestinely planned to make sure that although legal measures might have passed, local governments would not enforce the measures. In preparation for the upcoming conflict, Klan leaders infiltrated the Bogalusa city government as well as the police department. Their plan to neutralize the civil rights movement relied heavily on fear, intimidation, and coercion. But when national organizations such as CORE (Congress of Racial Equality) and the SNCC (Student Nonvi-

Lyndon Johnson with civil rights advocates at the White House in 1964 after signing the Voting Rights Act (National Archives, Washington, D.C.).

James Meredith being escorted by U.S. Marshals for his first day of registration at the University of Mississippi, 1962. Meredith became the first black student to register for classes at the university since the institution opened its doors in 1848 (National Archives, Washington, D.C.).

olent Coordinating Committee) focused on the area in their drive to register more black voters, the black population of the area felt empowered to aggressively resist the Klan's plan.

The new empowerment blacks felt was evidenced by the organization of a group known as the Deacons of Defense and Justice. At first, the Deacons organized roving patrols of armed men that would cruise black neighborhoods in Bogalusa to ensure the safety of its inhabitants. In the past, blacks had advocated civil disobedience, but the Deacons "were organized for mutual defense," whereas "The NAACP basically advocated the concept of non-violence." The Deacons' mantra dictated that members should not provoke violence, but rather strike in response to it. The Deacons practiced armed self-defense "in a visible and highly effective manner."[30] This strategy worked for a short time, but eventually the Deacons could not protect every black in the area; the Deacons served their purpose for a while and then disbanded a short time later.

The main conflicts in Bogalusa began when the previously mentioned national organizations (including the NAACP) attempted to force the integration of public schools, equal access to hotels and motels, and fair treatment of blacks by the main local employer for the town, Crown-Zellerbach. Crown-Zellerbach answered this call by forming "separate lines of progression" where whites saw no more upward mobility than blacks who competed for the same jobs and higher wages, but blacks would never serve in supervisory capacities over whites. In May 1964, Crown-Zellerbach instituted tests that workers had to take to receive promotions—another way to get around any fair-employment policies, as most of the black population in this rural area was unable to read and write.[31]

To quell the rising tide of tension in the area, the mayor of Bogalusa, Jesse Cutrer, extended an invitation to black leaders to sit on a biracial committee to examine how racial disputes could be settled more peacefully. Cutrer's efforts did not last long. Any gathering of the committee to discuss and resolve racial issues in Bogalusa would certainly require outside intervention. By the time the mayor organized this biracial committee, proponents of both sides of the racial issues had reached a critical mass, such that by the end of 1964, history would characterize the events that subsequently occurred as catastrophic.

As 1964 drew to a close and most looked forward to 1965, civil rights advocates became increasingly frustrated with the lack of attention paid to the course of their movement. Violence in Bogalusa escalated to the point where John J. McKeithen, governor of Louisiana at the time (1964–1972) and a stern segregationist, stated, "Louisiana citizens would not tolerate murder and mayhem ... while I disagree with the civil rights law, we don't resort to murder and mayhem, in any attempt to circumvent it."[32] In spite of the stance that McKeithen took regarding violence against blacks in the state (including the burning death of 51-year-old Frank Morris, a shoe repairman who was dowsed with gasoline and set ablaze in Ferriday, Louisiana, in December 1964; Morris died four days after the fire), clashes in Louisiana continued. As part of this movement, civil rights advocates descended on Bogalusa with a vengeance, determined to bring equality to the South.

In January 1965, in an effort to quell the racial distress, Bogalusa community leaders sponsored an interracial meeting to take place on January 4. When news of the meeting reached the ears of the local Klan leadership, they produced a pamphlet that "revealed the interracial nature of the meeting and nightly cross burnings followed at homes of the sponsors." The publication issued a threat to citizens who attended: "they will be tagged as integrationists and will be dealt with accordingly by the Ku Klux Klan."[33] The sponsors of the meeting acquiesced to the threat; they remained resolute in their quest, but vowed to fight at a different time.

Mayor Cutrer continued to assist with the struggle. In late January 1965, the city's chief executive helped the Voters League of Negro citizens "in their desegregation of 12 cafes, restaurants, drive-ins, two motion picture theaters, and the public library."[34] Cutrer and other city officials also questioned the motives of CORE representatives who made their way to the small town. When white members of the organizations unexpectedly paid a surprise visit to Bogalusa, they claimed they were brutally accosted. Two CORE members claimed a group of white men chased them through the streets of the city; the pursuers allegedly fired several gunshots at the young men, who subsequently sought refuge in a black barroom. One of the men alleged that the whites beat him viciously. William Jones Yates and Steve Miller, the reputed victims of the harassment, could not be found after the incident, however. Mayor Cutrer, in turn, dismissed the claims of the two men as a publicity stunt.[35]

The alleged incident with Yates and Miller frustrated local authorities, who had their hands full with real and justified concerns that seemed to intensify as the year progressed. Ralph Blumberg, the owner of a local radio station, WBOX, stated that on March 18, a woman who lived next door to the radio station heard a series of gunshots meant to destroy the transmitting equipment and disrupt broadcasting. According to Blumberg, "the Klan was behind the campaign to drive him out of town." The Washington Parish Sheriff's Office conducted an investigation, but leads proved elusive.[36]

In the spring of 1965, the flood of threatening events in Bogalusa reached a breakneck pace. On April 28, a clash between whites and blacks occurred at Cassidy Park in Bogalusa that prompted John Gallaspy, chairman of the Community Affairs Committee, to close the park indefinitely in an attempt to avoid any further violence. The Negro Voters League threatened to file a lawsuit unless Gallaspy and the committee reopened the park. Approximately a week after the riot, on May 3, a large group of whites broke through the gates to Cassidy Park and loitered around the area. The group of white citizens organized the break-in in protest of what they deemed "outsiders" interfering with Bogalusa's racial tensions. They vowed to keep James Farmer, the national director of CORE, from dictating racial policy to the whites of the city. Mayor Cutrer vowed to break the Klan's hold on the town; he announced he would "seek repeal of all segregation ordinances," and proclaimed he would "open all facilities to Negroes and would employ Negro policeman." The Washington Parish Sheriff's Office had already hired two black deputies a year earlier, in a move designed to appease blacks in the area. Cutrer wanted his proclamations to be more than a just a symbolic gesture, however: He wanted to break the grip that white supremacy had on his town and "lower racial barriers."[37] In the interim, Farmer and CORE wanted more action, and action sooner rather than later.

In an effort to compel more timely results, Farmer announced he would speak at a rally to be held at the Ebenezer Methodist Church in Bogalusa. Backed by Richard Haley, the southern director of CORE, and Robert Hicks, a vice-president of the Bogalusa Voters League, Farmer complained that virulent anti-black prejudice existed within the local police ranks, resulting in officers demonstrating a brutal ferocity when dealing with the black population of the town. Farmer "had no plans to meet with mediators trying to ease the racial situation," and, if the circumstances warranted, he planned to organize a demonstration the next day.[38]

Not too long after Farmer's announcement, police arrested two white men, William Blackwell and Richard Krebs, on suspicion of arson. According to Louisiana State Police Major Tom Bradley, law enforcement under his command witnessed a suspicious vehicle around the Ebenezer Church. Bradley's men "maintained security around the church where the rally was scheduled when the two passed in a car ... the pair saw a police car and [seeing] no one was in it they left, returning with a gallon of gasoline ... they circled the church three times before the city and state police stopped them."[39] Police later transported Blackwell and Krebs to the Washington Parish jail at Franklinton, where they stayed until they were arraigned. The two men were later released on $2,500 bond.

Frustrated by the constant criticism that he lacked either the ability or the desire to quash these incidents and diminish the potential for others to explode in an all-out race war, the mayor formulated a plan wherein he and the commission council "planned to repeal all ordinances requiring segregation, open public facilities [to blacks,] and see that all citizens get equal protection of the law." Farmer commended Cutrer's actions, but implored "decent white citizens" to voice their opinions about the injustices they had witnessed. The mayor hoped these resolutions would finally quell the tensions that plagued his city. In doing so, the mayor relied on his faith in his fellow human beings to exhibit some decency toward each other, whether black or white.

But the mayor's actions seemed too hesitant, especially to the Bogalusa Civic and Voters League (BCVL). Prior to Mayor Cutrer's declaration, these predominantly black organizations had threatened to protest in front of white businesses that refused to hire blacks. Although the BCVL declared a moratorium on protests in lieu of Mayor Cutrer's propositions, in not allowing the resolutions to run their course, the BCVL demonstrated an impatience that threatened the already volcanic atmosphere brewing in Bogalusa.[40]

The volcano slowly began spewing lava on May 24, 1965, when all control over the violence disintegrated. Twelve black protesters attempted to fight off scores of whites who descended upon Bogalusa's central business district. The demonstrators had gathered to protest the lack of jobs available for blacks at local businesses when "whites attacked them and the business section became a battleground." This incident followed another that had occurred earlier that week, when a group of whites chased Thomas Williams and Aaron

Griffith, two demonstrators, into a grocery store, beating them once they made their way inside. Moreover, in an attack reminiscent of a highly trained military unit executing an intricate tactical maneuver, "another fight broke out in front of a department store ... a large group of whites was milling about in Columbia Road when exploding firecrackers apparently signaled the start of the attack on the pickets. The firecrackers were used as a ruse to draw police to one end of the street while a white group attacked Negroes at the other end of the block."[41] Bogalusa police arrested those whom they believed responsible for the disturbances, but the violence continued with more abandon than ever. It seemed as if the opposing parties antagonized each other just to see who would go the furthest to achieve their objectives. It would not take long before one side crossed the imaginary line.

On May 29, 1965, Ronnie Moore, a CORE representative in Bogalusa, organized a meeting of blacks in the area and planned a demonstration march. He stated, "We are not going to march where the whites want us to march, but where we want to march." In preparation for what he suspected would be a bloody day, the Bogalusa police chief, Claxton Knight, "called for an additional 50 state troopers to augment the 30 already assigned here."[42] With the summer heat beginning to raise temperatures, the sweltering summer season promised to get even more incendiary.

In the face of the constant upheavals, local white leaders called for engaging the National Guard and declaring martial law to restore order. Business owners believed that calling in troops would damage "the image of the community." All during the day of May 30, small confrontations took place without larger riots occurring. Main Street was closed during the course of the day and at nightfall police noted the stillness that pervaded the town—an eerie calm, the one that many combat veterans attest comes before a large enemy assault. That attack would take place on June 2, 1965, breaking the uneasy tranquility.

At approximately midnight on the Wednesday evening, the two black Washington Parish deputies hired the year before, Oneal Moore and Creed Rogers, approached a railroad crossing at LA Highway 21 and Main Street in Varnado, Louisiana, just seven miles northeast of Bogalusa. As they crossed the railroad tracks, a late model pickup truck emerged from the darkness with two people in the bed of the truck. Traveling at a high rate of speed, the pickup truck also crossed the tracks and sped to catch up with the patrol car. Gunshots broke the night air, and Deputy Moore slumped forward onto the steering wheel. He had been struck with a shot to the back of the head, killing him instantly. The dead man's foot lodged on the accelerator, causing the vehicle to violently heave into an oak tree on the side of the road. Deputy Rogers also received a gunshot wound to the shoulder, and shards of glass penetrated both of his eyes. The pickup truck then sped into the night.

A short time later, police stopped a pickup truck near Tylertown, Mississippi, not far from the crime scene, that matched the description of the vehicle involved in the ambush of the deputies in Varnado. When police searched the vehicle, they found a .22-caliber handgun and a .45 automatic pistol. The marshal of Tylertown, Vern Brumfield, "stopped Ernest R. McElveen of Bogalusa on Highway 48 just inside the city limits."[43] Chief Deputy Doyle Holliday of Washington Parish arrived in Tylertown with other deputies from his department to question McElveen at approximately 1:00 a.m. After an interrogation that lasted into the early morning hours, local authorities believed that McElveen either was responsible for the murder of Deputy Moore and the wounding of Deputy Rogers, or possessed more information needed to identify the perpetrators. Due to the nature of the ambush, authorities believed that more than one assailant inflicted the injuries on the two lawmen.

On June 3, Washington/St. Tammany Parish District Attorney W. W. Erwin filed an affidavit and a warrant with the 22nd Judicial District Court for the arrest of Ernest McElveen. The suspect did not fight extradition from nearby Mississippi, and deputies from Washington Parish transported McEl-

At this railroad crossing in Varnado, Louisiana, on the night of June 2, 1965, Washington Parish deputies Oneal Moore and Creed Rogers drove into an ambush, crashing their car into the tree situated at the top right (Alan Gauthreaux collection).

veen to the jail in Franklinton. Immediately, officials from the parish called for the Federal Bureau of Investigation to become involved in the investigation.[44]

On the same day DA Erwin charged McElveen in the murder of Oneal Moore, Governor McKeithen called a special news conference to offer commentary on the attack on deputies Moore and Rogers. The state's chief executive characterized the ambush as a "dastardly, heinous, cowardly deed … the murder of this officer of the law and the attempted murder of his associate is a blot on our history and a disgrace to us all.… We shall not let this occur." Asked whether he believed one particular organization was responsible, Gov. McKeithen replied, "To my knowledge, there were no members of the Ku Klux Klan" responsible for the attack on the two deputies.[45] Although one suspect sat in jail under heavy suspicion of being involved in the crime, whispers among the citizenry pointed the finger at "nightriders," or affiliates with the Klan.

Governor McKeithen made that statement when the investigation was in its infancy. Therefore, his assessment of the facts seemed premature. On the night of June 4, the leading local investigator, Chief Deputy Doyle Holliday, sat in the living room of his home with his wife. At approximately 11:00 p.m., several gunshots rang out and penetrated the house, barely missing Mrs. Holliday. Chief Deputy Holliday grabbed a .357 magnum revolver he kept nearby when off-duty and rushed into the yard of his house. He unloaded the revolver at the fleeing vehicle, but later stated he did not know whether any of the rounds he fired found their mark.[46] After Holliday walked back into his house, the telephone rang and his 14-year-old son answered. On the other end of the line, the young man heard someone ask, "Did we hit anybody?" The caller then hung up. Chief Deputy Holliday believed the assault on his family was the Klan sending him a message about the Moore murder: Leave it alone![47]

After the incident at the Holliday residence, authorities increased their efforts in the Moore investigation. A witness came forward at this time who claimed to have been present at the scene of the ambush. The Varnado High School football coach, D. R. "Scrappy" Fornea, stated he had pulled his car into the garage of his residence, not too far from the railroad crossing where the incident took place, on the night in question. As he got out of his car, Fornea noticed the Washington Parish Sheriff's Office patrol car approaching the railroad crossing at LA 21 and Main Street in Varnado. Fornea also noticed a pickup truck following the patrol car. Fornea recalled, "as soon as the truck crossed the tracks, he heard some shots—he could not determine how many."[48] In describing the sounds of the gunshots, Fornea said that the report of the gunfire sounded like an M-1 Garand, the standard combat rifle of American infantrymen through World War II and the Korean Conflict.[49]

Fornea confirmed that he could not determine the color of the pickup truck because of the darkness. After he heard the shots, "the car veered off the road," and "he heard the tires run along a stretch of shells that comprise the shoulders of the highway." After the car crashed into a nearby oak tree, Fornea ran to the scene of the accident. Upon reaching the car, he recognized the passengers as Moore and Rogers, who they lived nearby. Rogers stated to Fornea that he believed his partner to be hurt. When Fornea looked over at Moore, he observed "a gaping wound in Moore's head."[50] Rogers then leaned on Moore's shoulder and pretended to be dead as well in case the assailants returned. While sitting next to his now-dead partner, according to Fornea, Rogers radioed to headquarters to report the incident.[51]

The tragic circumstances surrounding this brutal and unprovoked attack left Moore's wife, Mrs. Maevella Moore, the unenviable task of raising four children without their father. To complicate her bereavement further, the attorney general's office of Louisiana informed Mrs. Moore that she was not eligible for the $25,000 death benefit of her husband, even though he died in the line of duty. A new 1964 law provided that to warrant payment of this benefit, the officer "must be killed while 'engaged in the direct apprehension of a person during the course and performance of his duties.'" Technically, Moore died as a result of a routine patrol, but because he and Rogers were not apprehending a suspect, the law disqualified his family from receiving any compensation.[52]

To publicize the effect of Moore's death on the people of Louisiana (and understanding that the 1964 death benefit law demanded an amendment), Governor McKeithen offered a $25,000 reward "for the arrest and conviction of the murderer or murderers" of Deputy Sheriff Oneal Moore. In his statements, the chief executive also condemned the Holliday shooting on the night of June 4, and showed visible agitation at the press conference announcing the reward when he emphatically declared, "We're going to catch them.... We're going to catch them all."[53]

Gov. McKeithen wanted to be personally involved with the investigation into Moore's death and demanded frequent updates on the investigation from Colonel Tom Burbank of the Louisiana State Police and Dornan A. Crowe, the Washington Parish Sheriff. Col. Burbank informed the governor that he had contacted the FBI as soon as the incident occurred when he realized that the driver and passenger in the patrol car were the two black deputies. In a display emphasizing the personal nature of this loss, McKeithen sent a personal note of condolence and some flowers to Moore's widow.[54]

With the Moore investigation proceeding with all haste, the police found themselves stretched thin. Law enforcement continued to receive telephone calls in which citizens reported shootings in the northern black quarter of Bogalusa. One report indicated shots had been fired from a moving car. Officers, however, began to doubt the authenticity of the telephoned report. In a subsequent complaint, someone reported shots fired in the very location where the police had already converged from the previous call. Moreover, authorities had to deal with the ever-present Klan, who merely exacerbated the mayhem. St. Tammany Hospital located in Covington, just 30 miles southwest of Bogalusa, alerted police when staff members rushed out of the hospital on the night of June 5 to observe four burning crosses on the front lawn of the facility. This was the very same hospital where an ambulance delivered the lifeless body of Oneal Moore, and where the wounded Creed Rogers was

John J. McKeithen, governor of Louisiana during the civil rights era. Although McKeithen was a strict segregationist, he did make overtures to end racial discrimination within the state (courtesy of the New Orleans Public Library/Special Collections Division, Yvonne Loiselle, Archivist).

still being treated.[55] Even with these most recent incidents, authorities seemed reticent to accuse "nightriders" of culpability in Deputy Moore's murder, but the signs pointing to their complicity were hard to ignore.

One citizen opined on the incidents that occurred in Bogalusa, trying to comprehend the violence:

> Investigation of the nightrider attack in which one Negro deputy sheriff in Washington Parish was murdered and another gravely wounded ... encourage(s) the grim suspicion ... that the crime was the work of those who saw racial peace coming in the Bogalusa area and undertook to prevent it.... The exact relationship between his [Moore's] assassination and the subsequent firing on the home of the chief deputy of the parish, one of those directly in charge of the investigation, is not yet clear. But the second incident can only deepen alarm felt by all law-abiding citizens, hinting as it does of underground and possibly conspiratorial forces at work.[56]

The commentator vowed that the guilty parties would be brought to justice.

Efforts to apprehend Moore's assailant(s) became more concentrated as J. Edgar Hoover, director of the Federal Bureau of Investigation, assigned two seasoned investigators to the Moore case—Joe Sullivan and Joe Sylvester. Sullivan and Sylvester had worked tirelessly the year before in solving the murders of three civil rights workers in Philadelphia, Mississippi—James Chaney, Andrew Goodman, and Michael "Mickey" Schwermer. With 72 agents and the resources of the U.S. government at their disposal, local authorities and concerned citizens of Bogalusa and the state felt confident that a quick resolution of the case would be forthcoming.[57]

On June 9, 1965, funeral services for Deputy Sheriff Oneal Moore were held at 2:00 p.m. at the New Zion Missionary Church in Varnado, Louisiana. On that day, it rained incessantly, causing flooding in most of the city. Prior to the services, Mrs. Moore "asked that there be no motorcades or cavalcades at her husband's funeral." Representatives of CORE—specifically, Huge Robbins of San Francisco and James Farmer—planned a motorcade of their own and a walk after the services in direct contradiction to the widow's wishes. Neither Farmer nor Robbins had contacted Mrs. Moore since her husband's death, and she emphatically reiterated, through Sheriff Crowe, that "anyone can attend services that wishes, but I want no demonstrations or anything of that sort." Although some members of CORE stood in attendance at the funeral, no demonstrations or protests took place within close proximity to the funeral. After military and masonic honors were bestowed, pallbearers laid Deputy Sheriff Moore to rest at B. B. Moses Memorial Park.[58]

Instead of demonstrations and protests, CORE representatives Farmer and Robert Hicks, vice-president of the Bogalusa Voters League, held a rally on the night Moore was buried. Farmer exclaimed, "Deputy Moore was 'a casualty of hate and his death the Klan's bloody answer to the Bogalusa Voters

League request for police jobs in Bogalusa' for Negroes." After all the efforts of local authorities to solve the crime, including the Herculean efforts of Mayor Cutrer to ease racial tensions, Farmer merely added to the dissension with his vitriolic diatribe. Farmer, in an obvious attempt to incite agitation, made the unsubstantiated claim that the mayor "had sided with racists" to appease the belligerent whites in the area. Anyone who had paid attention to the mayor's actions during the events as they transpired knew Farmer's rhetoric merely sought to inflame blacks in Bogalusa and cast aspersions on the character of the city's chief executive. The authorities worked feverishly to solve the mystery surrounding Moore's death, but the distress caused by Farmer and others who descended on the area made the investigators' job that much more difficult. Turning Moore's death into an issue to advance the cause was not just deplorable, but disrespectful to the families involved. The desired result would be to lessen the sacrifice made by Moore and the advancements to that point for the sake of the movement.

Meanwhile, authorities continued to conduct their investigation, focusing on the man arrested on the night of the shooting. Ernest McElveen had sat in the Washington Parish jail in Franklinton since the early morning hours of June 2, repeatedly undergoing interrogations by the sheriff's office, the Louisiana State Police, and finally the FBI. Despite the incessant questioning that McElveen endured, the evidence to hold him as a suspect was circumstantial at best. On June 11, friends and relatives posted a $25,000 bond to secure his release. Ossie Brown, McElveen's defense attorney, argued that because his client did not fight extradition from Mississippi and "had recently undergone an operation and is still under a doctor's care," his client should be released on bond. The court agreed, and McElveen walked out of the jail. When he left, though, investigators decided to dig deeper into the insurance salesman's questionable affiliations.[59]

In addition to selling insurance, McElveen held an active membership in a white supremacist organization known at the time as the National States' Rights Party. Considering themselves a viable third party, the organization owed its beginnings to Judge Leander Perez, a St. Bernard Parish political boss and ally of the controversial progressive governor and U.S. Senator from Louisiana, Huey P. Long. Perez had laid the foundation for the party when he stated that Jews formulated integration as a plot to force mixing of the races. Perez continued on this theme: "I am un-compromisingly against forced integration, as sponsored by leading Zionist Jews in this country."[60] In the monthly newspaper of the National States' Rights Party, *The Thunderbolt*, subscribers were bombarded with anti-Semitic, racist, and nativist venom. Although the National States' Rights Party advocated stern resistance to integration policies, any violence (including murder) would have been carried out only by those with a history of such behavior, not those persons simply exercising their First Amendment rights. Even though McElveen appeared to have held his associations close to the vest and never spouted them to anyone, law enforcement kept close watch on him while the investigation continued in the atmosphere of continued racial clashes in Bogalusa.

On June 9, 1965, Farmer and Hicks announced a march and protest to take place at the state capitol in Baton Rouge. The two continued to blame government officials for the racial divisions that plagued Washington Parish. Farmer claimed to have received death threats for his continued magniloquence in Bogalusa and vowed that the cause demanded sacrifices. He would sacrifice himself if need be, he said. Farmer called the murder of Oneal Moore "the latest in a long list of martyrs in the cause," and further avowed, "We have got to make it clear to the authorities in Louisiana that the cowardly bums who shot Oneal Moore in the back must be punished." Again, Farmer blamed Mayor Cutrer for the ongoing violence in the area.[61]

The investigation of the Oneal Moore murder followed a familiar pattern that had been seen with similar incidents that occurred during this time period. That is, the murder occurs; local and state authorities "are bolstered by the Federal Bureau of Investigation" with all of the resources of the government at their disposal, demonstrating to the public that justice is only a matter of time; and a suspect is held, then put on trial and tried by an all-white jury, found not guilty, and released, if the investigation even goes that far. One editorial expressed the sentiments of blacks throughout the South concerning this inequitable process: "It is not our intention to pre-judge the Washington Parish case, but we do intend to continue viewing it in the light of a cold and barren logic with the consideration, of course, of what has been happening in similar type slayings in the Deep South."[62] Indeed, murders that occurred and had any affiliation with the civil rights movement followed the pattern previously mentioned—and the Oneal Moore case would not be the exception.

Racial clashes continued throughout the investigation on the streets of Bogalusa, and Moore's murder moved to the back papers of the day's media. More than a month elapsed, and the demonstrations and protests carried on, with no end in sight. Governor McKeithen, seeking a solution to the racial problems, organized a biracial advisory group; it was short-lived, however, and really did not solve the woes of Washington Parish. Eventually, with the assistance of the local and state authorities, racial tensions eased. Faced with a terminal investigation with no fresh leads, the Moore murder joined the myriad of unsolved civil rights cold cases; in effect, local authorities closed the file.

The death of Oneal Moore and the wounding of Creed Rogers proved to be a significant part of the civil rights struggle in Washington Parish. Many believed Moore to be a martyr to the cause, but ultimately he and Rogers were victims of the inequities. When Washington Parish Sheriff Crowe hired the first two blacks to join the department, he prohibited them from arresting whites who may have broken the law. Additionally, Moore and Rogers were not properly trained in standard police procedures. In essence, the appointments of the two officers proved more political than substantive. In the light of these facts, Moore and Rogers were set up for failure and their lack of training proved tragic.

Fifty years have passed since the murder of Oneal Moore, and the killer, or killers, have yet to be apprehended. Every few years, local newspapers commemorate the anniversary of the Moore's death and question whether the perpetrators will ever be caught. As time streams slowly by and racial tensions have waned, interest in the Moore case has recently been revived. In 2010, some 45 years after the crime, a witness came forward who claimed to have seen the whole attack.

Donald Seal, a long-time resident of Washington Parish, stated that while under an oak tree near Main Street in Varnado, Louisiana, around midnight on June 2, 1965, he saw Oneal Moore and Creed Rogers headed east in their patrol car. "I seen this pickup truck cut on his lights and pull in behind the patrol car ... and they crossed the railroad track and I seen two men stand up in back." Seal saw three men in the pickup truck, whom he recognized as members of his own family. One drove while the other two stood in the bed of the truck. As the truck gained ground on the patrol car, Seal saw one of the men in the bed of the truck lean over the side of the bed with what appeared to be a rifle. "I heard the gun go off," Seal claimed, "shot Oneal Moore and the other shot in the air." Seal identified Archie Roy Seal as the driver of the pickup; Shelley James Seal, Archie's brother, as the man who stood on the driver's side of the bed; and Robert "Bobby" Lang as the man who stood on the passenger's side of the truck's bed. Seal claimed Lang pulled the trigger in the shot that killed Oneal Moore. Although these three men had drawn the interest of authorities at the time of the offense and underwent extensive questioning, insufficient evidence existed (either then or now) to hold them accountable for the crime.[63]

Later research revealed that Donald Seal possessed a reputation for being a teller of tall tales and would do anything for attention. Current Washington Parish Sheriff Randy "Country" Seal elaborated on his distant cousin's dramatizations. According to the very congenial and professional chief lawman of the parish, "If you believe anything Donald Seal says, then you believe in Santa Claus and the tooth fairy."[64] Donald Seal had a history of making statements that held no weight and had numerous brushes with the law. To rely on the credibility of one so cavalier with the truth would be to play fast and loose with the facts.

A lasting remembrance of Deputy Oneal Moore (and the other deputies

The Washington Parish "Fallen Heroes" memorial, dedicated in 2012 by present sheriff Randy "Country" Seal to commemorate the service of those officers who perished in the line of duty. Contained in the memorial are likenesses of Deputy Delos Wood and Deputy Oneal Moore (Alan Gauthreaux collection).

who gave their last full measure, including Delos Wood) finally came to fruition on May 15, 2013. One mission that Sheriff Seal undertook when he was elected was to remember Moore and all the other deputies who lost their lives in the line of duty. The sheriff apportioned $12,000 for the construction of a monument inside the Washington Parish Sheriff's Office building located at 1002 Main Street in Franklinton, Louisiana. In a special place of prominence near the images of his fallen comrades, Oneal Moore's likeness appears in a bronze sculpture by artist Zach Slough. Maevella Moore viewed the homage to her deceased husband and solemnly said, "It's a long time coming ... but I still want to know who did it.... I don't know that ... that would wrap it up." In the initial dedication, Sheriff Seal used the most profound language when he lamented, "No sentiment can fully represent their bravery and their sacrifice; no memorial will ever be able to remember all of their courage."[65]

The memorial to the "Fallen Heroes" stands not only as a testament to the valor of the Washington Parish deputies who died in the line of duty, but also as a symbol of a community that deserved healing after its painful past. To this day, and after timeless openings and closings of the case over the last 50 years, no one has been charged with Moore's murder. Sheriff Seal believes that after so much time, the perpetrators either are deceased or will never be identified. Oneal Moore will be eternally remembered not as a martyr to the civil rights movement, but as a valorous individual who took an oath to protect and serve the citizens of Washington Parish at a trying time in Louisiana and American history.

Deadly Friendship

"If you tell the truth, you don't have to remember anything."—Mark Twain

During the course of many police homicide investigations, it becomes readily apparent that the crime scene and the stories of the participants suggest differing accounts as to what actually occurred. Therefore, it is incumbent upon the investigators to create an accurate depiction of the event based on the disparate information they may receive. When investigators arrive at a crime scene, particularly a homicide, they may determine fairly quickly the manner of death and the weapons used to dispatch the victim. But when human elements diverge, a witness's rendition of the events may be so convoluted with untruths or misstatements that the detection of the perpetrator of the crime may not be readily within the grasp of investigators.

Witnesses at a crime scene are interviewed immediately after an incident occurs; they retain a more recent recollection of their thoughts and the chronology of the events as they happened at that time, which should enable the investigators to determine the truth. But what if the witnesses to the incident present their versions and the evidence does not substantiate their recollections? And what if details added to their renditions at a later time lead to even more astonishment, confusion, and disbelief as part of an already expanding conglomeration of fabrications? Investigators and the judicial system in Jefferson Parish, just west of New Orleans, would have to decipher just such contradictory and confusing accounts in the case of the brutal beating of a young housewife and her toddler son in one of the most aberrant murder cases in Louisiana history.

On February 24, 1984, 911 operators received a call from a seemingly desperate man: "Please, somebody broke into my house and tried to kill me. I just stabbed him, 2232 Litchwood in Woodmere. Please, now, hurry."[1] Woodmere, a subdivision on the west bank of the Mississippi River from New Orleans, is regularly patrolled by members of the Jefferson Parish Sheriff's Office, 2nd District. The man on the telephone with the 911 operator went on to say that someone had broken into his house, and that he had stabbed the intruder. The man later identified himself as Kerry Myers. He reported he had arrived at his home at approximately 3:30 p.m. that same afternoon. According to Myers, he knew the man who attacked him, William Fontanille, and he knew that the latter had become depressed because Fontanille's wife had left him and took his toddler son with her a year before. According to Myers, when he walked into his house that afternoon, Fontanille attacked him with a baseball bat, ultimately shattering Myers's left arm. Fontanille subsequently gained possession of a knife. Myers claimed he spoke to Fontanille for an extended time, trying to calm him down. The conversation took several hours, but then the two began to struggle for the knife. Myers wrested the knife away and stabbed Fontanille, chasing his attacker with the knife in hand through the front door and into the street.[2]

Myers continued screaming into the phone to get the 911 operator to send an ambulance and then call his father. When prompted to check whether his children were safe, Myers went into another room and related what he saw: "Oh God, God, my God, my God, oh my God.... I think he killed my wife ... she's unconscious. There's blood all over. He said he didn't hurt her. He swore he didn't hurt her."

At this residence on February 24, 1984, Kerry Myers and William Fontanille fought for more than 10 hours, with both men subsequently disavowing knowledge of the carnage that police would discover in the living room (Alan Gauthreaux collection).

The operator dispatched an ambulance to the scene as well as the police. When they arrived, they found the house in shambles, with broken glass, overturned flower pots, and blood droplets all over the floor. When Detective Sergeant Robert Masson first arrived on the scene, the 11-year veteran of the Jefferson Parish Sheriff's Office walked through the foyer of the Myers residence and noticed two cardboard boxes along the east wall of the house. "Adjacent to the boxes and to the south, the officer observes the body of a white female."[3] Wearing purple leotards, blue shorts, white tennis shoes, and a striped, pullover shirt, she lay on her back, her face battered beyond recognition. Blood had coagulated in her brunette hair and tiny droplets of her blood appeared spattered all over the wall approximately two and a half feet above where she lay and on the ceiling. Both arms were positioned near her head, palms up, and a circular arch appeared near her right arm drawn in blood. A bloody and dented aluminum baseball bat stood against the loveseat

The body of Janet Myers as viewed by the crime unit of the Jefferson Parish sheriff's office on the morning of February 24, 1984. Notice the circular arc next to her left arm, indicating that she suffered in extreme agony before she expired (courtesy of the Jefferson Parish Sheriff's Office, Harry Lee, Sheriff).

of the Myers residence; a bloody knife lay on the kitchen counter; and several household objects, some shattered in numerous pieces, were strewn throughout the suburban home. It became apparent to crime scene investigators who arrived at the house on Litchwood that Janet Myers, who was assuredly in extreme pain and delirium, suffered horribly in her last moments of life. The evidence of her anguish can be seen in the crime scene photos taken that night—an arch on the carpet demonstrated that her right arm flailed in her own blood as she struggled to hang on to life.[4]

In addition to Kerry and Janet Myers and William Fontanille, Kerry Myers's two-and-a-half-year-old son, Ryan, and seven-week-old daughter, Sara, were at the back of the house at the time of the attacks. Myers claimed that the younger of the two had not been fed since 2:00 p.m. on the day of the attack. When police discovered the infant, other than being hungry and needing a diaper change, she appeared unhurt. The toddler had been bludgeoned just like Janet Myers, but he was still breathing when the ambulance arrived. An emergency medical unit urgently rushed the boy to West Jefferson Medical Center, noting at the time that blood ran from his ears and mouth. The medical examiner transported the body of Janet Myers to parish morgue.[5]

Assistant coroner Richard Tracy was the medical examiner assigned to perform the autopsy. In his initial findings, he stated that Janet Myers died as a result of blunt force trauma to the head and face, with brain hemorrhaging causing death (later, Dr. Tracy would amend his findings to say that Myers actually choked on her own blood). Closer examination of the woman's body revealed deep lacerations to the scalp and bruising to the inside and outside of the mouth; a deep tear to the area around her right ear, leaving the small appendage hanging from skin around the jaw; and "a y-shaped cut of the right cheek [that descended] to the soft tissue of the cheek, into the interior of the mouth," with "marked bruising present around the teeth."[6] Both of the victim's eyes exhibited swelling and purple bruising where hemorrhaging likely occurred. She also sustained what appeared to be several lost patches of skin from the knuckles of her right hand, which Dr. Tracy attributed to a possible postmortem attack by insects.[7] Dr. Tracy also noted that Mrs. Myers had a cesarean section scar across her lower abdomen that appeared pink, still healing, from her daughter's birth. The coroner found no evidence that the victim had sexual relations. A further examination of the autopsy report and the crime scene photos revealed the unbridled rage that had possessed the murderer of Janet Myers that night. Her death did not occur instantaneously, and she suffered intensely before finally expiring. Dr. Tracy determined that Mrs. Myers died sometime early or mid–Friday evening.[8]

On the next day, February 25, 1984, news reached Detective Sargent Masson that Fontanille had driven himself to Jo Ellen Smith Hospital in Algiers, Louisiana, approximately seven miles from the Woodmere subdivision to be treated for wounds he sustained in the altercation at the Myers residence. Det. Sgt. Masson interviewed Fontanille, who had known Kerry Myers since they attended Archbishop Shaw High School, an all-boys Catholic institution on the west bank of New Orleans. Fontanille had known the dead woman, Janet Myers, for approximately five years. Fontanille gave some background information to Masson, then explained that he went over to Kerry Myers's house in Woodmere to pick up a baseball bat he had left there the day before, which he needed to use as a cane because he had injured his back. Fontanille claimed to have been at the Myers residence twice the day before the murder. When he arrived there the first time at approximately 1:00 p.m., he claimed that Kerry Myers was at work and Janet was staying at home with the two children. Fontanille and the victim spoke at great length about Fontanille's separation from his wife and his job loss seven months before. Fontanille alleged that one thing led to another and while they talked, the two mutually agreed to have sexual intercourse in the baby Sara's room.

Fontanille left the Myers's residence at approximately 5:00 p.m. He later returned to hitch a ride with Kerry Myers to a basketball game with friends, but Myers did not exhibit any suspicion about the infidelity.

According to Fontanille, on the day of the murder he arrived at the Myers residence around 3:30 or 4:00 p.m. after parking his car down the street (Fontanille actually parked his car around the corner and 14 houses away from the Myers's residence).[9] He explained, "I didn't want to park my car in front of the house and have Kerry drive by. I wasn't sure if he suspected Janet and I had done what we did and I didn't want to cause any trouble."[10] When Fontanille walked to the front door of the residence after parking his car, he knocked on the front door and Myers opened the door to let him in the house. Fontanille claimed he took what amounted to two or three steps, then "it seemed like I was stabbed twenty times in the back." Myers chased Fontanille to the living room, where the bat he came to collect leaned against the loveseat. Fontanille picked up the bat when Myers ran into the room and repeatedly kept asking Myers why he was doing this to him. Myers, according to Fontanille, replied, "I'm doin' what I've got to do!" When Myers renewed his attack with the knife, Fontanille swung the bat wildly, connecting a few hard blows to Myers's upper body and shattering his left arm. After the struggle came to a stalemate, Fontanille sat on the floor and Myers sat on the couch, and they watched television for three or four hours.[11]

After watching various shows over an extended period of time, Fontanille told Myers that he had to relieve himself. Myers let him up from the floor to go to the bathroom, following his intended prey every step of the way. Myers suddenly lunged at Fontanille again, stabbing him two more times in addition to the initial wounds he had received when he walked through the door four hours earlier. The situation calmed down again, and Fontanille stated

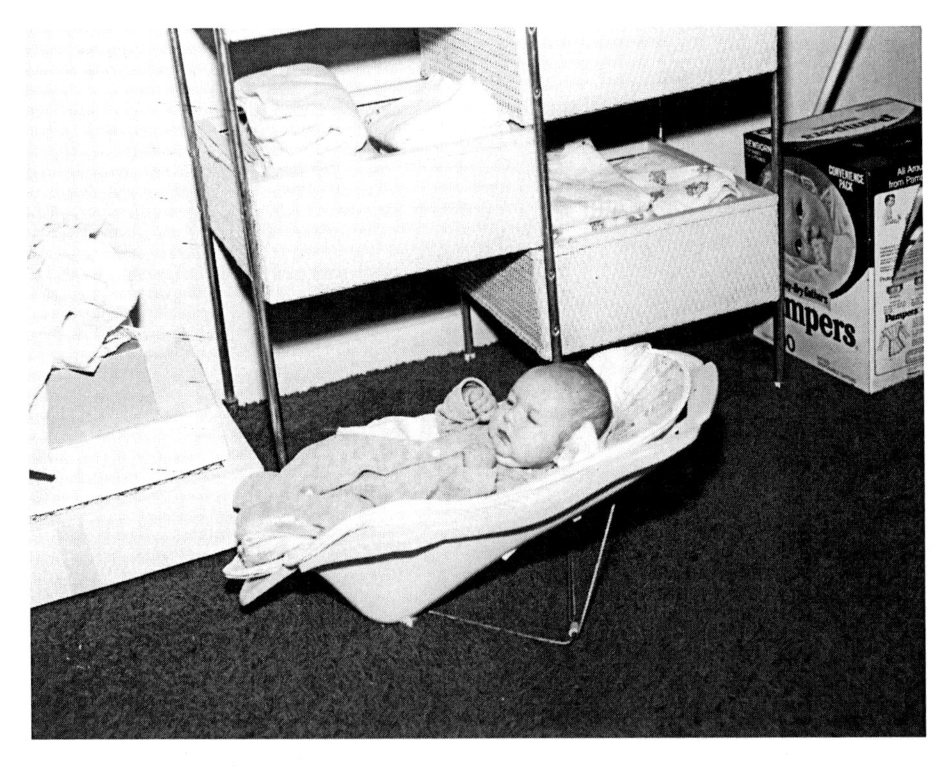

Sara Myers, two months old at the time of her mother's death, as she was photographed by the Jefferson Parish Sheriff's Office when officers arrived at the crime scene (courtesy Jefferson Parish Sheriff's Office, Harry Lee, Sheriff).

that he related to Myers his distress about not being able to see his son since the previous December. Myers seemed compassionate about his dilemma, and offered to go to wherever Fontanille's son was staying and steal him. Fontanille claimed he went along with the plan just to calm Myers down, while making plans to get away.

Finally, according to Fontanille, he and Myers struggled for the knife in a tussle that started in the hallway. When he felt Myers's grip loosen, he lunged toward the front door, hurriedly opened it, and escaped. During the whole time Fontanille and Myers struggled to gain control over the various weapons and circumstances, Fontanille allegedly saw neither Janet Myers, nor Ryan, nor Sara, although he did hear the seven-week-old child crying. Later, however, he claimed that he heard Janet Myers wheezing. During the entire encounter, according to Fontanille, Myers did not express any concern about his wife or his children.

Det. Sgt. Masson continued his interrogation of Fontanille and asked if he knew whether Myers had ever abused his wife. Fontanille responded,

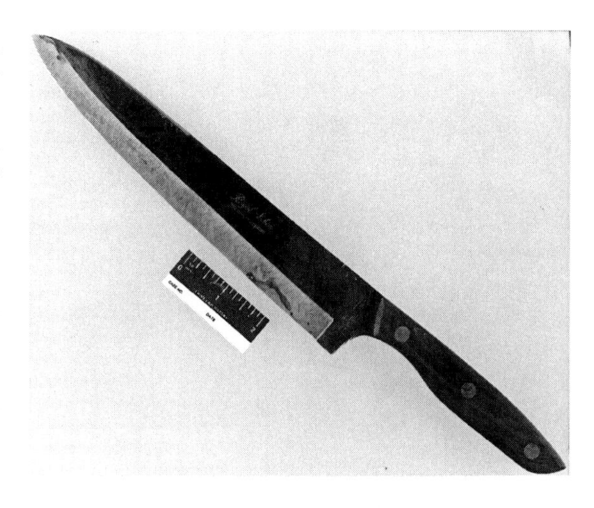

The kitchen knife allegedly used by both Kerry Myers and William Fontanille in their marathon struggle to stay alive (courtesy Jefferson Parish Sheriff's Office, Harry Lee, Sheriff).

"Before they were married, he abused her. I'm pretty sure he hit her several times. I know he did damage, physical damage to a trailer they were living in when they were in college. And I know he put her out on the highway one time, dropped her off on the interstate." Fontanille asserted that he did not kill Janet Myers and he did not know how she met her demise. Fontanille assumed, according to his statement, that Kerry Myers arrived at the home prior to his entering it, so the husband must be the culprit.[12]

Police relied on the coroner's report of the beating that Janet Myers took. In their review of the evidence they possessed up to this point, they decided the evidence pointed toward Fontanille as the perpetrator in the beating death of the young housewife and the assault on her young son, Ryan. Based upon the available evidence and the statement of Kerry Myers, on February 26, 1984, Jefferson Parish sheriff's deputies arrested William Fontanille for the murder of Janet Myers, the attempted murder in the beating of Kerry Myers, and the attempted murder of the couple's young son, Ryan.[13]

On March 14, 1984, Det. Sgt. Robert Masson interviewed Kerry Myers in the company of his attorney, Jack Rau. Myers appeared very eager to tell his story of what transpired the night of February 24 at 2232 Litchwood Lane. Myers claimed that when he arrived home from work on that Thursday between 3:30 and 3:45 p.m., he walked up to his front door, unlocked the door, and walked in. As soon as he turned to close the door behind him, Fontanille stood right there with the bat in his hands and swung it wildly at Myers. Myers attempted to deflect several of the swings that were directed at his head. In the melee, one of the blows shattered Myers's left arm. Fontanille then proceeded to grab Myers around the neck and hold him in a headlock. With his free hand, Fontanille grabbed at anything near and began smashing the items onto Myers's head. Myers pleaded with his attacker to let him go, and eventually Fontanille released his grip.[14]

During the course of the scuffle, Myers repeatedly asked if his wife and children were okay, but received no response from Fontanille. Myers heard

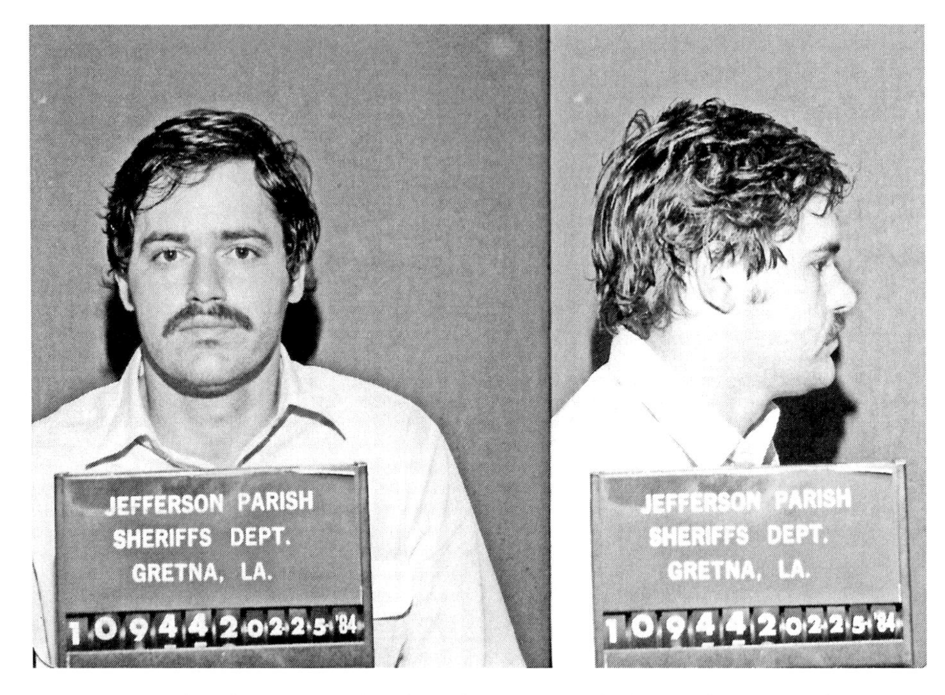

Mugshot of William Fontanille taken after his arrest for his involvement in the murder of Janet Myers and the attempted murder of two-year-old Ryan Myers (courtesy Jefferson Parish Sheriff's Office, Harry Lee, Sheriff).

groans coming from the living room, but Fontanille refused to let him ease his concerns. According to Myers, Fontanille stated that Janet Myers and the children were fine; in particular, he said he had tied up Janet with some cord and she was still alive. Subsequently, Fontanille helped Myers to a chair. As they both sat down, Fontanille began mumbling to himself that he needed to figure out what to do next and finally stated that he would leave when it got dark.

When sunset finally came, Myers reminded his attacker of the deadline. Each time Myers would bring it up, Fontanille became more agitated and finally said he wanted to watch a television program, *Magnum, P.I.* For some reason, even though the victim suffered through the constant ravings and changing of channels on the television set, Fontanille refused to leave and threatened to kill Myers if he attempted to check on his wife and children. During his statement to police, Myers kept reiterating that he tried desperately to get Fontanille to call for an ambulance to help him and his family, believing that his attacker had injured his wife and two children. Myers even tried to negotiate with Fontanille: "I kept telling him that if I'm the only one that is hurt, I won't press any charges.… I just want to get some help!"[15] Eventually,

Fontanille got up from the chair in which he was sitting and went into the kitchen. Myers believed he was calling for an ambulance. As time passed, however, Myers became worried that his captor had not called an ambulance.[16]

Myers continued:

> He said he wanted to go to the bathroom before he left, and that I was to go with him so I wouldn't try anything, because he was afraid I might do something to stop him. And as I got up, he made me walk in front of him. He grabbed me by the shoulder, which made me jump ... as I turned he tried to stab me with a knife in the back.

The struggle between the two was renewed after a respite of watching television, this time with a large kitchen knife. When Myers grabbed Fontanille's arm, the two men fell down on the floor. Myers grabbed the knife by the blade and gripped it tightly so that Fontanille could not wrest control of the weapon away from him. Subsequently, the two settled down and began talking again. Fontanille stated he had to come up with a plan. Myers suggested that Fontanille lock him in a room of the house so Fontanille could make his getaway. Myers thought about that suggestion for a minute, but then realized that none of the doors in his house locked from the outside. He then suggested that Fontanille lock him in the trunk of his car. Fontanille thought about that suggestion and then decided against it. At that point, Myers heard his son moan through the door of his room and yelled, "Ryan ... stay in the room ... don't come out. Lay back down and don't come out." The entire encounter was said to have lasted two or three hours, at the least.[17]

Fontanille seemed worried about whether young Ryan would open the door. Bloodied, in extreme pain, and exhausted, Myers then attacked Fontanille with the knife as Fontanille bent over to look through the crack at the bottom of the door leading to Ryan's room. According to Myers, he stabbed Fontanille twice in the back and attempted to lunge at him again. Myers knew he had drawn blood and screamed at Fontanille to get out of his house. Fontanille again put Myers in a headlock and smashed things over his head, and Myers tried to push his attacker toward the front door. Finally, Myers eluded his attacker and pushed him through the front door, claiming to have stabbed Fontanille again as he exited the house.[18]

After Myers forced Fontanille to leave the house, Myers claimed he put the knife on the kitchen counter, wet a kitchen towel to wipe the blood caked on his face from the protracted struggle, and grabbed a 12-gauge shotgun in which his attacker had chambered a round earlier in the evening. With a broken arm, in excruciating pain, and exhausted from the marathon confrontation, Myers claimed to have armed himself with the shotgun just in case Fontanille returned.[19]

When confronted with the claims about violence in his marriage, Myers admitted that he and Janet had arguments in the past that escalated to the point of being physical. In one incident that occurred when the two dated while attending Nicholls State University in Thibodaux, Louisiana, in the heart of bayou country, Myers lived in a trailer with a roommate, Chuck Kussard. Myers and Janet had fought, and she stepped outside of the trailer, picked up a rock, and threw it at the storm door on the trailer, shattering the full-length glass panel with that one throw.

In another instance a few years later, the two attended a Halloween party. Kerry Myers felt under the weather by the time he and Janet arrived at the party, not "like in a party mood." Janet seemed angered with her husband's disposition, and the two stepped outside of the party to continue their disagreement in a loud and animated manner.

In another incident preceding their marriage, Kerry and Janet had attended a softball game. While the couple were driving on the interstate highway, Kerry dropped Janet off on the interstate, then later went back to pick her up.

Myers claimed their arguments often became physical because nothing else seemed to calm Janet down. As the two yelled at each other, Myers slapped Janet, grabbed her by the shoulders, and told her to calm down so they could talk civilly.[20] Asked if he believed that Janet and Fontanille had engaged in some sort of liaison, Myers emphatically responded, "Absolutely not!" Myers trusted Janet and made sure that Masson knew that.[21] Like Fontanille, Myers claimed that he did not know how Janet Myers sustained the injuries that caused her death.

With both men's stories regarding what had occurred on that February evening now having been recorded, the evidence still supported Fontanille's culpability. On the day police arrested Fontanille for the murder of Janet Myers, Kerry Myers expressed feelings of guilt that he did not protect his family more diligently. Nevertheless, according to authorities, by March 1, partly due to investigators' zeal and partly because the investigation had not been concluded, Kerry Myers remained a viable suspect in his wife's murder. Forensic testing at the time had yet to determine which man murdered Janet Myers, but prosecutors at the Jefferson Parish district attorney's office expected to receive tests from the clothing worn by Kerry Myers on the night of the attack that would indicate whether Janet Myers's hair or blood was present. (At that time, DNA typing was not admissible in U.S. courts, and testing of blood, hair, and fiber evidence was the most technological certainty that investigators could hope for.) Other than speculation about the results of those tests and his statement, authorities possessed no conclusive evidence that Kerry Myers murdered his wife, yet the sheriff's office maintained that he was a viable suspect.[22] Later, after a careful reexamination of the crime scene, it would be the evidence—specifically, the blood evidence—that would show who ended Janet Myers's life and injured a defenseless little boy.

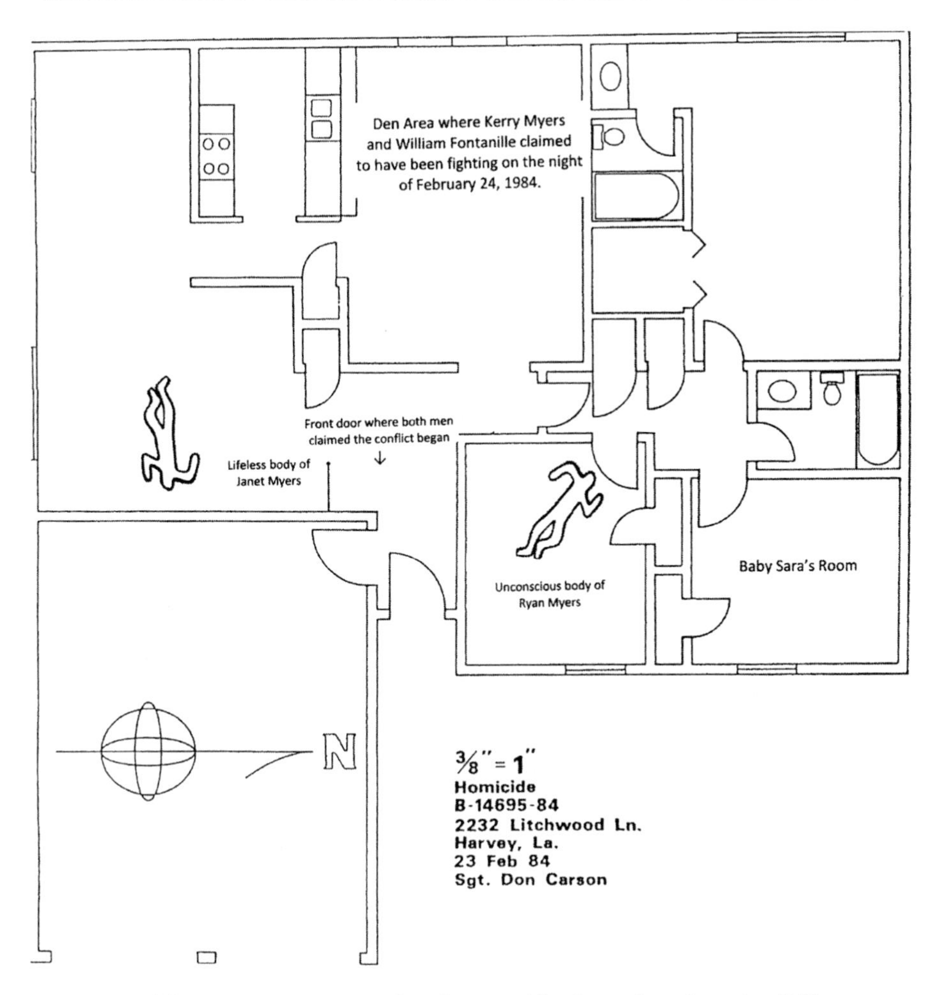

Diagram of the Myers crime scene. Supplemented by the authors (courtesy Jefferson Parish Sheriff's Office).

Until the police could investigate the case more fully, they proposed a few theories of their own as to what transpired that February night. Fontanille maintained that he and Janet Myers carried on an affair behind the back of her husband. Det. Sgt. Masson, the interrogating officer for both men, seemed convinced that Fontanille murdered Janet Myers based on the statements and the evidence obtained up to that point in time. Even though Myers and Fontanille implicated each other in the murder of Janet Myers, their stories differed only as to the person responsible for the beating that caused Janet Myers's demise and little Ryan's injuries.[23] Kerry Myers, though under intense scrutiny and suspicion, remained free while Fontanille remained ensconced in the Jefferson Parish Correctional Facility awaiting any adjudication. In the interim, authorities continued their investigation.

In March 1984, a grand jury refused to indict William Fontanille on the first-degree murder charge in the death of Janet Myers. Still refused bond, Fontanille remained incarcerated in the correctional facility until October 19, 1984, almost eight months to the day of his arrest, when the Jefferson District Attorney's Office empaneled a grand jury seeking an indictment against Fontanille.[24] District Attorney John M. Mamoullides maintained that Fontanille still had two charges of attempted murder pending against him, but the failure of the second grand jury to indict him elicited a confession from Mamoullides: "We are not going to prosecute him on those at this time if we are unable to get an indictment on the first-degree murder charge."[25] The case remained open.

The grand jury's refusal to indict and the DA's insistence that the case remain open did not assuage the frustration of Janet Myers's parents, Charles and Lorraine Cannon. The Cannons subsequently met with DA Mamoullides and Jefferson Parish sheriff Harry Lee for some reassurances that the case of their daughter's murder would not be forgotten. "I didn't want to mislead them," Sheriff Lee proclaimed. "It means that if something new comes to our attention, we will investigate it." Lee added, however, that his detectives would not actively pursue the investigation until that time. When Sheriff Lee's detectives discovered more evidence, Mamoullides promised, he would empanel a new grand jury and seek an indictment. Although the Cannons accepted Mamoullides's and Lee's promises, they remained skeptical about their validity: "[They're] politicians and I don't know if I can believe them, even when they look me in the eye and shake my hand."[26]

While Fontanille sat in jail, nearly two more years passed before a grand jury was empaneled to prosecute him for the first-degree murder of Janet Myers. On May 15, 1986, Jefferson Parish district attorneys presented more than eight hours of grand jury testimony, hoping that the jurors could determine whether the defendant killed the young mother of two and injured her young son. Both Herbert MacDonnel, a blood spatter expert, and former Det. Sgt. Masson testified within the grand jury chamber—the former regarding the blood patterns found at the scene and on the clothing of the principals involved, and the latter regarding his assessment of the case. Also called to testify were Mark Price and Curtis Jordan, friends of both Myers and Fontanille, who played basketball with them the night of the murder, as well as Joan Cannon Switzer and Jane Cannon Spears, sisters of Janet Myers.[27]

Perhaps the most interesting facet of that day's testimony came from MacDonnel's conclusion. Reading from his final report submitted after his examination of the clothing worn by both men, the blood spatter expert stated that the person who wore the clothing he examined had killed Janet

Myers. The clothing MacDonnel referred to was the clothing taken from William Fontanille at Jo Ellen Smith Hospital, where he went for treatment after the altercation. After careful consideration of the testimony and the evidence presented, the grand jury indicted William Fontanille on first-degree murder. Defense attorney Nick Noreia, Jr., and DA Mamoullides worked to set a trial date as soon as possible in front of Judge Alvin "Rudy" Eason, given that the defendant had already been sitting for nearly two years waiting for a determination.[28]

Noreia, an experienced criminal attorney, believed that at the trial his client would be exonerated once and for all. The confident jurist stated that the evidence would "discredit MacDonnel, the state's expert, and show that Fontanille had no motive." ADA Robert Pitre, who was appointed to supervise the state's case in conjunction with prosecutors Paul Connick and Art Lentini, claimed that Fontanille killed Janet Myers: "We simply have no case against Kerry Myers."[29] After jury selection, both prosecutors and defense counsel stood ready for trial. In the *State of Louisiana v. William Fontanille,* however, more questions would be raised than satisfactory conclusions reached.

On October 29, 1986, as the case of the *State of Louisiana v. William Fontanille* got under way, Noreia, Fontanille's attorney, asserted to the jury that the police committed errors in the collection of evidence from the crime scene. In particular, he alleged that the crime scene technician, Deputy William Viera, collected only "six blood samples from the house but admitted that blood was found on carpets and walls all over the house." The gore as a result of violence that February night became the major point of contention throughout the trial. Notably, it demonstrated flaws in the prosecution's case having to deal with the credibility of the witnesses and the evidence they presented.[30]

In more than five hours of testimony, a crime scene technician who specialized in blood analysis, Deputy Carol Dixon, explained how she discovered spots of Janet Myers's blood type ("A") on the jeans that Fontanille wore the night of the murder—specifically, on the right leg front of those pants—and on the purple leotard the victim wore that night. Furthermore, she found Kerry Myers's blood on Fontanille's jeans. More importantly, Dixon "found only blood types matching Kerry Myers and Fontanille on the husband's clothing, except indications of Janet Myers's blood on a t-shirt worn by Kerry Myers." Deputy Dixon explained this minute trace as occurring naturally through someone's sweat. After her long testimony, Dixon stumbled on some of her responses to Noreia's queries during defense questioning. Even though the court informed the jury that they must accept Dixon as an expert, her *curriculum vitae* stated she obtained a degree in marine biology with a minor in chemistry and worked as a bartender less than a year before the murder. Noreia's hammering on Dixon and her qualifications, therefore, highlighted for the jury the "expert's" lack of credibility.[31]

Herbert MacDonnel fared no better on the witness stand. He testified that the patterns of blood on the wall above Janet Myers head and the arc that her arm produced on the floor were consistent with the killer striking blows from a right-handed position, with a technical explanation of spatter physics that alienated the jury. MacDonnel then contradicted himself while under cross-examination by Nick Noreia. Ultimately, the witness lost all credibility with the triers of fact.[32]

With their experts apparently discredited and their case against William Fontanille seemingly disintegrating before their eyes, prosecutors Connick and Lentini called their star witness, Kerry Myers, to the stand. When prosecutors first questioned Myers about what occurred the night of February 24, 1984, they expected to hear the same rendition of events that the witness had repeated for the previous two years. For the most part, Myers met their expectations.[33]

At the conclusion of Myers's testimony, the prosecution rested and the defense called William Fontanille to the stand to testify on his own behalf. The defendant testified that he went to the Myers's residence on the day of the murder to retrieve the baseball bat he had left there the day before—the same bat he had used to assist him with walking after he claimed to have injured his back while playing sports. The witness added that he also went to the residence to end an alleged affair he and the victim had concealed from her husband. Contradicting Kerry Myers's testimony given earlier in the trial, Fontanille maintained that Myers had attacked him. After Fontanille concluded his testimony, defense attorney Noreia stated in his closing that the evidence supported his client's version of the events and that William Fontanille did not kill Janet Myers. With both sides rested after an exhausting trial, Judge Eason charged the jury and sent them out to begin their deliberations.[34]

"Following five hours and forty-five minutes deliberations," one account documented, "the jury of seven men and five women declared itself hopelessly deadlocked." Judge Eason had no choice but to declare a mistrial. Six of the jurors voted to convict Fontanille for Janet Myers's murder, and the other six members voted for acquittal. Although the jurors rushed from the court after being dismissed, dodging reporters as they exited, a few shed light on their conclusions. One trier of fact believed the state proved the case beyond a reasonable doubt with sufficient evidence to convict Fontanille of first-degree murder. Another juror, however, believed the case held a great deal of mystery and no amount of time would have determined the defendant's guilt or innocence. Meanwhile, Fontanille continued his residence in a correctional center cell while he waited for word as to whether he would face a new trial or a court would grant him bail.[35]

After two grand juries failed to indict Fontanille and the subsequent mistrial failed to produce a verdict, the mystery still perplexed those who were paying close attention to the case. If William Fontanille did not murder Janet Myers, who else would have had the motive and opportunity to do so? The evidence presented to the grand and the trial juries certainly added to the speculation as to what occurred on the night of February 24, 1984, culminating in the beating death of a young housewife and the bludgeoning into a coma of her toddler son. Some observers of the case believed authorities concentrated their investigation on the wrong suspect. Fontanille, incriminated through the physical evidence and the testimony of various witnesses, may have had a motive for the murder, but the rage exhibited by the killer pointed to another, more sinister motivation.

While Fontanille waited to hear his fate, the district attorney's office pondered whether prosecutors should try Fontanille again for the murder of Janet Myers. Nick Noreia, Fontanille's attorney, had a meeting to discuss the possibility of another trial. DA Mamoullides said without hesitation that "the case will be tried again," and the trial would likely begin in January 1987.[36]

It seemed as though the events themselves surrounding the case could not get any more bizarre, but approximately a week after the mistrial occurred William Fontanille and his attorney filed a $25 million federal lawsuit against the Jefferson Parish Sheriff's Office, Sheriff Harry Lee, and several deputies, alleging that the police "negligently failed to properly investigate the murder of Janet Myers" by not attempting to identify a handprint located on the wall just above Janet Myers's head. The suit alleged that the manner in which the police collected the evidence from the crime scene tainted any scientific testing on the clothing the defendant wore on the night of the murder.[37]

Given the questions about the very methods of evidence collection and police investigative work, one can understand the reticence of a jury to convict someone based upon the conclusions drawn as a result of those protocols. These accusations elicited responses from the very people accused of the malfeasance. Colonel Joseph D. Passalaqua (ret.), then a major and the commander of the Jefferson Parish Sheriff's Office Crime Scene Investigation Division, and an experienced crime scene investigator and Army Criminal Investigator, responded to the allegations by citing the investigative protocol. "It was a handprint," Col. Passalaqua maintained. "It was an outline on the wall and it was in blood.... I assure you that the outline of that hand was scrutinized by both the crime scene technician and the investigator involved." The handprint, according to Passalaqua, held no value whatsoever in determining the identity of Janet Myers's killer. When viewed in crime scene photographs, the impression appeared to have been made in a sliding motion downward toward the floor and "appeared fairly evident that it was a female's hand."[38]

Col. Passalaqua also pointed out that the local newspaper misstated some of the facts surrounding the case, but he did not blame the reporters for their lack of accuracy. The newspapers reported only the information they obtained themselves from sources close to the case. According to Passalaqua, the local media reported that the crime scene photographer and technician Deputy William Viera did not bring the handprint to anyone's attention at the time he discovered it. "That's not quite true," Passalaqua claimed. "He looked at it with the investigator and they both determined at that time that there was nothing there of value."[39]

Fontanille also alleged in his suit that the evidence collected from him at the time he arrived at Jo Ellen Smith Hospital on the night of the murder had been contaminated due to the collection method itself. The local media reported that Fontanille's clothing was placed in a plastic bag. "In fact," Col. Passalaqua noted, "the best method of transporting and carrying bloody clothing is placing each individual piece in regular old brown paper bags. That's what we use." Bloody articles of clothing collected from the two men on the night of the murder were collected in paper bags and then placed in a special dryer manufactured for that specific purpose. The evidence was then brought to the crime lab for analysis. "All evidence is done that way," Col. Passalaqua concluded.[40] The Fifth Circuit Court of Appeals eventually dismissed Fontanille's suit, although the doubts raised about the proper collection of the evidence remained a point of vigorous contention for the defense.

Despite Fontanille's federal lawsuit alleging the mishandling of the evidence, Fontanille remained locked in jail. Judge Rudy Eason denied a defense application for bail, stating, "There is sufficient evidence that Fontanille is potentially dangerous to himself and others." The defense, in its counterpoint, steadfastly argued that "there is no conclusive proof that Fontanille committed the crime and just as much evidence points to the husband."[41]

On May 4, 1987, the prosecution held a press conference and announced the selection of another jury for Fontanille's second trial. They claimed that, after a reinvestigation of the evidence, they possessed evidence that would prove beneficial to the defense. Prosecutors Paul Connick and Conn Regan had not produced the evidence for the defense and would not comment on the type of evidence they produced. All indications from the accounts given at the time, as well as the prosecutor's actions at a bond hearing for Fontanille, where the defendant sought to gain his release pending his second trial, showed that the evidence would not exonerate Fontanille, but instead warranted a charge of second-degree murder rather than first-degree murder as they originally speculated. Under Louisiana law, "second-degree murder is the killing of a human being when the offender has a specific intent to kill to inflict great bodily harm."[42] Judge Eason ultimately rejected Fontanille's request for release on a $250,000 bond guaranteed by his parents, nor would the jurist accept a bond signed by the defendant.

On June 3, despite Judge Eason's previous findings, Fontanille gained his freedom, if only temporarily.[43] His attorney, Nick Noreia, after being denied bail for his client, filed an appeal, in which he alleged that his client's Sixth Amendment right to a speedy trial had been violated. A month earlier, in a different case, the Louisiana Supreme Court had ruled that if Fontanille was not tried within 30 days, the Jefferson Parish authorities had to release him. On that hot, muggy Wednesday morning, Fontanille left the Jefferson Correctional Facility. In the meantime, Kerry Myers and Janet's family, the Cannons, would have to wait for a disposition in the case. Little did they know that more astounding surprises lay ahead as the reinvestigation of Janet's murder continued.

Under intense pressure from the families of Janet and Kerry Myers to find the truth, subsequent to the mistrial, the case circulated throughout the Jefferson Parish district attorney's office in search of a prosecutor willing to take on the daunting task of this perplexing conundrum. W. J. LeBlanc, who had until recently had worked in the juvenile division, wanted the case. The felony supervisor, Rob Petrie, called LeBlanc into his office and asked him, "Do you still want the Myers–Fontanille case?" LeBlanc responded, "Absolutely!" Petrie, with an "are you sure?" tone in his voice, matter-of-factly stated, "You know ... it's a loser." LeBlanc replied that he did not care, and added the case to his workload.[44] LeBlanc, a seasoned prosecutor, immediately asked Sheriff Lee to allow him to use another experienced veteran, Lieutenant Vince Lamia, of the Jefferson Parish Sheriff's Office Homicide Division, to assist with the new investigation; Sheriff Lee eagerly agreed and the two set out to reinvestigate the murder of Janet Myers.[45] LeBlanc and Lamia believed they could prove both Kerry Myers and William Fontanille killed Janet Myers and injured Ryan on that February night in 1984.

Lamia and LeBlanc's first area of concentration in the new investigation was the original 911 call that Myers made in the early morning hours after the murder. LeBlanc and Lamia repeatedly listened to the recording of the call, and questioned the sincerity of the caller. After spending hours parsing every syllable and inflection of Myers's voice, Lamia sent the recording of the call to a linguistics expert to ascertain the caller's earnestness. Several weeks passed until the linguistics expert contacted Lamia and LeBlanc and presented his assessment of the 911 call: Myers's attestations were "unabridged nonsense."[46]

Further scrutiny to the 911 call also revealed that during Myers's relating of the events to the operator, the "call waiting" feature on Myers's phone became activated. A few minutes passed, and then Myers returned to the line. Was it Fontanille calling to make sure the two had their stories straight before police got there? Or was it a call of penance, with Fontanille taking it upon himself to call and apologize for what he had done to the young housewife and Myers's son? The investigation continued and produced an unlikely line of inquiry culminating in the biggest disclosure in the case.

Another area of contention that LeBlanc and Lamia felt needed to be investigated further was why the prosecution in the first trial chose to utilize Kerry Myers as the star witness against William Fontanille. A few months before the trial, Myers took a polygraph test and showed deception when asked, "Did you kill your wife?" In well-settled law, a polygraph test or the results therefrom may not be used as evidence in a court of law because they are deemed unreliable; however, they have proven invaluable as an investigative tool. Given Myers's attempt at deception, he should not have been called as a witness in the first trial. However, owing to the conflicting statements and confusion about the events that transpired on the night of February 24, 1984, prosecutors had no choice if they wanted Fontanille to answer for the murder of Janet Myers. It became apparent to LeBlanc that the original prosecution team, in allowing Kerry's testimony, "just couldn't think of a scenario where both of them may have been involved in the killing."[47] No slight against the previous prosecution team was intended, but it seemed clear that the investigation into Janet's death needed a new set of eyes and ideas.

Driven by a new investigative team armed with a more plausible theory of the crime, on October 8, 1987, a grand jury astounded the Myers camp with an indictment of Kerry Myers for the murder of Janet Myers and for conspiracy with William Fontanille to kill both her and Fontanille's soon-to-be ex-wife, Susan Fontanille. On November 3, Myers appeared with his new attorney, Wiley Beevers, before Judge Rudy Eason and pleaded not guilty to the charges. Fontanille, arraigned later that month on November 12, also pleaded not guilty. Under intense pressure to secure a conviction, the district attorney's office indicted both men in the hopes that at least one would be convicted.[48]

After the arraignment and his release on $160,000 bond, Myers held a press conference at his attorney's office in Metairie, Louisiana. There, he emphatically proclaimed, "There is no evidence of a conspiracy," insisting that Fontanille actually murdered Janet Myers. Myers and his attorney strongly "urged the district attorney's office to prosecute Fontanille for second-degree murder instead of first degree, with the latter carrying the death penalty as a possible punishment."[49] Judge Eason, again presiding, set the trial date for May 1–6, 1988. Due to several legal challenges related to evidence in the prosecution's possession, the trial would not actually take place for another year.[50]

Based on the information that LeBlanc and Lamia had gathered during the renewed investigation, including statements Fontanille made at Jo Ellen

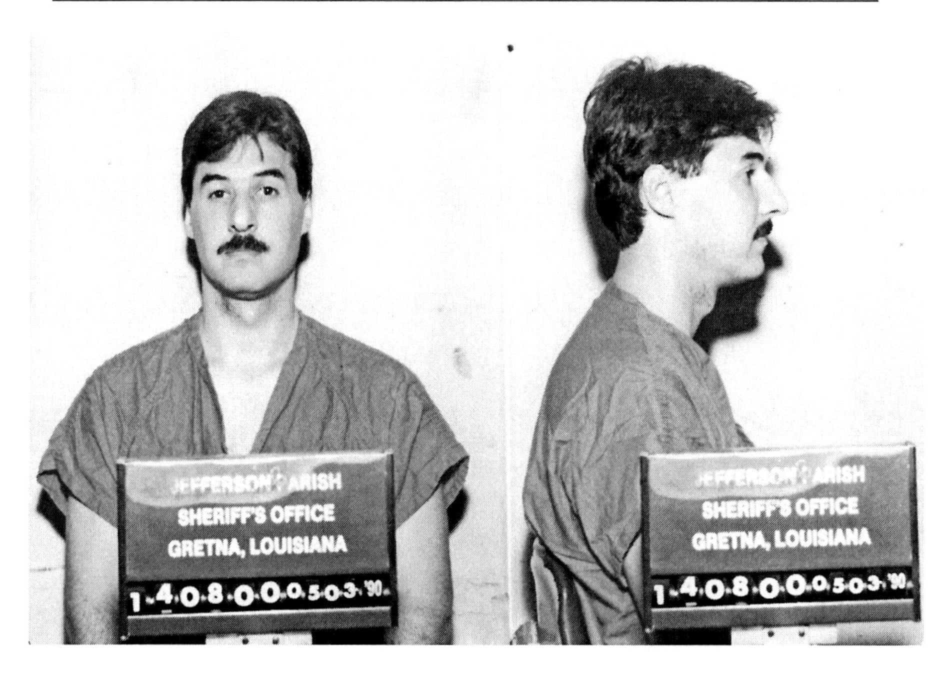

Mugshot of Kerry Myers taken after his arrest for his involvement in the murder of his young wife, Janet, and the attempted murder of their son, Ryan (courtesy Jefferson Parish Sheriff's Office, Harry Lee, Sheriff).

Smith Hospital, the two investigators theorized that Myers and Fontanille conspired to kill their respective spouses. Defense attorney Nick Noreia (Fontanille) and Wiley Beevers (Myers) filed motions to exclude the men's statements because the state failed to lay a predicate (i.e., show an evidentiary rationale) for their inclusion in the trial. In a hearing conducted on October 5, 1988, to prove that a conspiracy existed between the two men, the prosecution called three witnesses: Officer John Taylor, the officer on duty that night at Jo Ellen Smith Hospital when Fontanille arrived; Deputy Noel Adams, Jefferson Parish Sheriff's Office, who arrived at the same hospital later after being alerted by Officer Taylor that perhaps there had been two murders; and Det. Sgt. Masson, the officer who took Fontanille's statement the day after the murder and Myers's statement on March 14, 1984. The first witness, Officer Taylor, testified that when he first saw Fontanille, Taylor approached him and inquired about the amount of blood visible on his clothing. Taylor explained, "Fontanille then related his version of the events surrounding the murder of Janet Myers. He stated that Kerry Myers had told him [Fontanille] that he was going to blame the murder on him when he [Myers] called the police."[51] After being informed that two murder victims might be at the house located at 2232 Litchwood Lane, Officer Taylor called the Jefferson Parish

Sheriff's Office, and Deputy Adams arrived to speak with Fontanille at the hospital. Adams testified that he read Fontanille his rights and then collected a statement in which he repeated everything he told Taylor about the incidents of that night. Adams stated that Fontanille admitted that Myers formulated a conspiracy plot earlier that night, but "Fontanille did not state there was a conspiracy between the two"; rather, Fontanille was merely relaying what Myers had allegedly told him during the fight. Det. Sgt. Masson testified that the recordings of Myers and Fontanille were accurate reflections of the statements he took from both men. In open court, a New Orleans police officer, with no jurisdiction whatsoever in the case, testified that both men engaged in a conspiracy. One of the prosecutors at the first trial, W. J. LeBlanc, recalled that Fontanille's statement "certainly doesn't fit with the prosecution's theme [at the first trial] … and the defense can't use it because Fontanille was the one who said it."[52]

Judge Rudy Eason heard the arguments of counsel and listened to the taped statements of Myers and Fontanille before ruling that the state did not present a *prima facie* ("on its face") case of conspiracy and ultimately the statements of the defendants could not be used at their trials. In essence, with that ruling, the court held that a conspiracy did not exist simply because of an accusation made by one man (Fontanille) whose self-preservation depended upon the belief that another man (Myers) committed the crime. Because of Judge Eason's ruling, the state lost a vital piece of evidence in the case, leaving little or no evidence of a conspiracy between the two men. The Louisiana Supreme Court later agreed with Judge Eason's ruling and held that the statements taken from Myers and Fontanille did not prove collusion between the two men. Judge Eason subsequently released the jurors who had been chosen for the trial.[53]

Over the next year and a half, the legal system of Jefferson Parish and the state of Louisiana adjudicated various motions for the prosecution and the defense. The *State v. Kerry Myers and William Fontanille* for the murder of Janet Myers and the attempted murder of Ryan Myers finally commenced in the week of March 26, 1990, with the case to be tried in front of Judge Ernest V. Richards. Prior to the start of the trial, defense attorneys concurred on a motion to sever the cases of the two defendants. Judge Richards denied the motion, however—the two men would be tried together. But in a strange decision still pondered today, attorneys for Kerry Myers opted for a judge trial whereas those for Fontanille requested a jury trial. This procedural right granted to the defendants promised to elongate the length of the trial, as the jury had to be escorted from the courtroom so that defense attorneys could question the state's witnesses separately before the triers of fact.

At the start of trial, the defense attorneys adopted the strategy of blaming each other's client for the death of Janet Myers. The attempt to vigorously defend one's client against charges is one of the more admirable and noble aspects of the legal profession. However, in this instance, the strategy that Nick Noreia and Wiley Beevers adopted would only serve to confuse and confound the jurists who had to sit as the triers of fact to determine the guilt or innocence of their clients. Thus, the desired effect may have been lost in that confusion and the ploy may have boomeranged, causing justice to be forgotten and the courtroom dramatics to detract from the facts of the case. Meanwhile, prosecution attorneys W. J. LeBlanc and Howat Peters were at the helm of the state's case.

After opening arguments that featured opposing viewpoints by the defense and the prosecution and listening to the recorded statements of both defendants, the state called former Det. Sgt. Robert Masson (by then retired from the Jefferson Parish Sheriff's Office) to the stand. Masson testified that the impression of a handprint on the wall above Janet Myers, evident in photos taken at the crime scene, might have been properly identified with a different investigatory approach: "removal of the section of the wall with the print might have shed light on which of the two men might have been near the body, since both men claim they did not know the woman was dead."[54]

The prosecution then relied heavily on blood spatter evidence in an attempt to present an accurate scenario for the triers of fact of exactly what transpired on the night of the murder and to establish a visual map of the crime scene, as illustrated through diagrams and positioning of the subjects involved. In the first trial, blood spatter expert Herb MacDonnel had been unable to convince a jury that Fontanille killed Janet Myers. Because of a scheduling conflict, MacDonnel could not be called as a witness in the second trial. As an alternative, MacDonnel recommended Dr. Henry Lee, a noted blood spatter expert and author of more than 40 books on the subject of forensic science.

More concerned with presenting his findings in a more prosaic way instead of with the scientific confusion that MacDonnell had introduced to the jury in the first trial, Dr. Lee offered an abbreviated, yet understandable explanation of his dedicated, lifelong study of this forensic field. He then presented his conclusions based on a lengthy analysis of the evidence in the case to the triers of fact. This expert witness found that the blood-soaked jeans Fontanille wore on the night of the murder had more than 1,000 spatters; indeed, if Lee had to type every spatter, he said, "It would take the rest of my life." Dr. Lee stated he found Janet Myers's blood (type A), along with spatters from the two defendants, on those jeans as well. The lower part of the jeans proved the most telling, as Lee pronounced, "Fontanille must have been standing near Janet Myers because of the pattern of the spurted bloodstains on his jeans." Moreover, Fontanille's sweater contained two head hairs that were distinctive to someone with Janet Myers's blood type. Of the dress pants

Kerry Myers wore on the night of the murder, Dr. Lee opined that they had spatters of blood and smears. For the stains to appear in the pattern that the expert described, "the person wearing the pants had to be near the person spattering the blood."[55] However, in later testimony, with reference to the T-shirt that Kerry Myers wore on the night of the murder, Lee testified that the apparent bloodstains had been considerably diluted with water, so that he was unable to definitively type those stains.[56] Prior to the widespread reliance on DNA, Dr. Lee's conclusions were the best the prosecutor could hope for in terms of science-based analysis at that time. (While the defense teams engaged a blood spatter expert of their own, she never testified at the trial, leaving prosecutors to surmise that she agreed with Dr. Lee's findings.[57])

Wiley Beevers, defense attorney for Kerry Myers, presented an argument that the smears and drips of blood on the pants Myers wore on the night of the murder could have been placed there by transfer of the blood already on the bat after Fontanille killed Janet Myers, when Fontanille attacked Myers from behind when he came through the front door when entering the house. Dr. Lee's repudiation of the counselor's argument came swiftly and decisively: "The smear on Myers's pants could not have been caused by a dripping bat because it was not a vertical smear."[58]

With Dr. Lee's testimony, the prosecution and the defense also hoped to clarify the mysterious handprint discovered in crime scene photographs on the wall above Janet Myers's head. The expert inspected an enlarged photo of the area in question and determined that "while she was on the floor she reached up to the wall with her left hand and it slid down the wall to the right." The singular most important piece of testimony that prosecutors hoped for during the entire direct and cross-examination of the witness could not be resolved with the blood evidence, as Dr. Lee refused to opine as to which defendant the blood evidence implicated as the killer.[59]

The prosecution called one more witness before resting its case. Patricia Murphy, an emergency medical technician who was on duty the night Myers called for help, remembered speaking with the defendant in the ambulance on the way to hospital. Myers, she testified, claimed that he came home from work early and found his wife in bed with a neighbor. Under cross-examination, however, Murphy corrected herself and stated that Myers did not say he caught them in bed together.

Defense attorney Beevers called his final witness. Ryan Myers had been two and a half years old at the time of the attack, so investigators raised questions as to the reliability of his recollection of the events on the night of the murder. Agatha T. Zeilinger, a child and family therapist, took the stand and stated she began seeing Ryan when he reached the age of six, three years after the murder of his mother. Six months after Ryan recovered from the massive blows he suffered on the night of the murder, Ryan saw two psychiatrists, both of whom stated he had no memory of the incident, partly because his mind mobilized a defense mechanism to protect his psyche from the trauma experienced. Zeilinger quoted from her notes on the stand, revealing that at the beginning of her association with Ryan, the two discussed the events of the night he was injured. Ryan stated that "the man was tall, strong and had flat hair," and he struck Ryan "with a baseball bat."[60] Zeilinger emphasized that when conducting therapy sessions with Ryan, he reiterated that the man was big and remembered that "the man and his mother [Janet] were sitting at the dining room table talking, and the man told him he would hurt him if he did not keep the secret." Zeilinger did not elaborate on the secret that Ryan was supposed to keep.[61]

Defense attorney Noreia called his final defense witness as well. Ernest Barrow, attorney at law, testified that Janet Myers came to see him approximately two months before her death. She had questions as to "the legal consequences of legal separation such as child support, alimony, and community property."[62] Noreia hoped that Barrow's testimony would deflect suspicion away from Fontanille and toward Myers, as the history of violence in the Myers marriage might combine with Barrow's testimony to prove Kerry Myers's motive in killing his wife.

After all of the witnesses' testimony, the jury, attorneys, and judge went to the crime scene to examine for themselves the site of Janet Myers's murder. On April 4, 1990, after both sides rested their case, the time came for closing arguments—the last opportunity for the prosecution and the defense to convince the jury of their respective positions. W. J. LeBlanc rose to speak for the prosecution, summarizing the statements of the two men that the jury had heard during the trial. LeBlanc asserted to both the jury and Judge Richards that "the two men killed Janet, thought they killed two-and-a-half-year-old Ryan Myers, and then spent almost the next 10 hours concocting a story."[63] The defense attorneys summarized their evidence as well, with Noreia and Beevers arguing and hurling accusations that each other's client had killed Janet Myers and injured Ryan. Judge Richards subsequently charged the jury concerning second-degree murder and the jury went into deliberations.

On April 5, 1990, Judge Richards received word that the jury had reached a verdict in Fontanille's trial. Judge Richards held the verdict for Kerry Myers sealed in an envelope to be read in front of the court at the same time Fontanille's verdict would be revealed. In front of all counsel, defendants, jurors, and a crowded gallery, the foreman handed Judge Richards the jury's verdict for their portion of the trial: William Fontanille, guilty of manslaughter. Judge Richards then opened the envelope he had prepared with the verdict for Kerry Myers: Kerry Myers, guilty of second-degree murder. Both the Myers and

Fontanille families wept at the verdicts, and some shook their heads in disbelief. Judge Richards quieted the crowded gallery and then excused the jury, thanking them for their service.

In keeping with the verdicts, Judge Richards sentenced Fontanille to a maximum 21 years in prison, and Myers received a life sentence without the possibility of parole. The long process of appeals then began. Fontanille contended that he was denied to right to a speedy trial, improperly denied a motion to sever the trial, had some questionable evidentiary rulings, and had insufficient evidence to support his convictions. The higher courts denied the motions. Kerry Myers sought similar relief from the courts, but the issues raised in his appeal were also quickly dispatched. The Department of Corrections assigned Fontanille to the Louisiana State Correctional and Industrial Institute, while Myers went to Angola State Penitentiary.

While in prison, Fontanille gained a little weight and began working out. He gave very few, if any, interviews and was released in 2011. He now lives somewhere in Mississippi.

Myers started working in the printing department at Angola State Penitentiary (which is the official state printer of Louisiana) and eventually became assistant editor, then editor, of *Angolite*, the award-winning prison newspaper. He has been described by Warden Burl Cain as a model prisoner, and currently there is an effort under way to secure his release from prison through a gubernatorial pardon.

The murder of Janet Myers and the wounding of her son, Ryan, concluded with the convictions of Kerry Myers and William Fontanille, two men who, as the prosecution stated on numerous occasions, tried to outwit the system to escape justice. The case made headlines for almost six years, yet the truth never surfaced as to who actually murdered Janet Myers. To decipher what may have occurred that cool February evening in 1984, a series of seemingly deceptive events brought together in a logical sequence brings the truth closer to exposure for those who may seek it.

Two logical theories emerged as to what how Janet Myers met her demise: (1) from a seasoned investigator close to the case (who chooses to remain anonymous for fear of retribution) and (2) from the prosecutor who finally convicted the men responsible for her death, W. J. LeBlanc.

According to the investigator, Fontanille, who had been *personae non grata* for a little over a year, mysteriously appeared before his friends a few days before the murder. Fontanille considered himself a ladies' man, but since his separation from his wife Susan a little less than a year before the murder, he had sought a variety of female company to satisfy himself sexually. As Fontanille had no job, he sought an easy target: Janet Myers. After all, Janet had always showed Fontanille friendly compassion regarding the trials of his marriage and the custody battle he had to endure to see his son. On the day in question, Fontanille drove his car to the vicinity of the Myers home, parking nearly two blocks away in an attempt to remain undetected. He walked to the Myers home and knocked on the door, and the unsuspecting Janet opened the door.[64]

For a time, Fontanille and Janet Myers sat at the kitchen table talking. During the conversation, young Ryan walked in, seeking his mother's attention. Fontanille called the boy over to him and whispered in the boy's ear that he would hurt him if he told their secret—the secret being that Fontanille visited the Myers home without Kerry being there.

Despite his statement to the police to the contrary, Fontanille next moved on the primary intention of his visit. After Ryan left the room, Fontanille tried to seduce Janet Myers—gently at first, but then with more determined and forceful advances. Seeing that his strategy contained flaws, Fontanille finally attempted to force himself on to Janet. She fought back. To fend off Fontanille's attack, Janet Myers picked up the closest weapon she could find—a large kitchen knife. Fontanille then looked for a weapon he could use to defend himself from the thrusts of the kitchen knife. He found the aluminum baseball bat he had left at the residence the day before located near the front door. Fontanille raised the bat to strike Janet; fearing for her life, Janet lunged at Fontanille and connected, ever so slightly, slicing him in his upper torso. Of the many knife wounds he received that day and evening, one was located just above the navel. Fontanille, who was much larger and stronger than Janet despite having complained of an injured back, raised his bat again. Janet ran into the living to escape the blows from Fontanille's weapon.

Simultaneously with the assault of Janet Myers, little Ryan ran into the room and clung to her right leg. Missing several times with the swing of the baseball bat, Fontanille swung wildly, missing Janet and striking her son Ryan as he tried to protect his mother from the larger aggressor. The child lay unconscious. Fontanille's next swing did not miss, hitting Janet in the head. In a frenzied, violence-induced rage, he bent down next to her, choked his grip on the baseball bat, and continued to strike the young housewife until she stopped moving.[65]

After beating Janet Myers incessantly, and thinking she was dead, Fontanille next turned his attention to the unconscious Ryan. He dragged the toddler's body from the living room and into one of the back bedrooms of the house. At that point, panic engulfed him. The situation clearly would be extremely difficult for anyone to explain.

As he heard the key in the lock of the front door, his mind raced. Grabbing the baseball bat, he stood poised waiting for the door to open. When Kerry Myers entered the residence, Fontanille swung the bat at his intended victim's head. Myers put his left arm up to block the blow, shattering the bones of his lower forearm. In excruciating pain and bewilderment as to why one of his friends would do such a thing, the two began an awkward struggle that lasted most of the night, with both of them receiving various wounds about their heads and bodies.[66]

Fontanille knew that Janet Myers was either dead or struggling to stay alive and that Ryan lay badly wounded in one of the back bedrooms. He refused to let Myers see either of them. During the course of the conflict, at the point when they claimed to have rested and watched television, Myers arose from his seated position in the television room to use the restroom. Fontanille followed Myers carefully down the hallway and attacked him with the kitchen knife. Finally, Myers, wounded and in intense agony, managed to stab Fontanille with the kitchen knife after disarming Fontanille, and chased him from the house.[67]

According to W. J. LeBlanc, the prosecution's theory in the last trial has more credibility given the forensic evidence that ultimately convicted the two men. "My theory of the case was this was supposed to look like a burglary," LeBlanc remembered. "It was supposed to look like a burglary gone bad." As seen in the crime scene photos, each of the rooms was in disarray, especially the master bedroom. "Bill Fontanille was supposed to go there, kill her, make the crime scene look like that and then take off … walk around the corner and get into his car and leave. That way, nobody could testify about the car." LeBlanc contends that Fontanille and Myers planned the whole thing, but when little Ryan stepped in the middle of the assault on Janet Myers, Kerry Myers became angry; the injuring of his son was not part of the concocted plan.[68] The problems for the two men began, LeBlanc surmised, when they "boxed themselves into this position that they never saw the child … that they never saw her [Janet Myers]."

Three years after the conclusion of the Myers-Fontanille murder trial, and because the case drew nationwide attention, it did not take long for either an enterprising exposé writer or Hollywood to recognize the commercial value inherent in the sensationalism of the case. Joseph Bosco, a writer of predominantly sports books, wrote a "tell-all" book entitled *Blood Will Tell: The Story of Deadly Obsession in New Orleans.* Lacking objectivity (and listing the wrong location in the book's title), in addition to being abrasive in his telling of the story, Bosco relied heavily on the hearsay surrounding the case. The author also used rumors as a basis for his thesis rather than analyzing the aspects that would have demonstrated he clearly cared about the result of the trial. Although authorities granted Bosco unlimited access to evidence and documentation concerning the case, the author chose to try the two men through rumors from unsubstantiated sources to produce a popular and untrained perspective on the crime. Readers were left with the sense that Bosco served his own agenda in attempting to look like an omnipotent, literary sleuth who claimed to have solved the case. The author's attempts to make one of the men appear guiltier than the other falls short of the intended mark owing to his use of unreliable information and hyperbolic stylings.

While Bosco's book reached a sizable audience, it attracted even more publicity when Fontanille's defense attorney, Nick Noreia, filed a motion for a new trial. This motion, filed in early 1993, alleged that former Det. Sgt. Robert Masson gave a copy of Fontanille's statement to Myers prior to interviewing Myers. Noreia stated that this information came to light as a result of Bosco's manuscript; the author, he claimed, held interview tapes in his possession in which Myers made the assertion about the statement. Noreia claimed that the information came to light as a result of the publication of Bosco's manuscript, where the author cited interview tapes with Myers in making his assertion against Masson. When called to the stand in a hearing on the defense's new motion on November 4, 1993, Kerry Myers testified that no detectives at the time of his questioning showed him a copy of Fontanille's statement. Nevertheless, the witness thought, "he was either told or shown a portion of the Fontanille statement dealing with the time of day that Fontanille claimed to have been at the Myers's home before the murder."[69] When Masson took the stand, he denied any claims that he provided Myers with a copy of Fontanille's statement or informed Myers of its contents.[70]

Judge E. V. Richards ordered Bosco to take the stand, but when questioned as to whether he interviewed Myers, Bosco steadfastly refused to respond. Defense attorney Noreia immediately requested the court to hold the author in contempt for not answering the defense's questions. Judge Richards proffered to hold his decision for a later date. The prosecution, under the direction of W. J. LeBlanc and Terry Boudreaux, stated that Noreia did not file his motion for a new trial in a timely fashion and contended that the motion should be dismissed. Subsequently, Bosco admitted that the tapes and his notes from the Myers interview had been destroyed after the book's publication. Judge Richards ultimately ruled that Bosco enjoyed a "journalistic privilege" and, therefore, would not have to produce the tapes.[71]

In addition to Bosco's book, a made-for-television movie appeared shortly after the second trial, *Murder Among Friends* (1992). It took so much dramatic license that the story was unrecognizable to those who had lived through it. Additionally, the producers fabricated incidents that had not occurred during the course of the case and that slandered the reputations of the investigators and prosecutors who had so earnestly sought the truth surrounding the death of Janet Myers and the beating of Ryan Myers. The producers of the film diluted the facts to make the story more macabre, but the truth got in the way.

Ryan Myers never testified in his father's murder trial or the trial of William Fontanille. It seemed that he did not suffer any lasting effects from the night he was almost beaten to death, with the exception of short-term amnesia. After the trial and his father's sentencing, he grew up in relative obscurity. Ryan later joined the U.S. Army. In 2005, Sgt. Ryan Myers returned from Afghanistan as a distinguished veteran of the conflict there. Ryan currently lives in the Midwest with his wife and young child.[72]

Baby Sara, who was two months old at the time of her mother's murder and was unhurt on that night, lives on the west bank of New Orleans. As of this writing, she is married and the mother of two children of her own.

Kerry Myers and William Fontanille were "thicker than thieves" from the time they attended high school together until this incident saw their friendship dissolve through a blanket of lies and deceit and, finally, forensic evidence. With the murder of a young, vibrant Janet Myers and the nonsensical beating of her young son, Ryan, the situation gave meaning to the old adage, "The truth shall set you free." Certainly, the truth in this case would have set either William Fontanille or Kerry Myers free. Unfortunately, neither one of them could bring themselves to convey what happened on that February night in 1984 without suffering the consequences of implication.

The Final Broadcast

"Conceit, more rich in matter than in words,
Brags of his substance, not of ornament:
They are but beggars that can count their worth."
—William Shakespeare

In our respective lives, we have all known individuals who might be described as human beings of incredible virtue and conduct. Selfless individuals do exist, whose actions and manners go beyond the normal human response to tragedy, pain, and comfort, epitomizing the description of "a gift to mankind." In demonstrating the traits of virtue, individuals give of themselves in an altruistic manner, making the world a better place for both them and those around them. Furthermore, these individuals are willing to give more of themselves in a manner that goes unappreciated—in fact, that may even be exploited as a weakness. This is the story of such a spirit: a woman who gave everything to her family, friends, and love interests, only to be discarded by the one person who claimed to adore her most, with this all done in the interest of an over-inflated sense of notoriety and the conceit that results from such an embellishment. One hot summer Louisiana day, such a spirit was lost as a result of an incident that shocked and surprised those living in the New Orleans area and confirmed suspicions about a narcissistic personality once thought to be laughable.

On August 31, 2006, at approximately 3:37 p.m., Mary Elizabeth "Liz" Norman Caruso Marinello left an office building at 433 Metairie Road, just a short distance from the New Orleans city limits. Finishing an afternoon appointment with her counselor, she was approaching her car when a scruffy, bearded, homeless man approached her on a red bicycle. As the derelict peddled next to her, he stopped. Caruso was searching for the keys to her car in her purse, and she turned and looked at the man. The gruff stranger raised a .38-caliber revolver up to her face and fired two shots at point-blank range. After she fell to the ground, barely breathing and clutching her purse, the stranger peddled his bike to the edge of the parking lot, where he stopped at a used White Ford Taurus. The perpetrator then dismounted the bicycle, placed it in the trunk of the car, and drove away. Caruso lay in the parking lot for a brief moment before a passerby who heard the shots called emergency medical technicians. She was brought to Elmwood Emergency Trauma Center, where emergency surgeons worked feverishly to save her life. Liz Caruso died as a result of her injuries at approximately 2:00 a.m. the next morning.[1]

Mary Elizabeth Norman Caruso worked as a respiratory therapist at Children's Hospital in New Orleans for more than 10 years. She came to New Orleans at age 19, from Purvis, Mississippi. Liz was a trusting soul who loved children, family, and friends, giving her love to all those who asked. In her occupation at the hospital, she calmed the fears of the children to whom she administered respiratory treatments and became friends with the parents of her patients; friendliness was a trait she exhibited genuinely and effortlessly. Liz gave everyone the benefit of the doubt, almost to the point of naiveté, which proved to be a weakness upon which one individual in particular played.

In 2004, Liz was newly divorced from her husband, Peter Caruso, and living in Harahan with her daughter, 10-year-old Claire. At that point in her life, she did not expect the attentions of a much older, overzealous suitor. One night in January 2004, Liz, her mother Bertha Norman, and Claire

Liz Marinello left her therapist's office through this back door, walked a few feet, and then confronted the man who shot her and rode away on a red bicycle (Alan Gauthreaux collection).

arrived at an Elvis impersonators competition at a local hangout, the Rock-n-Bowl, for an innocent night out on the town.

"She told me the next day that some old guy was following her and kept bugging her for a date," one friend said. "It was a whirlwind romance," said another who observed the two that night. After asking Liz to dance, the mature stranger stressed how attractive and intriguing the young divorcee appeared to him. The dance was short, and the two soon parted company. Over the next few days, however, Liz received flowers at work from the man, who was named Vince Marinello. According to friends, she appeared flattered, but noted that the man who danced with her and sent her flowers was 20 years older than her. Liz approached the situation with some caution.

Vincent Marinello, the man who approached Liz and then sent her flowers, had achieved local notoriety as a sports personality with a thick New Orleans accent. He appealed to many viewers in the city with his "native" delivery and cartoon-like toupee. Although trusted with his reporting of local sports, in particular the New Orleans Saints football team and the horse racing venue at the Fairgrounds, his semi-intelligent commentary made for great conversation among those who tuned into whatever station Marinello found himself employed. Always dapperly dressed, Marinello conveyed the image of someone with no financial problems or difficulties on the horizon.

Graduating from St. Aloysius High School in New Orleans, Marinello grew up in the upper Ninth Ward of New Orleans, an area that saw heavy flooding during Hurricane Katrina in August 2005. Marinello played baseball and basketball at the school, but also took a strong interest at an early age in horse racing. Likewise, he took an interest in boxing, which was an important sport during the era in which Marinello matured. In the 1970s, alongside colorful sports commentator Bernard "Buddy" Diliberto, another local broadcasting favorite, Marinello worked as a sports reporter until the news anchor, local Alec Gifford, left for another station, WDSU, taking Diliberto and Marinello with him. Later, Diliberto and Marinello moved to radio, where they reigned as the primary sportscaster personalities in the area. Marinello's flamboyance and arrogance did not go unnoticed.

In addition to utilizing his personality-driven persona as a broadcaster, Marinello had self-proclaimed connections to the local Mafia, or so he told his co-workers and friends. He dressed in very dapper style wherever he went, in a signature suit, tie, and conspicuous toupee; people immediately recognized him as a gentleman and fashionable local celebrity. Marinello also claimed to have a law degree from Louisiana State University, and no one doubted that, given his wealth of sports knowledge, he possessed a mind sharp enough to study law as well.

Liz and Vince, from all appearances, seemed to share some chemistry. Eventually, albeit reluctantly, Liz accepted an invitation for a date to take place on Valentine's Day 2004. From that point onward, the courtship proceeded at a dizzying pace. On October 24, 2004, the two were married. Soon after the marriage, Marinello related to his new bride that he had more than $3 million in bearer bonds in safekeeping with a friend in New York City. Marinello stated that when the bonds matured, he would financially take care of Liz and her daughter, Claire, for life. To the newly married Mrs. Marinello, this seemed too good to be true.[2] But, since she had grown to love the older man, she thought nothing of it at the time. Marinello also stated to Liz, in a rather veiled manner, that he had "connections" with a local mob family in the New Orleans area and that he envied them.[3]

Soon after the honeymoon, the relationship between Liz and Vince Marinello began to deteriorate rapidly. Marinello possessed an ego of a size usually reserved for those who performed his occupation at the national level. One observer pointed out that at the Marinello wedding, "Vinnie wore a lot of pancake makeup and had a makeup artist following him around [the wedding reception] to touch up any problems."[4] Marinello often scolded Liz for not complimenting him on his appearance.

Moreover, Marinello never completely moved out of the house that he used to share with his ex-wife, Andrea (another untruth he told was that he had been divorced from Andrea before marrying Liz). He brought clothing to Liz's residence in Harahan, but never fully moved into the house they allegedly shared. Additionally, Marinello would write little notes to his wife complaining that she spent more time with her daughter than she did with him. Liz wanted to believe everything that Marinello told her over the course of their courtship and short marriage about having a secure financial future, but something inside her begged to know the truth.

In search of that truth, Liz and Marinello scheduled a trip to New York. Prior to their scheduled departure, Marinello started an argument with Liz on purpose and then stayed home. Liz took her daughter, Claire, and sought out a relative of Marinello—his estranged brother, Peter. When asked about the myriad of tales that Marinello had shared with her, Tony stated that his brother had no $3 million in bonds; in fact, all of the financial resources he had were his salary from the radio station and his Social Security check. Peter also stated that his brother might have had connections with the Mafia earlier in his life, but at the time of the New York trip, those connections existed only in Marinello's mind. Liz also learned that Marinello had never divorced his previous wife. All of these facts, combined with the gambling receipts she had discovered, the house in Lakeview that Marinello had never relinquished, the discovery that he never went to college, much less law school, the constant verbal abuse, and the outsized ego, were enough for Liz to file for divorce. She did just that soon after returning from New York on July 6, 2006.

After she filed for divorce, Liz suspected that Marinello had begun stalking her. She noticed him following her wherever she went and shadowing her every move. Liz complained to a friend, "I feel as though he [is] going to kill me."[5] Even persons who knew Marinello from his old Ninth Ward neighborhood agreed that "Vinnie was no good," and should be avoided at all costs.[6] But Liz never called the police to register a complaint or state that Marinello had been stalking her. She believed herself to be safe.

When they first looked at the shooting death of Liz Marinello, investigators of the Jefferson Parish Sheriff's Office believed it was a random occurrence—an attempted robbery that had gone terribly bad. But later, after questioning Marinello, the authorities grew suspicious that a more nefarious incident had occurred that required more digging.

On September 2, 2006, three days after the murder, Vince Marinello telephoned Colonel John Fortunato of the Jefferson Parish Sheriff's Office, a man whom the former considered a friend, and volunteered to give a statement to the detectives investigating the case. Many saw this as a preemptive strike of sorts, with the volunteer questioning whether police looked at him as a viable suspect in his wife's murder. While speaking with detectives, Marinello disclosed that he and Liz were engaged in an "acrimonious divorce," and things got heated. There had also been a "history of domestic disturbances," according to Sheriff Harry Lee, and Liz had just recently discovered that Marinello "was still married to his first wife when the couple wed in October 2004." Sheriff Lee did not want to cast any suspicion on Marinello as a prime suspect, but did say, "It's standard procedure for spouses to be considered suspects in murder cases and most are usually exonerated."[7]

Marinello gave an alibi as to his whereabouts when Liz had been shot: He was traveling to Jackson, Mississippi, where the New Orleans Saints were to play a preseason game. He stated that he arrived at a friend's house there sometime around 4:30 p.m. on August 31, 2006. According to his attorney, Marinello could not have committed the murder and gotten to the game at the time witnesses saw the broadcaster there. He also made a cell phone call during the time that he traveled on the road that appeared to substantiate his story. Marinello stated he went to the game and then returned to his home in Lakeview, a Federal Emergency Management Agency (FEMA) trailer where he resided due to the unrepaired condition of his home, which had been damaged in Hurricane Katrina. His story seemed credible, especially when investigators questioned witnesses at the scene of the shooting, who attested that a "scruffy-looking man clad in [a] black, blue, green shirt" was seen peddling a red bicycle away from the shooting.[8]

Relatives who learned of Liz's death immediately began to question the authorities' assumption that the crime was a robbery gone badly. When Liz was found lying in the parking lot, her keys to her truck were in her hand and her credit cards were still in her purse; there was also no signs of a struggle. Liz's sister, Claudia Labue, and brother, Dwayne Norman, would not cast aspersions on Marinello, but the relatives knew that the relationship between the two soured.[9] There also remained the very manner in which the perpetrator committed the crime: Firing two shots into someone's face at point-blank range suggests a more personal motive, rather than a random act. In the 1970s, when the federal government utilized the Racketeer Influenced and Corrupted Organizations (RICO) Act to engage informants against organized crime, those who were about to testify against their former bosses often did not make it to the witness stand, as they suffered the same fate as Liz Marinello. This history also raised suspicions about the motive behind the murder.

As the investigation ensued, Liz's family members went to the house that the couple shared in River Ridge (Harahan) to sort through the possessions of their loved one and discovered some disturbing material. Several letter notes Marinello wrote to Liz demonstrated a sense of insecurity as well as jealousy. Less than a year after they married, Marinello reprimanded his newlywed bride, accusing her of selfishness and acerbity and claiming that these attributes became "aggravating."[10] Later in the same note, he chastised her for not complimenting him for a new shirt he had worn the night before. This note and others like it revealed "the poisonous relationship that [Liz] endured until a few weeks before she was fatally shot."[11]

Bertha Norman, Liz's mother, stated that her daughter played detective when she went to New York. Uncovering the truth about her husband, she perceived, was tantamount to escaping the abuse she suffered at the hands of Marinello. In addition to learning that Marinello did not have Mafia ties and had not yet divorced his wife Andrea before marrying Liz, she discovered that his former wife, Andrea, had filed a lawsuit against Marinello in which she claimed "he forged her name on $126,000.00 in loans secured with her certificates of deposit." Relatives noticed that when she learned the truth, Liz's personality changed and the discoveries had "a profound effect on her typically buoyant spirit."[12] Learning the truth may also have had something to do with a domestic disturbance in which Liz actually got angry enough to fight back. According to Marinello, his wife attacked him, leaving scratches and punching him during a fight. But if the fight had been really serious, why did he wait two months before he claimed he was a victim of her domestic abuse? More credible sources stated that Marinello had become enraged with Liz and pinned her against a wall in the house they shared in River Ridge, Louisiana. To break his grip, Liz was faced with no other choice but to slap and scratch until she could get away from him. Marinello waited until the scratches disappeared before he filed charges with the Harahan Police Department. Friends witnessed the bruises on Liz's shoulders just weeks before her death.[13] Marinello's attorney spun the perception that Marinello abused his new wife as "a sign that he retained deep affection for his wife, even after their love died out."[14]

On September 7, 2006, despite the protestations of Marinello and his attorney to the contrary, Jefferson Parish sheriff's deputies and New Orleans police arrived at his FEMA trailer in front of his Lakeview suburb residence to conduct a search for any evidence in the murder of his wife, Liz. Police maintained they were searching for ammunition for a .38-caliber revolver and a disguise that Marinello might have worn while killing his wife. Detectives for the Jefferson Parish Sheriff's Office, it seemed, believed that the murder looked more like a "hit" than a botched robbery. Their suspicions were confirmed when the search turned up part of a disguise, a special type of ammunition consistent with a .38-caliber revolver and, surprisingly, a piece of paper that appeared to be a "to do" list for a murder.

After considering the evidence they had up to that point, Jefferson Parish detectives issued a warrant for the arrest of Vince Marinello. Advised that police had made a determination that the evidence implicated him as the killer, the 69-year-old broadcaster turned himself in to authorities at 3:00 p.m. on September 8, 2006. Although investigators had not discovered the full disguise or the weapon used in the crime, Sheriff Lee believed that the evidence they obtained from the suspect's trailer would serve to convict him.[15] Bertha Norman, mother of Liz Marinello, learned of Marinello's arrest through the Internet. She stated that the family strongly suspected that Marinello had something to do with her daughter's murder, but did not think he had the intestinal fortitude to commit the murder himself.[16]

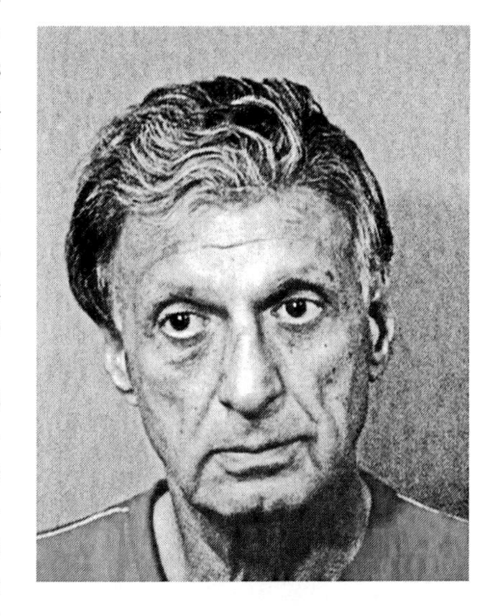

Vince Marinello, a popular sportscaster whom the people of New Orleans had grown to trust, pictured here in his mugshot having been arrested and charged with the murder of his estranged wife, Liz (courtesy Jefferson Parish Sheriff's Office).

Although the search of Marinello's living quarters revealed a wealth of evidence against the broadcaster, the motive for the murder eluded investigators. Family members speculated that Marinello wanted Liz silenced "before she spread the word that he was a bigamist, an allegation sure to surface during the pair's divorce proceedings."[17] Furthermore, the web of untruths that Marinello had spun during their marriage would damage his reputation as a trusted sportscaster. Knowing his level of vanity, even among his true friends and colleagues, the threat of exposure seemed too great a risk for someone whose reputation relied on the public trust.

To execute the crime, authorities speculated, Marinello drove his white Ford Taurus to within three blocks of the office building where Liz had a standing appointment with a therapist whom she had been seeing to deal with the problems in her marriage. Marinello had knowledge of this standing appointment. Once he arrived at a local school in the area, he donned a disguise and retrieved a red bicycle from the trunk. He rode the bicycle to 433 Metairie Towers on Metairie Road and went to the back parking lot. He located Liz's truck and waited until she came out of the building. In the video surveillance tapes from the office building, a scruffy man with a beard and baseball cap can be seen pacing in the back parking lot. After shooting Liz twice in the face, Marinello mounted the red bicycle and rode back to his car, and according to a witness near the school, placed the bicycle into the trunk and drove off.[18] In confirming this scenario, investigators relied upon the testimony of two witnesses. First, a local costume shop employee stated that a man fitting Marinello's description came into his shop and purchased a moustache. When asked if he needed a beard, the customer stated that he already had one. Second, a Jefferson Parish gunshop owner stated that a man also fitting Marinello's description came into his shop to have a weapon test-fired and to purchase some ammunition for the weapon—special Nyclad bullets. The type of ammunition that Marinello allegedly purchased was extremely "special" and rarely purchased by owners of .38-caliber guns. Marinello, however, denied that he owned a .38-caliber weapon.[19]

More surprisingly, Marinello's alibi of his whereabouts at the time of the shooting disintegrated. The couple whom Marinello allegedly visited in Jackson while attending the Saints game "first told authorities Marinello arrived in town at 6:30 p.m., not enough time to gun down his wife at 4 p.m., bicycle two blocks and drive 185 miles to Jackson." Later, the couple who provided his alibi changed their story, stating that Marinello arrived after 7:30 p.m., when the Saints game had already started.[20]

Another piece of evidence that proved equally damning demonstrated that even a disguise could not hide personal mannerisms that identify someone with a notably distinctive physical appearance. Videotape from the crime scene prior to Liz's shooting portrayed a scruffy man with his arms folded, pacing back and forth. His gait showed someone of mature years as he walked nervously around the outside camera near the parking lot.

When authorities arrested Marinello in September 2006, the criminal clerk of court set his bond at $250,000. At this time, the suspect's attorney, criminal lawyer Donald "Chick" Foret, began calling his client's friends to secure enough of a percentage of the bond to allow Marinello's release. For four days, Marinello spent time in the Jefferson Correctional Facility on a suicide watch. When he turned himself in, the suspect had given no indication that he suffered from any type of depression or remorse that his soon-to-be ex-wife had been murdered. Yet, the parish resources were devoted to making sure that he did not hurt himself while in their custody.

Vince Marinello walked out of the correctional center a free man on September 11, at least for the time being. As a condition of his release, in addition to providing the security for a $500,000 bond, Marinello would be under house arrest, wearing an ankle monitor.

Further examination of the evidence found in the suspect's trailer showed a determination to accomplish his mission with the utmost deception and calculation. Marinello knew his wife would be at Metairie Towers for the standing appointment with her therapist, as he had attended several meetings with her at that very address. From these visits, Marinello likely knew where the video surveillance cameras recorded happenings in and around the building. The "list" found in the trailer revealed a drawing of the very parking lot where the shooting occurred, with exits for a quick departure clearly marked. At the bottom of the list, and as a complete surprise to everyone, Marinello wrote the name of Sheriff Harry Lee. He also wrote a note to himself to dispose of the weapon near his mother's residence.

At the time that the police searched Marinello's trailer, they also possessed a warrant to search a residence owned by David Daniels, located at 6705 Vicksburg, New Orleans, in the Lakeview section of the city. Daniels and his wife still owned the house, but they had recently moved to Jackson, Mississippi; the couple had established Marinello's alibi on the day of Liz's murder, only to have that alibi later crumble under law enforcement scrutiny. Authorities could not find the weapon that Marinello may have used to kill his wife within his trailer, but they learned that the Daniels couple had a .38-caliber gun they kept hidden in their bathroom closet away from the prying hands of their young grandchildren. When police searched the house, the weapon was missing—but the couple maintained that Marinello knew where they kept the weapon.[21] A search of the radio station where Marinello worked produced no usable evidence.

Even though the police felt they could demonstrate the means by which Marinello committed this ghastly and unnecessary crime, fans, colleagues, and friends of the broadcaster expressed disbelief as to how this incident unfolded. His friends stated that Marinello would do anything for a friend; his fans felt reassured after listening to his post–Katrina broadcasts; and his colleagues thought his manner to be very professional. Not one of the groups believed him to be a cold-blooded killer who would go to such great lengths to keep his public reputation intact. Bob Mitchell, Marinello's on-air partner, expressed the view that if Marinello did not commit the crime, "then I hope God will lead investigators to the guilty person.... If he's not [innocent], and he did the crime, then he should pay the price, whatever it is."[22] Marinello stayed at his mother's condominium in Metairie, Louisiana, just outside of New Orleans while investigators continued to build their case.

During his stay at his mother's residence, Marinello received a call from Dave Selmo and Bob Mitchell to see if he wanted to visit for a while. Marinello indicated that Mitchell and Selmo could pick him up from his mother's residence. Dave Selmo would prove beneficial to the prosecution owing to certain information he obtained through conversations with Marinello prior to the murder. But at this encounter, Mitchell and Selmo arrived in the early afternoon approximately a week after Marinello bonded out. Selmo and Mitchell sat in the front seat and Marinello got in the backseat of the car. According to Selmo, Marinello was not especially talkative—that is, until they made their way to the trailer the police searched a few days before. Marinello sat in the FEMA trailer with Mitchell and Selmo. Marinello told the two that he had no respect for a man whose wife would not put his house up for bail for a friend (a remark directed at Mitchell). "If a friend of mine had shot the Pope, I'd still bail him out!" Selmo recalled Marinello saying at the meeting.[23]

During the long wait until the arraignment, Sheriff Harry Lee drew criticism for remarks he had made prior to Marinello's arrest. During the initial phase of the investigation, Sheriff Lee went to the crime scene with his detectives. He immediately assumed that Liz Marinello had become the random victim of a robbery, and believed that the crime was one of opportunity for the armed gunman. In another statement, Lee described the video from the surveillance camera at the crime scene as "useless because it was aimed into the glare of the late-afternoon sun."[24] Later, Lee claimed that he did not want to give any indication to the perpetrator of the crime that they were looking for a murderer; rather, he wanted to let his constituents know that the police were searching for a robber. In regard to the videotape, Sheriff Lee and his investigators wanted to make sure they could use the tape in building a case against Vince Marinello. Sheriff Lee later corrected his initial misstatements without entering an apology.

The investigation continued, with new details coming to light. On the back of the checklist found at Marinello's trailer, the detectives discovered a sketch of the murder scene. Moreover, Marinello had a schedule of the appointments that Liz Marinello kept with her therapist at the office she visited on the day she was murdered. In addition, as part of information gathering through interviews with witnesses who came forward later, police took the statement of a person who first saw a scruffy-looking man taking a red bicycle from the trunk of a Ford Taurus and then later saw the same disheveled man putting the bike into the trunk of the car and driving off. Marinello owned a white Ford Taurus similar to the one in this witness's descriptions.

On December 7, 2006, Marinello once again stood on front of a judge in Jefferson Parish; his first appearance was for his indictment for second-degree murder, and the second for a hearing on an increase in his bail amount. Judge Joan Benge set Marinello's bond at $750,000. As a condition of his bail, Marinello had to agree to house arrest. When the now-defendant appeared in Judge Benge's court, his attorney, Donald "Chick" Foret, "disclosed publicly that he was no longer representing Marinello." Instead, the court appointed a public defender to represent Marinello due to his insistence that he had no further financial resources to hire his own attorney.[25]

On February 16, 2007, Marinello had a new defense team. Because of his allegedly indigent condition, Paul Fleming, Jr., and Sam Scillitani were appointed to represent Marinello. Both attorneys had experience with capital murder cases. One of their first orders of business was filing for a change of venue for the trial of Vince Marinello due to the excessive press coverage and the well-known identity of their client. The defense also moved that the district attorneys assigned to the case recuse themselves because of an apparent relationship Marinello had with the Jefferson Parish District Attorney's Office prior to his wife's murder. Over the course of several meetings and conversations with various assistant district attorneys, Marinello toyed with the idea of whether he should press charges against his deceased wife. According to Assistant District Attorney David Wolff, in January 2006, Marinello wanted to place a restraining order against his wife's ex-husband for abuse against her. In July, his tune seemed to change when Marinello expressed interest in filing charges against his wife "after their marriage started to erode, alleging his wife beat him May 29 in their Harahan home."[26] Marinello also considered getting a restraining order against Liz as a result of the alleged beating. But, according to Wolff, "he [Marinello] did not qualify for one through criminal means." It appeared that he tried to make his soon-to-be ex-wife miserable through a series of antagonistic legal maneuvers. The day after Marinello filed for divorce, July 7, 2006, he claimed that his wife slapped him while he slept and he sought a criminal complaint against her. Then, strangely, Marinello seemed contrite and wanted to salvage what he had left of his marriage with Liz. Subsequently, police arrested Liz, but never pursued the charges against her for domestic violence.

Even more twists would occur and delay justice. The chief prosecutor in the case, Assistant District Attorney Roger Jordan, suddenly and abruptly took a leave of absence without giving any reason for his departure. All of the cases he worked on then had to be placed with other members of his office. Additionally, Jordan's absence coincided with evidentiary hearings that proved integral to the prosecution of Marinello for his wife's murder. Despite the chaos, District Attorney Paul Connick reassured the public and the victim's family that with Jordan's replacement, Ken Bordelon, who was just as capable and determined to try the case, justice would be served.[27]

The trial date was set for February 25, 2008. Then, in a show of dramatics, the defense announced they would be filing a continuance because a new attorney would be joining the defense team. Lee Faulkner, Jr., became the third member of Marinello's defense. Judge Conn Regan, in a hearing on February 16, 2008, stated that this case had been waiting almost two years for adjudication; he would reluctantly grant the continuance, but he would not entertain any further motions that sought to delay the trying of the case.[28]

One editorialist made reference to Marinello (and U.S. Representative William Jefferson, who was being tried on bribery charges during the same time period and secured several delays in his trial) when he opined, "There is nothing like a long-drawn out case to test the public's faith in the criminal justice system ... following the postponement that leaves Marinello waiting trial under house arrest at his mother's apartment." A citizen even complained about the delay: "It shows that persons of power, influence, and status can manipulate the system to delay both of their and the public's day in court time and time again.... The Constitution requires a fair trial, not a perfect one, and if Jefferson and Marinello are the measure, perhaps it doesn't require any trial at all."[29]

The legal wrangling continued. The defense lost its battle to recuse the district attorneys assigned to the case because of their previous dealings with the defendant, but eventually won a motion for a change of venue to a court in Lafayette, Louisiana, 230 miles to the southwest of Metairie.[30] The prosecution and the defense both sought to have a jury from Jefferson Parish transported to the new trial jurisdiction, but Judge Regan determined that because Marinello was not charged with a capital crime (one that carries a death sentence should he be convicted), a jury would be picked from the citizens of the new venue.[31]

Even in Lafayette, the defense team delayed the proceedings at every turn before the trial began. The prosecution, as a matter of law, supplied the defense team with all of the documentation they needed to conduct their portion of the trial. However, a DNA report, which stated no DNA from Marinello could be gathered from the mysterious bicycle allegedly used in the crime, had to be examined. After Judge Conn Regan had ruled in a previous hearing that there would be no more continuances, he felt compelled to grant this one in the interests of fairness and justice. Instead of the trial starting on May 12, 2008, it would be at least another week before a jury selection began. These delay tactics seemed to take their toll on Liz's family, even though they were certain that in the end, justice would come. With the exposure of the DNA report, however, it would not be until the fall of 2008 that the case would be tried before a jury.[32] Prosecutors hoped that no further delays would occur and the court would not grant the defense any further continuances, as the new trial date, September 15, was fast approaching.

With so many delays and attempts to keep the former sportscaster out of jail, the right to a speedy trial seemed to have gone out the window. From the time of Marinello's arrest until the scheduled start of his trial, a span of 20 months would have passed. The point of the Constitutional guarantee did not escape one citizen: "One can be sure it will be very difficult for police and witnesses to accurately recollect events of almost two years ago."[33]

Another forthcoming delay had nothing to do with legal jousting. With forecasts predicting the landfall of two hurricanes, Gustav and Ike, on or about September 15, 2008, the defense motioned for another continuance. Fortunately, by the time of the trial, forecasters predicted the storm would make landfall in Texas. However, meteorologists later predicted that Ike would make landfall somewhere between Galveston, Texas, and Morgan City, Louisiana, which could have brought wind speeds in the area to 65 miles per hour. Once again, Judge Regan felt compelled to select a new trial date.[34] All those concerned chose December 1, 2008.

In more pretrial motions, the defense sought to have the second-degree murder charges dismissed because they asserted that a grand juror on the panel that indicted Marinello could be called as a witness in his murder trial. The juror in question worked at the office building where Liz was shot, and was there on the day of the crime. The prosecution also made a motion that evidence proving Marinello to be a bigamist should be introduced, as it was part of the motive in the murder of Liz Marinello. Moreover, the prosecution sought to prevent the defense from besmirching Liz's reputation by introducing evidence of her previous marriage and child custody battle with her former husband, Peter Caruso. Judge Regan determined that the evidence of her prior court actions regarding her divorce would not be discussed because they were irrelevant to the present case.[35]

In addition to evidence in the form of the checklist with the notes to himself to throw the gun away, the map of the murder scene, the eyewitness accounts that placed Marinello at the scene of his wife's murder, and a messy divorce under way, police concentrated on the accused man's alibi for the day of the murder. Marinello maintained that he traveled from his home in Lakeview to Byram, Mississippi, to view a New Orleans Saints preseason game at the residence of David and Annette Daniels, who had been displaced there as a result of Hurricane Katrina. Marinello stated that he left his Lakeview residence at approximately 4:10 p.m., and making his way to Fluker, Louisiana, exited the highway some time before 5:16 p.m. At that time in the afternoon, a local news crew conducted a test in which they made the same journey. From the time they left the Marinello residence, it took them 1 hour and 45 minutes to arrive at the Fluker exit—much longer than the time that Marinello claimed it took him to make the trip.[36] The prosecution, in attempting to establish that either Marinello lied or his alibi witnesses were not being totally truthful, referenced the defendant's cell phone records as a means to destroy the alibi.

With all of these points in mind, the prosecution stood ready for trial. They felt confident that even though they possessed only circumstantial evidence of the defendant's guilt, the jury would do the right thing and convict Marinello of second-degree murder.

The testimony in the case of the *State v. Vincent Marinello* began on December 3, 2008. When attorney Paul Fleming made his opening remarks to the jury, he clearly stated that Marinello did not shoot his wife and that all of the evidence in the possession of the prosecution could be clearly explained. Fleming tried to influence the jury's perceptions of the "checklist" by questioning when the note was written: "Was it before or after the wife had been shot?" District Attorney Tommy Block, for his part, stated that Marinello was the killer who planned the murder of Liz Marinello, buying a disguise and ammunition specifically to accomplish that objective. The checklist, he said, merely laid out the plan visually.[37]

In the prosecution's case, the first witness called to testify was Peter Caruso, who described how he heard of Liz's demise. He also noted that Claire, the couple's adopted daughter, had to undergo 13 weeks of intensive therapy to cope with her mother's death. Marinello frequently discussed his marital woes with Caruso, especially on the morning of the murder, and expressed despair that Liz Marinello had refused to give Claire a stuffed teddy bear that Marinello had purchased for the child's 10th birthday.[38]

The prosecution then called fellow employees from the radio station where Marinello worked. On the day of the murder, Todd Menesses, WWL-Radio 870's assistant program director, testified that Marinello showed up at the radio station "wearing 'ratty' shoes and a stained shirt." The next day, after Menesses learned of Liz Marinello's murder and heard the description of the man whom witnesses stated was in the area at the time of the shooting, he telephoned Marinello's supervisor, Diane Newman, and told her that he thought Marinello might have shot his wife. The defense attempted to counter this testimony by stating that Marinello's colleagues never saw what the sportscaster wore when not at the station.[39]

Despite the testimony and the fact that he could spend the rest of his life in prison, Marinello relished in the comfort with which he had been viewing the trial. He often bragged about his hotel room, where he had numerous pillows, a Jacuzzi tub, and a microwave, never once showing any remorse for the death of his former wife. One reporter commented, "He had better get the most out of it on account of the accommodations at the state penitentiary are somewhat less plush." Marinello also displayed an interest in learning the outcomes of races at the New Orleans Fairgrounds, where he had earned extra money as a handicapper. Even as the evidence mounted against him, he continued to display an air of unconcern, much less any type of contrition.[40]

On the third day of testimony, the prosecution called Tracy Andre, a radiofrequency engineer from AT&T. Andre testified that Marinello's cell phone records for the day of the murder showed "Marinello was near Pontchatoula [Louisiana] 54 minutes after Liz Marinello was shot." Andre emphatically insisted that there was no way that the call Marinello claimed he made from Mississippi could have been made from that location.[41] Moreover, the cell phone records indicated that Marinello was within a half-mile of the crime scene two hours before the shooting.[42]

Various other witnesses testified that day as well, including David Selmo. The prosecution wanted this witness to elaborate on the conversations that took place between him and defendant before and after the murder. Selmo, a former Special Forces member and Army Ranger, testified about when he first met Marinello. When Marinello discovered Selmo's experience with weapons, he inquired as to whether a .38-caliber gun could be outfitted with a silencer. The witness also testified that Marinello related a story concerning a famous Mafia hitman, Anthony "Tony Pro" Provolone, who, Marinello claimed, could execute a hit in Detroit in the morning and be back in New Orleans "by the end of the day."[43] Although sources at the time could not substantiate Marinello's claims about the elusive hitman, an individual by the name of Anthony Provanzano, known for being a *caporegime*, or captain in the Genovese crime family, had ties to various unions in the northeastern United States, including connections to Teamsters union president Jimmy Hoffa and even the president of the United States, Richard M. Nixon. However, Provanzano never dirtied his hands with contract murders; he hired someone else to do the work. In any case, Selmo attributed Marinello's story to urban legend until after Liz Marinello's death. He then asked one of the prosecutors whether he should go into hiding until after the conclusion of the trial for fear of Mafia retribution. Marinello never confided to Selmo that he had done anything illegal; therefore, prosecutors determined Selmo was safe from any retribution.[44]

One of the most important witnesses of the trial was Annette Daniels, Marinello's alibi witness. She testified that when Marinello arrived at her apartment, the game had already started. Daniels had originally told sheriff's deputies that when Marinello arrived at her residence, he wore a white T-shirt, blue jeans, and a pair of white tennis shoes; this matched the description given to police of the scruffy man who was seen riding a bicycle near the crime scene. Later, the witness changed her testimony to say that Marinello wore a pair of dark pants to her residence on the night of the murder. When Daniels notified Marinello that Liz had been shot, he simply shook his head from side to side, yet continued to watch the Saints game on television. As far as she knew, during the course of the night Marinello made no effort to determine the well-being of either his estranged wife or her daughter.

The prosecution also questioned Annette Daniels concerning the .38-caliber revolver that she and her husband allegedly gave Marinello as a gift in 1985. During the 1980s or 1990s, Daniels testified that Marinello gave the weapon back to the couple "for her protection during a drive to Dallas to visit her ill father." After returning from the trip, Annette Daniels hid the weapon in the bathroom of the house she owned prior to Hurricane Katrina. The gun was still there when the floodwaters from the storm overwhelmed the area, including her home. She never saw the weapon again. In a strange twist on the usual procedure, Daniels testified in part with the jury out of the courtroom: During this testimony, she claimed that Jefferson Parish Sheriff Harry Lee personally called her and wanted her to tell him that "Mrs. Daniels gave Marinello the weapon in question," or he would see to it that his detectives would arrest her as an accessory to the murder. The witness then claimed that she told Sheriff Lee she would not do that.[45]

By the time the prosecution rested its case, the evidence, though circumstantial, had mounted to a level that removed any reasonable doubt of whether Marinello had killed his wife for anyone who had been listening to the three days of testimony and the introduction of physical evidence. The defense strategy appeared to be largely damage control. As Paul Fleming had stated at the beginning of the trial, "The evidence will not show Vince Marinello is guilty. Can I prove he's innocent? Probably not. But I can try." It became obvious throughout the trial, as the defense attempted to discredit the prosecution's case, that an uphill battle awaited the defendant's attorneys. Defense attorney Fleming tried to blame the police, alleging that their probe did not reach deep enough before Marinello became the prime suspect in his wife's murder. For example, the defense maintained that the Jefferson Parish Sheriff's Office did not make an adequate attempt to determine whether Marinello's fingerprints appeared on the bicycle that officers retrieved. The crime scene technician at the time, Lt. Kelly Carrigan, stated that there were no fingerprints to be found. This is easily explainable, as the perpetrator wore gloves. Still, to focus on such a small scintilla of evidence when there were greater obstacles to conquer to obtain an acquittal for the defendant seemed a trivial pursuit to those observing the trial.

The defense continued in their quest to instill reasonable doubt into the minds of the jurors. The "scruffy man" identification was held in doubt by the defense, even though two witnesses had stepped forward identifying Marinello as the hobo who rode the bike in the Old Metairie neighborhood both prior to the shooting and on the day of the shooting. Lauren White, an elementary school physical education coach, remembered seeing a man matching the description of the shabbily dressed man riding a bicycle up and down Metairie Road just a few blocks from the murder scene. She witnessed the man she later identified as Marinello "for four consecutive days passing Metairie Academy" where she supervised children's physical activities in the front of the school. White claimed, "The last time she saw him was the day Liz Marinello was shot." Her identification of the defendant stemmed from the fact that she was so close to the bicycle rider that she saw his eyes. When she saw Marinello's booking photo, she made a positive identification.[46]

With the mounting evidence against him, in a not-so-intelligent move on the defense's part, Marinello took the stand in his own defense on December 12, 2008. During the more than six hours of his testimony, Marinello presented himself as a "well-connected career newsman," and attempted to rationalize why he wrote the checklist that detectives found in his FEMA trailer. The defendant reasoned with the court that he formulated the checklist to clear his name. He knew he was being considered a suspect and wanted to examine the motives that the police might cite for him to kill his wife. Marinello stated that he assembled the thoughts on the checklist because he suspected he would have to clear his name as a suspect. With reference to Sheriff Harry Lee's name being at the bottom of the list, Marinello stated that he compiled an evidence list that he would later present to the now-deceased sheriff.[47]

In reference to the gunshot residue found in his car, Marinello explained that it was left over from a time when he test-fired a 9-mm pistol he had recently purchased. The witness claimed that when he purchased the weapon, the store clerk chambered a round and let him leave the store with the gun in his hand. In reference to the ammunition used to kill Liz Marinello, the defendant stated that he had never fired a weapon in his life, but then contradicted himself by admitting that he test-fired the 9-mm weapon near his FEMA trailer. Moreover, prior to Marinello taking the stand in his own defense, Allen Reese, an employee at the gun store where Marinello stated he purchased the 9-mm pistol, had testified that the defendant also purchased a box of .38-caliber Nyclad bullets. These particular rounds had a blue covering and were very distinctive in their appearance. A bullet of this type was removed from Liz Marinello's skull during her autopsy. Vincent Marinello also testified that he had Reese test-fire an old .38-caliber revolver in July 2006—the same type of weapon used to shoot and kill Liz Marinello. With Annette Daniels testifying that she and her husband gave Marinello a .38-caliber Charter Arms revolver for a Christmas present in 1985, it became incumbent upon the jury to determine whether Marinello used that same weapon to murder his wife.[48]

Marinello maintained a sense of arrogance throughout his testimony. When it ended, the defense rested. Every piece of evidence that the prosecution had produced demonstrating his guilt, Marinello explained away as mere happenstance. It appeared that he was not worried about what the jury thought: He would be walking out of the Lafayette courtroom a free man—or so he thought and confidently portrayed as the expected outcome throughout his examination and cross-examination. When the defense rested its case, however, the wait began to see if Marinello would be convicted of the second-degree murder of his wife.

On Saturday, December 14, 2008, at 5:00 p.m., after 90 minutes of deliberation, the jury came back into the courtroom with a unanimous verdict—guilty of second-degree murder in the death of Liz Marinello. After pronouncing their verdict, Judge Conn Regan thanked the jurors for their service during this difficult trial and excused them from the courtroom. As soon as the court announced the verdict, deputies from the Lafayette Parish Sheriff's Office confiscated Marinello's jewelry and other personal items, while a deputy from Jefferson Parish frisked the newly convicted murderer for any hidden objects. The trial that was delayed for so long and the justice that Marinello sought to escape finally caught up to the once-beloved and trusted sportscaster.[49]

After the trial concluded, members of the prosecution team and Liz Marinello's family gathered outside the courtroom to field questions from the press. Tommy Block, the assistant district attorney for Jefferson Parish, stated in all of his years of practicing law, he had never met someone "more egotistical, self-centered, and narcissistic" than Vince Marinello. Block also related that he could not understand how Marinello could have expressed such loathing for someone he avowed to adore. The family members reiterated that they had believed Marinello's guilt from the start, from the moment they received word that Liz had been shot.[50]

Debra Schmidt, the forewoman of the Marinello jury, kept telling herself that Marinello was innocent until proven guilty. In examining the evidence, Schmidt and her fellow jurors took special notice of the videotapes shown by the prosecution. When they compared the Vince Marinello from the district attorney's office visit with the scruffy man in the parking lot of the Metairie Towers building, the two matched perfectly—it was the same man! The arrogance that Marinello displayed to the jury and anyone else in the courtroom during the trial lent credence to the belief that he was a cold-blooded murderer. It became glaringly obvious to the jury, according to Schmidt, that Marinello valued his reputation more than the life of his wife.[51]

During the whole process of the trial, the Norman family—the relatives of Liz Marinello—were noticeably disturbed by the evidence presented. Once the jury verdict was announced, the jurors expressed an interest in meeting the family. They wanted to offer their condolences at the loss to the family members as well as shake hands and share an emotional moment that the trial had finally concluded. "Even the most macho men on the jury cried" as the jury formed a line to meet with Liz's family, remembered Debra Schmidt.[52] The Normans then retired to their hotel and toasted the verdict. It was not a happy celebration, but rather one of relief that Vince Marinello would be spending the rest of his life behind bars without the benefit of parole or probation for the senseless murder of a mother, sister, niece, and daughter who would be remembered as a caring, thoughtful, and selfless woman who lost her life at the hands of a narcissistic man with no reason to exhibit that type of conceit.

Marinello's sentence was officially confirmed on January 22, 2009. At that hearing, Liz Marinello's family members lashed out at the inmate, who arrived in court dressed in an orange jumpsuit, convict shower shoes, and no toupee, with his hands shackled to his waist. As he stood before the court to receive his sentence, according to one eyewitness, Marinello "offered no expressions of remorse or words of condolence" to the Norman family. After several of the family members stated their opinions of the defendant, Judge Regan pronounced the sentence: Marinello would spend the rest of his life behind bars, without the benefit of parole or probation. Given his advanced age at the time of his conviction (Marinello was 71), he would probably die behind bars unless he were granted a new trial. Judge Regan believed that Marinello received a fair trial, so there was hardly any doubt that a higher court would grant such a request.[53]

After his conviction and incarceration, Marinello continued to insist he did not shoot his former wife and questioned the methods employed by his defense team. Marinello criticized Paul Fleming for refusing to question a ballistics report about the powder residue found in his car and for not hiring an image expert to contest the similarities between the video from the district attorney's office and the video from Metairie Towers. These issues were reiterated on appeals filed in the Louisiana court circuit, but were denied as baseless.[54] As of this writing, Marinello still protests his innocence and continues to file appeals, which are repeatedly denied.

Vince Marinello was a legend in his own mind who thought he could transcend the reach of justice. Because of his comical appearance (some have made the reference that without his toupee he resembled the character of "Mr. Burns" from *The Simpsons*) and insistence on being the center of attention wherever he appeared, the public never took him seriously enough to believe him capable of such a heinous crime. After he shattered that laughable reputation with a history of bigamy and pathological lies, a jury saw through the veil and found him guilty of murder.

Chapter Notes

The First Godfather

1. "Italian Immigrants," *Daily Picayune*, New Orleans, December 27, 1888; Elizabeth Cometti, "Trends in Italian Immigration," *Western Political Quarterly*, 11, no. 4 (December 1958): 820–834, 821; Humbert S. Nelli, *From Immigrants to Ethnics: The Italian Americans* (Oxford, UK: Oxford University Press, 1983), 81.

2. Michael Hunt and Martha Macheca, *Deep Water: Joseph P. Macheca and the Rise of the Mafia* (New York: iUniverse Publishing, 2004), 50–51; Napier Bartlett, *Military Record of Louisiana* (Baton Rouge: Louisiana State University Press, 1964), 238.

3. David L. Chandler, *Brothers in Blood: The Rise of the Criminal Brotherhoods* (New York: E. P. Dutton & Co., 1975), 74.

4. Bennett Wall et al., *Louisiana: A History* (Arlington Heights, IL: Harlan Davidson, 1984), 201.

5. John Sacher, *A Perfect War of Politics: Parties, Politicians, and Democracy in Louisiana, 1824–1861* (Baton Rouge: Louisiana State University Press, 2007), 293.

6. Michael Kurtz, "Organized Crime in Myth and Reality," *Louisiana History: The Journal of the Louisiana Historical Association*, 24, no. 4 (Autumn 1983): 361.

7. Kurtz, "Organized Crime in Myth and Reality," 361.

8. Wall et al., *Louisiana: A History*, 201–202; Robert Somers, *The Southern States Since the War, 1870–1871*, introduction by Malcolm C. McMillan (Tuscaloosa, AL: University of Alabama Press, 1965), 228.

9. Henry Clay Warmoth, *War, Politics, and Reconstruction: Stormy Days in Louisiana* (New York: Negro University Press, 1970), 33.

10. Wall et al., *Louisiana: A History*, 203.

11. Ted Tunnell, *The Crucible of Reconstruction: War, Radicalism, and Race in Louisiana, 1862–1877* (Baton Rouge, LA: Louisiana State University Press, 1992), 193–195; Anne Campbell, *Louisiana: The History of an American State* (Atlanta: Clairmont Press, 2007), 361–364.

12. James K. Hogue, *Uncivil War: Five New Orleans Street Battles and the Rise and Fall of Radical Reconstruction* (Baton Rouge: Louisiana State University Press, 2006), 128.

13. "The Italians; They Meet and Define Their Position on the White League Question," *The New Orleans Times*, July 24, 1874, p. 4.

14. Editorial: "The League Movement," *The New Orleans Times*, July 17, 1874, p. 2.

15. "Telegraph; Foreign News," *The New Orleans Times*, September 2, 1874, p. 1; Ella Lonn, *Reconstruction in Louisiana After 1868* (New York: Russell & Russell, 1918), 265; George C. Rable, *But There Was No Peace: The Role of Violence in the Politics of Reconstruction* (Athens: University of Georgia, 1984), 135.

16. "More Arms Seized; Detectives Take Three More Boxes of Arms from Oliver's Gun Store, Seventy-Two Muskets," *The Daily Picayune*, New Orleans, September 11, 1874, p. 1; "Editorial: Who Are the Violators of the Constitution?" *The Daily Picayune*, New Orleans, September 11, 1874, p. 3.

17. "The Arms Seizure; A *Times* Reporter Interviews Governor Kellogg on the Subject, His Views in Regard to the Law and the Facts," *The New Orleans Times*, September 14, 1874, p. 1.

18. Thomas Hunt and Martha Macheca, *Deep Water: Joseph P. Macheca and the Birth of the American Mafia* (New York: iUniverse

Publishing, 2004), 102–103; "A Mass Meeting," *The New Orleans Times*, September 14, 1874, p. 4; "War; Uprising of the Citizens," *The Daily Picayune*, New Orleans, September 15, 1874, p. 1.

19. Hunt and Macheca, *Deep Water*, 102–103.

20. "War; Uprising of the Citizens," *The Daily Picayune*, New Orleans, September 15, 1874, p. 1; 102–103.

21. "War; Telegram of Acting Gov. Penn to President Grant," *The Daily Picayune*, New Orleans, September 15, 1874, p.1.

22. "The Outlook," *The New Orleans Times*, September 16, 1874, p. 2; "About Town," *The Daily Picayune*, New Orleans, September 17, 1874, p. 8; "Exodus; The Prologue," *The Daily Picayune*, New Orleans, September 18, 1874, p. 1; Rable, *But There Was No Peace*, 135–140; Ella Lonn, *Reconstruction in Louisiana After 1868* (New York: Russell & Russell, 1918), 268–290.

23. "Where They Were on the Night of the Matranga," *The Daily States*, New Orleans, May 6, 1890, p. 3; 1–2; Tom Smith, *The Crescent City Lynchings* (Guilford, CT: Lyons Press, 2007), 41–42.

24. John E. Coxe, *The New Orleans Mafia Incident* (Unpublished master's thesis, Louisiana State University, 1928), 1072; "Where They Were on the Night of the Matranga Trouble," *The Daily States*, New Orleans, January 22, 1891, p. 3: 1–2.

The Other Assassinated Chiefs

1. Alan Gauthreaux, *Italian Louisiana: History, Tradition, and Heritage* (Charleston, SC: History Press, 2014), 38–39, 59–62.

2. Jennifer Gardner, *The Murder of Patrick Mealey: Police Chief of New Orleans, 1880–1888* (Unpublished master's thesis, University of New Orleans, 2001), 3.

3. "Murdered; Hon. Patrick Mealey Shot Down in Cold Blood," *The Daily Picayune*, New Orleans, January 2, 1888, p. 1: 5–7, 2: 1–3; "Mealey Murder Trial; The Fifth Day's Proceeding," *The Daily Picayune*, New Orleans, November 3, 1888, p. 2.

4. "Murdered; Hon. Patrick Mealey Shot Down in Cold Blood," p. 1: 5–7, 2: 1–3.

5. "Murdered; Hon. Patrick Mealey Shot Down in Cold Blood," p. 1: 5–7, 2: 1–3.

6. "Murdered; Hon. Patrick Mealey Shot Down in Cold Blood," p. 1: 5–7; 2: 1–3.

7. "Murdered; Hon. Patrick Mealey Shot Down in Cold Blood," p. 1: 5–7, 2: 1–3.

8. "Mourned," *The Daily Picayune*, New Orleans, January 3, 1888, p. 1: 3–5.

9. "Mourned," p. 1: 3–5.

10. "Mourned," p. 1: 3–5.

11. "Murdered; Hon. Patrick Mealey Shot Down in Cold Blood," p. 1: 5–7, 2: 1–3.

12. "Murdered; Hon. Patrick Mealey Shot Down in Cold Blood," p. 1: 5–7, 2: 1–3.

13. "The Killing of Patrick Mealey," *The Daily Picayune*, New Orleans, January 2, 1888, p. 4: 2.

14. "The Killing of Patrick Mealey," p. 4: 2.

15. "The Killing of Patrick Mealey," p. 4: 2.

16. Gardner, *The Murder of Patrick Mealey*, 14; *Criminal District Court for the Parish of Orleans*, Section "A", Judge Alfred Roman presiding, Arraignment Hearing, February 21, 1888.

17. "Mealey Murder; Claire, Gibson, and Feehan on Trial for Their Lives," *The Daily Picayune*, New Orleans, October 31, 1888, p. 8.

18. "Mealey Murder," p. 8; Gardner, *The Murder of Patrick Mealey*, 11–12.

19. Madelon Powers, *Faces Along the Bar: Lore and Order in the Workingman's Saloon, 1870–1920* (Chicago: University of Chicago Press, 1998), 76–133.

20. *Criminal District Court for the Parish of Orleans*, No. 207, Case #10321, *State of Louisiana v. Louis Claire, John Gibson, and William Feehan*, Docket #1267.

21. *Criminal District Court for the Parish of Orleans*, No. 207, Case #10321, *State of Louisiana v. Louis Claire, John Gibson, and William Feehan*, Docket #1267.

22. "The Mealey Murder; Seventh Day of the Trial of Claire, Gibson, and Feehan," *The Daily Picayune*, New Orleans, November 6, 1888, p. 8.

23. "The Mealey Murder; Seventh Day," p. 8.

24. "The Mealey Murder; Seventh Day," p. 8.

25. "The Mealey Murder; Seventh Day," p. 8.

26. "Claire Convicted; Trial of Mealey Murders Completed," *The Daily Picayune*, New Orleans, November 7, 1888, p. 8.

27. "Claire Convicted," p. 8; "Shot after Conviction," *Philadelphia Inquirer*, November 9, 1888, p. 1.

28. "The Mealey Murder," *The Daily Picayune*, New Orleans, May 21, 1889, p. 6.

29. "The Mealey Tomb," *The Daily Picayune*, New Orleans, June 21, 1889, p. 2.

30. "Funeral of the Late Police Chief to Be Held Saturday," *The Daily Picayune*, New Orleans, August 4, 1917, p. 5: 4–5.

31. "Pathetic Scenes Feature Funeral of Police Chief," *The Times Picayune*, New Orleans, LA, August 5, 1917, p. 3: 1–5.

32. "James W. Reynolds, Head of Police Force, Murdered by Madman," *The Daily Picayune*, New Orleans, August 3, 1917, p. 1: 1, 1–5.

33. "Probe of Chief's Murder Begins Monday," *The Daily Picayune*, New Orleans, August 4, 1917, p. 1: 1, 5: 1–5.

34. "Terence Mullen, Murderer of Chief, Strapped to Bed," *The Daily Picayune*, New Orleans, August 6, 1917, p. A-1: 2–3.

35. "Terence Mullen, Murderer of Chief, Strapped to Bed," p. A-1: 2–3.

36. "Board Takes First Step in Probing Assassination," *The Daily Picayune*, New Orleans, August 7, 1917, p. A-1: 2.

37. 'Witnesses Unable to Recognize Men Who Sought Cover," *The Daily Picayune*, New Orleans, August 14, 1917, p. 4: 3.

38. "Charges Against Police Made by Chief Mooney," *The Daily Picayune*, New Orleans, August 15, 1917, p. 1: 1, 4: 2–7.

The Madam's Last Will

1. Al Rose, *Storyville, New Orleans* (Tuscaloosa: University of Alabama Press, 1974), 5.

2. Herbert Asbury, *The French Quarter: A History of the New Orleans Underworld* (Atlanta: Mockingbird Books, 1963).

3. The district between Decatur Street and North Rampart and Canal and Esplanade comprised the district known as Storyville. Named for City Alderman Sidney Story, this was the district in which the New Orleans City Council voted to tolerate prostitution in 1897.

4. Asbury, *The French Quarter*, 68.

5. Rose, *Storyville*, 6–7.

6. "Carved to Death; Terrible Fate of Kate Townsend, at the Hands of Troisville Sykes," *The Daily Picayune*, November 4, 1883, p. 11.

7. "Our New Orleans Letter," *West Feliciana Sentinel*, St. Francisville, LA, July 14, 1977, p. 1.

8. "Sykes Slips; How He Got Away with $9,000 of Townsend's Money," *The New Orleans Daily Democrat*, January 15, 1879, p. 8.

9. "Sykes and Townsend," *The Daily Picayune*, New Orleans, August 10, 1879, p. 2; "Carved to Death," p. 11.

10. "Kate Townsend Killed," *The Daily Telegraph*, Monroe, LA, November 3, 1883.

11. Report of Coroner's Inquest of Kate Townsend, November 3, 1883, p. 374, Orleans Parish Coroner Inquests and Views, New Orleans Public Library, Special Collections Division, Loyola Branch, Ms. Irene Wainwright, Head Archivist.

12. "Carved to Death," p. 11.

13. "Carved to Death," p. 11.

14. "Killing of Kate Townsend; Testimony Taken before the Coroner," *The Daily Picayune*, November 8, 1883, p. 2.

15. "Killing of Kate Townsend; Testimony Taken Before the Coroner," p. 2.

16. "Before Recorder Davey; Sykes Appears, Waives Examination, and Returns to Parish Prison," *The Daily Picayune*, New Orleans, November 11, 1883, p.11.

17. "Townsend Laid to Rest," *The Daily States*, New Orleans, November 6, 1883, in Robert Tallant, *Ready to Hang: Seven Famous New Orleans Murders* (New Orleans: Pelican Publishing, 2012), 15.

18. Tallant, *Ready to Hang*, 18.

19. "Kate Townsend's Will," *The Daily Picayune*, New Orleans, November 13, 1883, p. 2.

20. "Troisville Sykes," *The Daily Picayune*, New Orleans, November 21, 1883, p. 2.

21. Sykes' defense team comprised A. D. Henriques, Charles Luzenberg, Lionel Adams, and Arthur Gastinel. All of these men would be involved in the infamous "Italian Mafia Trial" of March 1891. *See* Alan Gauthreaux, *Italian Louisiana: History, Heritage, and Tradition* (Charleston, SC: History Press, 2014), 39.

22. "Troisville Sykes; On Trial in Judge Roman's Court for the Murder of Kate Townsend," *The Daily Picayune*, New Orleans, January 29, 1884, p. 1.

23. "Troisville Sykes," *The Daily Picayune*, January 30, 1884, p. 6.

24. "The Sykes Case; Statement of the Accused and the Arguments of the Lawyers in the Case," *The Daily Picayune*, New Orleans, January 31, 1884, p. 1.

25. "Troisville Sykes; Second Day of the Trial of the Kate Townsend Murder Case," *The Daily Picayune*, New Orleans, January 31, 1884.

26. "Troisville Sykes; Second."

27. "The Sykes Case; The Statement of the Accused and the Argument of the Lawyers in the Case," *The Daily Picayune*, New Orleans, January 31, 1884, p. 1.

28. "The Sykes Case," p. 1.

29. "The Sykes Case," p. 1.

30. "A Murderer Acquitted; Troisville Sykes Set Free by a Considerate Jury," *The New York Times*, February 2, 1884.

31. Tallant, *Ready to Hang*, 31.

32. "Sykes Dismissed; From the Executorship of the Estate of Kate Townsend," *The Daily Picayune*, New Orleans, February 19, 1884, p. 2.

33. "Sykes Dismissed," p. 2.

34. "Romance of Kate Townsend; Further Examination of the Alleged Sister in Judge Houston's Court," *The Daily Picayune*, New Orleans, November 12, 1885, p. 3; "The Kate Townsend Estate," *The Daily Telegraph*, Monroe, LA, June 30, 1886, p. 2.

35. "The Kate Townsend Estate," p. 2.

36. "Sykes in Prison; Committed by Judge Houston until He Produces Kate Townsend's Jewelry," *The Daily Picayune*, New Orleans, February 19, 1886, p. 3.

37. "Sykes in Prison," p. 3.

38. "For the State; Judge Houston Decides the Famous Kate Townsend Will Case," *The Daily Picayune*, New Orleans, June 30, 1886, p. 6.

39. "The Townsend Estate; Judge Poché Reads an Elaborate Opinion," *The Daily Picayune*, New Orleans, November 22, 1887, p. 1.

40. "Tangled Accounts," *The Daily Picayune*, New Orleans, October 10, 1888, p. 8.

41. *St. Tammany Farmer*, Covington, LA, November 24, 1888, p. 1.

42. Joy Jackson, *New Orleans in the Gilded Age: Politics and Urban Progress, 1880–1896* (Lafayette, LA: ULL Press, 1969), 179–180.

43. *The Bienville Democrat*, Acadia, LA, December 11, 1919, p. 1.

The Case of the Human Five

1. "Whole Family Murdered," *Le Macébé*, Lucy, LA, February 11, 1911.

2. "Whole Family Murdered."

3. *Reports on Clementine Barnabet*, Records of the Lafayette District Court, in Federal Writers' Project, No. 45, Northwestern Louisiana University, Walton Memorial Library, Henry Research Center, Mary Wernet, Archivist, p. 1.

4. "Negro with White Wife and Children Murdered," *The Bryan Daily Eagle*, Bryan, TX, March 22, 1911, p. 1; "Race Prejudice Causes Murder; Entire Family Murdered Supposedly by Fanatic in Texas Town," *Bismarck Daily Tribune*, Bismarck, SD, March 29, 1911, p. 8: 2.

5. *Reports on Clementine Barnabet*, p. 1.

6. *Reports on Clementine Barnabet*, p. 2.

7. *Reports on Clementine Barnabet*, p. 2.

8. *Reports on Clementine Barnabet*, p. 3.

9. *Reports on Clementine Barnabet*, p. 4.

10. "Family of Six Butchered in Bed; Lafayette Stirred by a Second Horrible Murder," *The Daily Picayune*, New Orleans, November 28, 1911, p. 1: 6, 3: 1.

11. "Family of Six Butchered in Bed," p. 3: 1.

12. "Negress Laughs at Charge of Sextuple Murder," *The Bellingham Herald*, Bellingham, WA, November 28, 1911, p. 7; *Reports on Clementine Barnabet*, p. 5.

13. *Reports on Clementine Barnabet*, p. 6.

14. "Young Negress Perpetrator," *The Daily Picayune*, New Orleans, November 29, 1911, p. 1: 7, 2: 3.

15. "Lafayette; Father and Daughter Accused of Butcheries in Separate Prisons," *The Daily Picayune*, New Orleans, December 1, 1911, p. 16: 5.

16. "Meeting of Order Held Night of Randall Killing Near Scene of Crime," *The Daily Picayune*, New Orleans, January 21, 1912, p. 16: 5.

17. "Negro Family Killed in Crowley," *The Lafayette Advertiser*, Lafayette, LA, January 23, 1912, p. 1.

18. "Sacrifice Sect Slaughters 26," *The Daily Picayune*, New Orleans, January 22, 1912, p. 1: 5, 3: 5; "Second Arrest Made of Negro Preacher in Connection with Human Sacrifices," *The Daily Picayune*, New Orleans, January 27, 1912, p. 16: 3.

19. "Lake Charles; Woman Held in Connection with Wholesale Murder of Negroes," *The Daily Picayune*, New Orleans, January 30, 1912, p. 6: 1; "Opelousas: Negro Carpenter Warned to Prepare for Departure—Words in Blood," *The Daily Picayune*, New Orleans, January 31, 1912, p. 16: 5.

20. "Breaux Bridge; Frenzied Negroes Refuse to Sleep Without Weapons Nearby," *The Daily Picayune*, New Orleans, February 10, 1912, p. 14:2.

21. "Colored Citizens," *The Lafayette Advertiser*, Lafayette, LA, February 12, 1912, p. 2.

22. "Ax Fiend at Beaumont; Mother and Three Children Killed While They Slept," *The Lafayette Advertiser*, Lafayette, LA, February 23, 1912, p. 1.

23. *Reports on Clementine Barnabet*, p. 9; "Negress Confesses; Clementine Barnabet Gives Detailed Account of Ax Murders in Rayne Crowley and Lafayette," *The Lafayette Advertiser*, Lafayette, LA, April 5, 1912, p. 1.

24. *Reports on Clementine Barnabet*, p. 10.

25. *Reports on Clementine Barnabet*, p. 9.

26. *Reports on Clementine Barnabet*, p. 9.

27. "Says She Slew Twenty Blacks," *The Daily Picayune*, New Orleans, April 2, 1912, p. 1: 7.

28. "Officials Think That Woman Had Accomplice; Only Part of the Story Told by Clementine Barnabet Credited," *The Daily Picayune*, New Orleans, April 3, 1912, p. 1: 2, 2: 6–7.

29. Parish of Lafayette Criminal District Court Records, No. 2900, 2905, 2914, 2915, April 4, 1912, Louisiana State Archives, Dr. Florent Hardy, Archivist.

30. "A Negro Charm Seller Held in the Ax Cases," *The Daily Picayune*, New Orleans, April 4, 1912, p. 1: 2, 13: 4.

31. *Reports on Clementine Barnabet*, p. 13.

32. "Ax Man Again," *Lafayette Advertiser*, Lafayette, LA, August 20, 1912, p. 1.

33. *State of Louisiana v. Clementine Barnabet*, Eighteenth Judicial District Court, Parish of Lafayette, State of Louisiana, Record No. 2900, October 16, 1912.

34. *Report of the Findings to the Court of Psychiatric Evaluation of Clementine Barnabet*, October 21, 1912, Records of the Lafayette District Court, in Federal Writers' Project, No. 45, Northwestern Louisiana University, Walton Memorial Library, Henry Research Center, Mary Wernet, Archivist.

35. *State of Louisiana v. Clementine Barnabet*, Eighteenth Judicial District Court, Parish of Lafayette, State of Louisiana, Record No. 2900, October 26, 1912; "Life Term for Murderer," *Rock Island Argus*, Rock Island, IL, October 26, 1912, p. 1; "Negress Given Life Sentence," *Miami Herald*, Miami, FL, October 26, 1912, p. 1.

36. "Three Murdered By Sacrifice Sect," *The Kingston Daily Freeman*, Kingston, KY, November 23, 1912, p. 12; "Family Slain with an Ax," *Mexico Missouri Message*, November 28, 1912, p. 12.

37. Records of Angola State Penitentiary, pp. 24–25, Louisiana State Archives, Dr. Florent Hardy, Archivist, Baton Rouge, LA.

38. Louisiana Legislative Acts of 1902, Act 160, Amending §2, §6, and §8 of Act 112 of 1890, pp. 305–306.

39. The Lavoisier Reports: "My Secret, My City: The Legend of Clementine Barnabet," http://ireport.cnn.com/docs/DOC-563081, accessed June 3, 2014.

40. The Lavoisier Reports: "My Secret, My City."

41. "The Lavoisier Reports: "My Secret, My City."

Respectable Poisoner

1. "Annie Crawford Confesses She Poisoned Her Sister," *The Daily Picayune*, New Orleans, September 28, 1911, p. 1: 6–8.

2. "Annie Crawford Confesses She Poisoned Her Sister," p. 1: 6–8.

3. "Annie Crawford Confesses She Poisoned Her Sister," p. 1: 6–8.

4. "Annie Crawford Confesses She Poisoned Her Sister," p. 1: 6–8.

5. "Annie Crawford Was Arraigned," *The Daily Picayune*, New Orleans, September 29, 1911, p. 1: 7, 5: 5–7.

6. "Annie Crawford Was Arraigned," p. 1: 7, 5: 5–7.

7. "Annie Crawford Was Arraigned," p. 1: 7, 5: 5–7.

8. "Crawford Family Industrious and the Members Well Known," *The Daily Picayune*, New Orleans, September 29, 1911, p. 12: 4–5.

9. "Girl Cannot Give Bail," *Belleville News-Democrat*, Belleville, IL, October 3, 1911, p. 6.

10. "Murder Indictment for Annie Craw-

ford," *Gulfport Daily Herald*, Gulfport, MS, October 10, 1911, p. 8.

11. "Anna Crawford Goes to Trial; Three Jurors Sworn for the First Day," *The Daily Picayune*, New Orleans, March 13, 1912, p. 7: 1–2; "On Trial for Her Sister's Death," *Kansas City Star*, Kansas City, MO, March 13, 1912, p. 2; "Three Jurors Selected for Crawford Trial," *The Macon Daily Telegraph*, Macon, GA, March 13, 1912, p. 11.

12. "Anna Crawford Goes to Trial; Three Jurors Sworn for the First Day," *The Daily Picayune*, New Orleans, March 13, 1912, p. 7: 1–2.

13. "The Annie Crawford Jury Completed; Taking of Testimony Begins Today," *The Daily Picayune*, New Orleans, March 15, 1915, p. 7: 1–2.

14. "State's Witnesses on in the Crawford Trial," *Macon Daily-Telegraph*, Macon, GA, March 16, 1912, p. 1.

15. "State's Witnesses on in the Crawford Trial," p. 1.

16. "Sensation in Crawford Case," *The Daily Picayune*, New Orleans, March 19, 1912, p. 1: 7, 6: 1–3.

17. "Sensation in Crawford Case," p. 1: 7, 6: 1–3.

18. "Sensation in Crawford Case," p. 1: 7, 6: 1–3.

19. "Sensation in Crawford Case," p. 1: 7, 6: 1–3.

20. "Counsel Clash after Crawford Trial Ends," *The Daily Picayune*, New Orleans, March 21, 1912, p. 1: 6–7, 7: 1–8; "Fight Features Crawford Trial," *The State*, Columbia, SC, March 21, 1912, p. 6; "Encounters at the Crawford Trial," *Dallas Morning News*, March 21, 1912, p. 18.

21. "Adds Forgery to the Murder Charge," *The Salt Lake Tribune*, March 22, 1912, p. 2: 6.

22. "State Seeking Murder Motive," *The Daily Picayune*, New Orleans, March 22, 1912, p. 1: 7.

23. "State Seeking Murder Motive," p. 1: 7.

24. "State Seeking Murder Motive," p. 1: 7.

25. "State Seeking Murder Motive," p. 1: 7.

26. "Crawford Defense Trying to Prove Girl Killed Self," *Fort Worth Star-Telegram*, Fort Worth, TX, March 23, 1912, p. 1.

27. "Annie Crawford Tells Her Story," *Columbus Daily Enquirer*, Columbus, GA, March 24, 1912, p. 1.

28. "Jury Disagrees in Case of Girl Held for Murder," *Fort Worth Star-Telegram*, Fort Worth, TX, March 26, 1912, p. 1; "Girl on Trial for Poisoning Sister Expects Aquittal," *Fort Worth Star-Telegram*, Fort Worth, TX, March 25, 1912, p. 2; "Mistrial Announced of Alleged Sister Slayer," *Philadelphia Inquirer*, March 27, 1912, p. 1; "Crawford Jury Unable to Agree and Mistrial Ends Famous Case," March 27, 1912, p. 1; *True Democrat*, St. Francisville, LA, March 30, 1912, p. 1.

The Mysterious Case of Dr. Weiss

1. Letter from Marie de Bethanie to Dr. and Mrs. Carl Weiss, Sr., September 11, 1935, Historic New Orleans Collection, Weiss Family Papers, Accession Number 89-37-L.

2. Telegram from "Seven Friends" to the Weiss Family, Historic New Orleans Collection, Weiss Family Papers, Accession Number 89-37-L.

3. Thomas O. Harris, *The Kingfish: Huey P. Long Dictator* (Baton Rouge: Claitor's Publishing Division, 1968), 12–13; Richard D. White, Jr., *Kingfish: The Reign of Huey P. Long* (New York: Random House, 2006), 8–9.

4. White, *Kingfish*, 8.

5. White, *Kingfish*, 9–11.

6. White, *Kingfish*, 10–11.

7. Harris, *The Kingfish*, 12–13.

8. Harris, *The Kingfish*, 24–27.

9. Arthur M. Schlesinger, "The Messiah of the Rednecks," in *The Louisiana Purchase Bicentennial Series in Louisiana History. Volume VIII: The Age of the Longs, 1928–1960*, ed. by Edward F. Haas (Lafayette, LA: Center for Louisiana Studies University of Louisiana at Lafayette, 2001), 49.

10. Schlesinger, "The Messiah of the Rednecks," 49; John Kingston Fineran, *The Career of a Tinpot Napoleon: A Political Biography of Huey P. Long* (New Orleans: John Kingston Fineran, 1932), 60–61.

11. White, *Kingfish*, 62–63.

12. George Vandervoort, "Solons Testify Long Offered Bribes to Gain Support," *The Times Picayune*, New Orleans, April 4, 1929, p. 1: 7.

13. "House Votes First Impeachment Count in Stormy Session," *The Times Pica-*

yune, New Orleans, April 7, 1929, p. 1: 7; 14A: 1–2.

14. Schlesinger, "The Messiah of the Rednecks," 49.

15. Schlesinger, "The Messiah of the Rednecks," 49.

16. White, *Kingfish*, 144.

17. White, *Kingfish*, 162.

18. *Address to the Legislature, Convening May 9, 1932, "The Strange Case of Louisiana and Huey P. Long,"* published April 20, 1932, Federal Bureau of Investigation, Huey P. Long File, Item No. 62-27030.

19. *Address to the Legislature, Convening May 9, 1932.*

20. Open Letter from Shirley G. Wimberly, Attorney at Law, to Members of the Senate and the Press, March 28, 1933, Federal Bureau of Investigation, Huey P. Long File, Item No. 62-28479-1.

21. White, *Kingfish*, 176–178.

22. Schlesinger, "Messiah of the Rednecks," 56–57.

23. "Call for Troops to Guard Polls Hinted by Long," *New York Herald Tribune*, December 4, 1933, Federal Bureau of Investigation, Huey P. Long File, Item No. 62-28479-A.

24. Drew Pearson and Robert S. Allen, "The Daily Washington Merry Go Round," *New York Daily Mirror*, April 23, 1934, p. 8.

25. White, *Kingfish*, 200–201.

26. White, *Kingfish*, 204–205.

27. Teletype transmission to Federal Bureau of Investigation, New Orleans to Washington, D.C., Federal Bureau of Investigation, Huey P. Long File, August 1, 1934, Item No. 62-27479; White, *Kingfish*, 208–209.

28. Letter from Seth Guion to U.S. Assistant Attorney J. Warren Coleman, New Orleans, August 25, 1934, Federal Bureau of Investigation, Huey P. Long File, Item No. 62-32509-28.

29. "Long Will Direct Investigation of City Government," *The Times Picayune*, New Orleans, August 19, 1934; White, *Kingfish*, 218–219.

30. "Long Will Direct Investigation of City Government"; White, *Kingfish*, 218–219.

31. White, *Kingfish*, 222–223.

32. Death Certificate of Carl Austin Weiss, 10 September 1935, Baton Rouge, Louisiana, Registration No. 10563, Louisiana State Archives, Huey P. Long Assassination Collection, P1993-193.

33. David Zinman, *The Day Huey Long Was Shot, September 8, 1935* (New York: Ivan Obelensky, 1963), 51–53.

34. Zinman, *The Day Huey Long Was Shot*, 54–57.

35. Zinman, *The Day Huey Long Was Shot*, 60.

36. Hermann Deutsch, *The Huey Long Murder Case* (New York: Doubleday and Company, 1963), 71–72.

37. Deutsch, *The Huey Long Murder Case*, 72; Zinman, *The Day Huey Long Was Shot*, 77–78.

38. Zinman, *The Day Huey Long Was Shot*, 80–81.

39. Zinman, *The Day Huey Long Was Shot*, 80–81; White, *Kingfish*, 161.

40. Zinman, *The Day Huey Long Was Shot*, 80–81; White, *Kingfish*, 161.

41. Zinman, *The Day Huey Long Was Shot*, 81–82.

42. White, *Kingfish*, 261–262; Zinman, *The Day Huey Long Was Shot*, 17–18.

43. White, *Kingfish*, 262.

44. "Long Bodyguards and Others Tell of Weis Slaying in Capitol Hall," *The Times Picayune*, New Orleans, September 17, 1935, p. 1: 1, 3: 1–7.

45. "Long Bodyguards and Others Tell of Weis Slaying in Capitol Hall," p. 1: 1, 3: 1–7.

46. "Long Bodyguards and Others Tell of Weis Slaying in Capitol Hall," p. 1: 1, 3: 1–7.

47. "Long Bodyguards and Others Tell of Weis Slaying in Capitol Hall," p. 1: 1, 3: 1–7; White, *Kingfish*, 263.

48. Jim Beam, "Long's Assassin Wasn't Armed," *Lake Charles American Press*, Lake Charles, LA, August 15, 1999, p. 3.

49. Michael C. Trotter, "Huey Long's Last Operation: When Politics and Medicine Don't Mix," *The Ochsner Journal* 12, no. 1 (Spring 2012): 9–12, 10; Zinman, *The Day Huey Long Was Shot*, 175–176, 270–274.

50. Trotter, "Huey Long's Last Operation," 12.

51. Trotter, "Huey Long's Last Operation," 12.

52. "President Is Grieved," *New York Times*, September 10, 1935, p. 1: 4.

53. Trotter, "Huey Long's Last Operation," 11.

54. "House Inquiry Urged to Find Those 'Instigating' Long Shooting," *New York Times*, September 10, 1935, p. 1: 507, 3: 4.

55. "House Inquiry Urged to Find Those 'Instigating' Long Shooting," p. 1: 507, 3: 4.
56. Deutsch, *The Huey Long Murder Case*, 127.
57. "Long Bodyguards and Others Tell of Weiss Slaying in the Capitol Hall," p. 3: 1–7.
58. "House Inquiry Urged to Find Those 'Instigating' Long Shooting," p. 1: 507, 3: 4.
59. "House Inquiry Urged to Find Those 'Instigating' Long Shooting," p. 1: 507, 3: 4.
60. "House Inquiry Urged to Find Those 'Instigating' Long Shooting," p. 1: 507, 3: 4.
61. "House Inquiry Urged to Find Those 'Instigating' Long Shooting," p. 1: 507, 3: 4.
62. "Father Denies Weiss Killed Senator Long," *Washington Herald*, January 16, 1936, p. 2, Federal Bureau of Investigation, Huey Long File, Item No. 62-32509-A.
63. Letter to Rose Long from an anonymous author, New Orleans, Louisiana, September 30, 1935, Louisiana State Archives, Huey P. Long Assassination Collection, P1993-193.
64. Report to General Louis Guerre, October 23, 1935, Louisiana State Archives, Huey P. Long Assassination Collection, P1993-193; White, *Kingfish*, 256–259.
65. White, *Kingfish*, 259.
66. White, *Kingfish*, 259.
67. "Bodyguards Deny They Killed Long," *Washington Herald*, January 18, 1936, Federal Bureau of Investigation, Huey P. Long File, Item No. 62-32509-A.
68. "Long Aide Told to Send Proof of Plot to DOJ," *Washington Herald*, September 18, 1935, Federal Bureau of Investigation, Huey P. Long File, Item No. 62-32509-A; "No US Inquiry into Long Plot," *New York Evening Journal*, September 18, 1935, Federal Bureau of Investigation, Huey P. Long File, Item No. 62-32509-A.
69. Final Report of Lieutenant Don Moreau, Louisiana State Police, April 20, 1992, Louisiana State Archives, Huey P. Long Assassination Collection, L1993-193; Bruce Eggler, "Long's Killer Was Weiss, Probe Finds," *The Times Picayune*, New Orleans, June 6, 1992.
70. Final Report of Lieutenant Don Moreau; Eggler, "Long's Killer Was Weiss, Probe Finds"; Zinman, *The Day Huey Long Was Shot*, 300–302.
71. Final Report of Lieutenant Don Moreau; Eggler, "Long's Killer Was Weiss, Probe Finds."
72. David Zinman, "The Meteoric Life and Mysterious Death of Huey P. Long," *American History Illustrated* 28, no. 3 (July/August 1993): 24–37, 32–33; Frances Frank Marcus, "Researchers Exhume Doctor's Grave to Resolve Part of Huey Long Legend," *New York Times*, October 21, 1991, p. 5.

Louisiana Burning

1. "Bloody Scenes of the Race War; Fully Twelve People Known to Be Dead or Dying," *Idaho Statesman*, Boise, ID, October 30, 1901, p. 1.
2. "Thirty-Four Killed in Louisiana Race War; Negroes and Whites Clash at a Country Camp Meeting," *New York Times*, October 29, 1901, p. 1; "Race War Reported," *Idaho Daily Stateman*, Boise, ID, October 19, 1901, p. 2; "A Race Riot in Louisiana," *Charleston Oberver*, Charleston, SC, October 29, 1901, p. 1; "Race War Breaks Out," *Grand Forks Daily Herald*, Grand Forks, ND, October 29, 1901, p. 1; "War between the Races," *Dallas Morning News*, October 29, 1901, p. 1; "Sheriff Calls for Troops," *Omaha World Herald*, Omaha, NE, October 29, 1901, p. 2.
3. "Race War Reported," p. 2.
4. "War between the Races," p. 1.
5. "About Thirty Already Dead," *Columbus Daily Enquirer*, Columbus, GA, October 29, 1901, p. 1.
6. "Endorsed by Grand Jury; No Condemnation for Men Who Burned Negro at the Stake," *Aberdeen Daily News*, Aberdeen, SD, December 6, 1901, p. 3.
7. "Afro-Americans Seek Fair Play," *The Philadelphia Enquirer*, December 9, 1901, p. 2.
8. "Murder Case Presents New Evidence," *Louisiana Weekly*, New Orleans, November 3, 1935, p. 1:1; 4:5.
9. F. J. Montegut, "19 Arrested for Death of Dep. Sheriff," *Louisiana Weekly*, New Orleans, August 4, 1934, p. 1: 6; p. 6: 5.
10. Montegut, "19 Arrested for Death of Dep. Sheriff," p. 1: 6.
11. Montegut, "19 Arrested for Death of Dep. Sheriff," p. 1: 6; Adam Fairclough, *Race and Democracy: The Civil Rights Struggle in Louisiana, 1915–1972* (Athens, GA: University of Georgia Press, 2008), 28.

12. Orin Blackstone, "Coroner's Jury Says Woods Slain Performing Duty," *The Times Picayune*, New Orleans, July 23, 1934, p. 1: 4, 4: 1–2.

13. Blackstone, "Coroner's Jury Says Woods Slain Performing Duty," p. 1: 4.

14. Blackstone, "Coroner's Jury Says Woods Slain Performing Duty," p. 1: 4.

15. "Rites for Deputy Held; Jury to Act on Slaying Today," *The Times Picayune*, New Orleans, July 24,1934, p. 2: 3.

16. Sam Lang, "Murder Charged to Trio in Killing of Deputy Wood," *The Times Picayune*, New Orleans, July 25, 1934, p. 1: 2.

17. D. W. Taylor, "Franklinton Youth Sentenced to Hang for Defending Self," *Louisiana Weekly*, New Orleans, August 4, 1934, p. 1: 6.

18. "Seek New Trial for Franklinton Man Now Sentenced to Hang," *Louisiana Weekly*, New Orleans, August 11, 1934, p. 1: 1.

19. "We Must Act Immediately" [Editorial], *Louisiana Weekly*, New Orleans, September 1, 1934, p. 8:2.

20. "Murder Case Presents New Evidence," *Louisiana Weekly*, New Orleans, November 3, 1934, p. 1: 1, 4: 5.

21. "Murder Case Presents New Evidence," p. 1: 1, 4: 5.

22. "Wilson Gets New Trial," *Louisiana Weekly*, January 12, 1935, p. 1: 5.

23. "Killer of Deputy Slain by Band in Franklinton Jail," *The Times Picayune*, New Orleans, January 12, 1935, p. 7: 1.

24. "Killer of Deputy Slain by Band in Franklinton Jail" p. 7: 1; "Negro Is Lynched in Louisiana Jail," *New York Times*, January 12, 1935, p. 5: 1.

25. "There Wasn't Any Lynching" [Editorial], *Louisiana Weekly*, New Orleans, January 19, 1935, p. 8: 1.

26. "There Wasn't Any Lynching," p. 8: 1.

27. Executive Order 9981, Harry S. Truman Presidential Library. http://www.trumanlibrary.org/9981.htm. Accessed November 24, 2014.

28. *Brown v. Board of Education of Topeka*, 347 U.S. 483 (1954).

29. Mary Lee Muller, "New Orleans Public School Segregation," *Louisiana History: The Journal of the Louisiana Historical Association* 17, no. 1 (Winter 1976): 69–88, 69.

30. Author interview, Dr. Raphael Cassimere, Jr., November 20, 2014, Kenner, LA.

31. Fairclough, *Race and Democracy*, 345.

32. James McClean, "Governor Decries Racial Violence," *The Baton Rouge Advocate*, December 19, 1964, p. 1-A: 4–5.

33. "Interracial Meeting Dropped in Bogalusa," *The Baton Rouge Advocate*, January 6, 1965, p. 1-A: 2, 8-A: 7.

34. "Interracial Meeting Dropped in Bogalusa," p. 1-A: 2, 8-A: 7.

35. "Two CORE Workers Pay Surprise Visit," *The Baton Rouge Advocate*, February 4, 1965, p. 1-A: 4.

36. "Radio Building Hit by Bullets," *The Times Picayune*, New Orleans, March 23, 1965, p. 3: 2.

37. "Park Gates at Bogalusa Ripped Down," *The Baton Rouge Advocate*, May 5, 1965, p. 1-A: 3.

38. "Farmer Plans Bogalusa Talk," *The Times Picayune*, New Orleans, May 22, 1965, p. 2: 8.

39. "Park Gates at Bogalusa Ripped Down," p. 1-A: 3.

40. "Bogalusa Mayor Outlines Plan to Bring City Peace," *The Times Picayune*, New Orleans, May 24, 1965, p. 1: 4, 11:1; Gibbs Adams, "Mayor of Bogalusa Announces Program to End Racial Strife," *The Baton Rouge Advocate*, May 24, 1965, p. 1-A: 6–7; "Bogalusa Group Ends 'Cool Off,'" *The Times Picayune*, New Orleans, May 25, 1965, p. 1: 5; "Bogalusa Mayor Pledges to Curb All Race Bias," *Louisiana Weekly*, New Orleans, May 29, 1965, p. 3: 1.

41. "Fight Rocks Bogalusa," *Louisiana Weekly*, New Orleans, May 29, 1965, p. 1.

42. John Fahey, "Negroes Study March Plans," *The Times Picayune*, New Orleans, May 30, 1965, p. 1: 2.

43. "Deputy Slain," *The Baton Rouge Advocate*, June 3, 1965, p. 1-A, 10-A: 8.

44. Wiley S. Masters and John Fahey, "Police Charge Man in Slaying of LA Deputy," *The Times Picayune*, New Orleans, June 4, 1965, p. 1: 1, 5: 2, 13: 1.

45. "McKeithen View of the Killing," *The Times Picayune*, New Orleans, June 4, 1965, p. 1: 2.

46. Gibbs Adams, "Chief Deputy's Home Riddled by Gunfire," *The Baton Rouge Advocate*, June 5, 1965, p. 1-A, 10-A: 6.

47. Author interview with Winola Holliday, November 18, 2014, Kenner, LA.

48. "Witness Reported to Deputy Slain,"

The Times Picayune, New Orleans, June 5, 1965, p. 1: 1, 19: 1.

49. "Witness Reported to Deputy Slain," p. 1: 1, 19: 1.

50. "Witness Reported to Deputy Slain," p. 1: 1, 19: 1.

51. "Witness Reported to Deputy Slain," p. 1: 1, 19: 1.

52. "Deputy Moore's Widow Ineligible, Says Ruling," *The Times Picayune*, New Orleans, June 5, 1965, p. 19:2.

53. John Fahey, "$25,000 Is Offered in Deputy Slaying," *The Times Picayune*, New Orleans, June 6, 1965, p. 1: 1, 14: 1; Gibbs Adams, "Murder Reward Offered," *The Baton Rouge Advocate*, June 6, 1965, p. 1-A: 2, 10-A: 6–7.

54. "Deputy Moore's Widow Ineligible, Says Ruling," *The Times Picayune*, New Orleans, June 5, 1965, p. 19: 2.

55. Adams, "Murder Reward Posted," p. 10-A.

56. "Louisiana Is Shocked" [Editorial], *The Baton Rouge Advocate*, June 6, 1965, p. 4-B:1.

57. Gibbs Adams, "Probe of Deputy's Slaying Is Intense," *The Baton Rouge Advocate*, June 9, 1965, p. 1-A: 6.

58. John Fahey and Joseph A. Lucia, "Tuesday Hearing for Slay Case Suspect," *The Times Picayune*, New Orleans, June 10, 1965, p. 8: 1; Fahey, "$25,000 Reward Offered in Deputy Slaying," p. 14: 1.

59. "Man Charged in Negro Deputy Slaying Case Is Free on Bond," *The Baton Rouge Advocate*, June 12, 1965, p. 1-A: 6, 12-A: 7.

60. *The Thunderbolt* (Birmingham, AL) 25 (January 1961): 2.

61. Gibbs Adams, "Bogalusa Negroes to Picket Capitol," *The Baton Rouge Advocate*, June 10, 1965, p. 1-A: 6, 12-A: 3.

62. "Look Out! Here Comes Justice!" [Editorial], *Louisiana Weekly*, June 26, 1965, p. 4:2.

63. "An Eyewitness in the Oneal Moore Case," *Injustice Files: Discovery Communications*, hosted by Ken Beauchamp, 2010. http://www.investigationdiscovery.com/tv-shows/injusticefiles/videos. Accessed September 9, 2014.

64. Author interview, Washington Parish Sheriff Randy "Country" Seal, December 15, 2014, Franklinton, LA.

65. "Washington Parish Deputies Honored in Memorial," WDSU-TV, Heath Allen reporting, May 15, 2013.

Deadly Friendship

1. 911 Transcript of February 24, 1984, Kerry Meyers, Jefferson Parish Sheriff's Office, Operator 73.

2. 911 Transcript of February 24, 1984, Kerry Meyers.

3. Jefferson Parish Sheriff's Office, Crime Report, Sec. A, Item # B-14695-84, February 14, 1984.

4. Alan Shields, "Who Killed Who in the Louisiana House of Horrors?" *Startling Detective* 82, no. 2 (March 1992): 20–21, 33–37.

5. "Mom Beaten to Death, 2½-Year-Old in Coma," *The Times Picayune*, New Orleans, February 25, 1984, p. 1: 1, 4.

6. Autopsy Protocol, Janet Myers, February 24, 1984, Dr. Richard E. Tracy, Medical Examiner.

7. Autopsy Protocol, Janet Myers.

8. Autopsy Protocol, Janet Myers; Shields, "Who Killed Who in the Louisiana House of Horrors?," p. 34.

9. Author interview with W. J. LeBlanc, September 22, 2014, Kenner, LA.

10. Statement of William A. Fontanille. February 25, 1984, Jefferson Parish Sheriff's Office, Homicide Unit, Gretna, LA, p. 1–3.

11. Statement of William A. Fontanille, p. 4.

12. Statement of William A. Fontanille, p. 6–11.

13. "Family Friend Booked in Beating Death," *The Times Picayune*, New Orleans, February 26, 1984, p. 1, 4.

14. Statement of Kerry Myers, March 14, 1984, Jefferson Parish Sheriff's Office, Homicide Unit, Gretna, LA, p. 5–7.

15. Statement of Kerry Myers, p. 5–7.

16. Statement of Kerry Myers, p. 5–7.

17. Statement of Kerry Myers, p. 5–7.

18. Statement of Kerry Myers, p. 10–13.

19. Statement of Kerry Myers, p. 15–17.

20. Statement of Kerry Myers, p. 15–17.

21. Statement of Kerry Myers, p. 19.

22. "Husband a Suspect, Jeff Prosecutor Says," *The Times Picayune*, New Orleans, March 1, 1984, p. 1, 4.

23. "Trial May Unravel Puzzle of Slaying,"

The Times Picayune, New Orleans, October 26, 1986, p. B: 1.

24. Sandra Barrier, "Slay Probe Doesn't Yield Indictment," *The Times Picayune*, New Orleans, October 22, 1984, p. A: 9.

25. Barrier, "Slay Probe Doesn't Yield Indictment," p. A: 9.

26. Richard Boyd, "Parents Beg to Keep Daughter's Case Alive," *The Times Picayune*, New Orleans, October 24, 1984, p. A: 2.

27. "Testimony Heard in Baffling Case of Wife's Murder," *The Times Picayune*, New Orleans, May 16, 1986, p. H: 30; "Suspect: Unaware Woman Was Dead," *The Times Picayune*, New Orleans, July 3, 1986, p. B: 1, 10.

28. "Testimony Heard in Baffling Case of Wife's Murder," p. H: 30; "Suspect: Unaware Woman Was Dead," p. B: 1, 10.

29. Richard Boyd, "Trial May Unravel Puzzle of Slaying," *The Times Picayune*, New Orleans, October 26, 1986, p. B: 1.

30. Richard Boyd, "Jeff Jurors Relive Tragedy of Woman's Death on Tape," *The Times Picayune*, New Orleans, October 29, 1986, p. A: 1, 3.

31. Richard Boyd, "Jeans Had Spatters of Blood," *The Times Picayune*, New Orleans, October 30, 1986, p. B: 1, 5; Joseph Bosco, *Blood Will Tell* (New York: William Morrow, 1993), 144.

32. Bosco, *Blood Will Tell*, 152–153.

33. Boyd, "Jeans Had Splatters of Blood," p. B: 1, 5; "Victim's Mate: Defendant Hoped to Kill Ex-Wife," *The Times Picayune*, New Orleans, October 31, 1986, p. B: 1, 2.

34. "Fontanille Murder Trial Goes to the Jury," *The Times Picayune*, New Orleans, November 1, 1986, B: 1.

35. "Fontanille Murder Case Ends in Mistrial," *The Times Picayune*, New Orleans, November 2, 1986, p. B: 1, 6.

36. "2nd Trial in Killing Likely in January," *The Times Picayune*, New Orleans, November 7, 1986, p. B: 1, 2.

37. "Defendant Sues Sheriff Over Evidence," *The Times Picayune*, New Orleans, November 11, 1986, p. B: 3.

38. Interview with Major Joseph D. Passalaqua, Commander, Jefferson Parish Sheriff's Office Crime Scene Investigations Unit, August 14, 1991, Metairie, LA.

39. Interview with Major Joseph D. Passalaqua.

40. Interview with Major Joseph D. Passalaqua.

41. Richard Boyd, "Slay Defendant Will Stay in Jail Until the Second Trial," *The Times Picayune*, New Orleans, January 6, 1987, p. B: 1.

42. La. Revised Statutes Title 14 § 30.1.

43. Richard Boyd, "Evidence Twist Might Add Murder Suspect," *The Times Picayune*, New Orleans, May 5, 1987, p. B: 1.

44. Author interview with W. J. LeBlanc.

45. Shields, "Who Killed Who in the Louisiana House of Horrors?," p. 36.

46. Shields, "Who Killed Who in the Louisiana House of Horrors?," p. 36; Bosco, *Blood Will Tell*, 87.

47. Author interview with W. J. LeBlanc.

48. Richard Boyd, "Man Pleads Innocent to Beating Murder of Wife," *The Times Picayune*, New Orleans, November 4, 1987, p. B: 4.

49. Boyd, "Man Pleads Innocent to Beating Murder of Wife," p. B: 4.

50. Richard Boyd, "Joint Trial Set for Two in Slay Conspiracy," *The Times Picayune*, New Orleans, March 2, 1988, p. B: 3.

51. *State of Louisiana v. Kerry Myers and William Fontanille*, 545 So.2d 981 (La. 1989), 982.

52. Author interview with W. J. LeBlanc.

53. *State of Louisiana v. Kerry Myers and William Fontanille*, 982–984; *William Fontanille, Petitioner-Appellant versus Steve Rader, Warden, Louisiana State Correctional Facility and Industrial School and Richard P. Ieyoub, Attorney General, State of Louisiana, Respondents-Appellees*, No. 92–3558, June 28, 1993, unpublished opinion; Richard Boyd, "Judge Throws Out Conspiracy Charge in Killing," *The Times Picayune*, New Orleans, October 6, 1988, p. A: 22; author interview with W. J. LeBlanc.

54. "Myers' Account of Fateful Night Heard in Court," *The Times Picayune*, New Orleans, March 31, 1990, p. B: 1, 2.

55. "Expert: Blood Spatters Tie Both to Killing," *The Times Picayune*, New Orleans, April 1, 1990, p. B: 1, 4.

56. "Expert: Blood Spatters Tie Both to Killing," p. B: 1, 4; *State v. Myers*, No. 90-KA-539 (Fifth Circuit Court of Appeals, State of Louisiana (1991); Richard Boyd, "Blood on Pants Was Diluted, Expert Testifies," *The Times Picayune*, New Orleans, April 2, 1990, p. B: 1, 3.

57. Author interview with W. J. LeBlanc.

58. "Blood on Pants Was Diluted," p. B: 1, 3.

59. "Blood on Pants Was Diluted," p. B: 1, 3

60. "Jury Gets Fontanille Murder Case," *The Times Picayune*, New Orleans, April 5, 1990, p. B: 1, 2.

61. "Jury Gets Fontanille Murder Case."

62. *State v. Myers*, No. 90-KA-539 (Fifth Circuit Court of Appeals, State of Louisiana , 1991).

63. "Jury Gets Fontanille Murder Case."

64. Author interview, anonymous source, September 15, 2014, Metairie, LA.

65. Author interview, anonymous source.

66. Author interview, anonymous source.

67. Author interview, anonymous source.

68. Author interview with W. J. LeBlanc.

69. Richard Boyd, "Author Risks Jail Over Recordings; Refuses to Release Talks with Killer," *The Times Picayune*, New Orleans, November 5, 1993, p. B: 1.

70. Boyd, "Author Risks Jail Over Recordings," p. B: 1.

71. Joe Darby, "'Blood Will Tell' Author Won't Have to Testify," *The Times Picayune*, New Orleans, April 9, 1994, p. D: 1.

72. Author interview, anonymous source, 15 September 2014, Metairie, LA.

The Final Broadcast

1. *State of Louisiana v. Vince Marinello*, No. 09-1260, (Ct. of Appeals, 3rd Cir. 2010); Michelle Hunter, "Radio Host Questioned in Wife's Killing; Old Metairie Victim in Bitter Divorce with Marinello," *The Times Picayune*, New Orleans, September 2, 2006, A:1.

2. Anonymous interview with author, July 28, 2014, Metairie, LA.

3. Anonymous interview with author, July 28, 2014.

4. Anonymous interview with author, July 28, 2014.

5. Anonymous interview with author, July 28, 2014.

6. Anonymous interview with author, July 28, 2014.

7. Hunter, "Radio Host Questioned in Wife's Killing."

8. Hunter, "Radio Host Questioned in Wife's Killing."

9. Hunter, "Radio Host Questioned in Wife's Killing."

10. Meghan Gordon, "Family Dissects Marinello Marriage; Spark Turned Cold—They Say," *The Times Picayune*, New Orleans, September 6, 2006, B:1.

11. Gordon, "Family Dissects Marinello Marriage."

12. Gordon, "Family Dissects Marinello Marriage."

13. Anonymous interview with author, July 28, 2014.

14. Gordon, "Family Dissects Marinello Marriage."

15. Michelle Hunter, "Marinello Booked with Wife's Murder," *The Times Picayune*, New Orleans, LA, September 8, 2006, A:1.

16. Hunter, "Marinello Booked with Wife's Murder."

17. Hunter, "Marinello Booked with Wife's Murder."

18. Hunter, "Marinello Booked with Wife's Murder."

19. Hunter, "Marinello Booked with Wife's Murder."

20. Hunter, "Marinello Booked with Wife's Murder."

21. Drew Broach, "Details Emerge in Marinello Case; Sketch of the Murder Site on the Checklist, Officials Say," *The Times Picayune*, New Orleans, September 20, 2006.

22. Mary Foster, "From Lovable New Orleans Sportscaster to Murderer? Friends and Fans Find It Hard to Believe," *Associated Press*, September 8, 2006, n.p.

23. "Vince Marinello Trial Special," WWL-870 AM Radio, December 17, 2008, New Orleans, LA.

24. Drew Broach, "Lee Fibs to Reel in a Murder Suspect," *The Times Picayune*, New Orleans, LA, September 18, 2008, B:7.

25. Paul Purpura, "Marinello Put Under House Arrest; Ex-Sportscaster Staying at Condo Overlooking Scene of Wife's Killing, *The Times Picayune*, New Orleans, LA, December 28, 2006, A:1.

26. "Marinello Prosecutors Testify About Involvement," *The Times Picayune*, New Orleans, LA, July 3, 2007.

27. Andrea Shaw, "Prosecutor's Sudden Leave Raises Questions," *The Times Picayune*, New Orleans, LA, November 26, 2007, B:2.

28. Paul Purpura, "Marinello Trial Moving to May 12; New Lawyer Needs Time to Review Metairie Murder Case," *The Times Picayune*, New Orleans, LA, February 16, 2008, A:1; A:11.

29. James Gill, "Lady Justice Drags Her Feet," *The Times Picayune*, New Orleans, LA, February 27, 2008, B:7; Mary Alice Lange, "A Trial Needn't Be Perfect," editorial in response to "Lady Justice Drags Her Feet," *The Times Picayune*, New Orleans, LA, February 29, 2008, B:6.

30. "Marinello Prosecutors Testify About Involvement," *The Times Picayune*, New Orleans, LA, July 3, 2007, A:1; A:11; "DA Wins Round in Marinello Case; But Defense Given Time to Appeal Ruling," *The Times Picayune*, New Orleans, LA, July 13, 2007, B:1; B:2; "Conflict Won't Stall Marinello Trial," *The Times Picayune*, New Orleans, LA, August 10, 2007, A:1; A:6; "Imported Jury for Marinello Trial Rejected; Murder Trial to Move from Jefferson Parish," *The Times Picayune*, New Orleans, LA, April 3, 2008, A:1.

31. WDSU-TV, Channel 6 News Report, "Change of Venue in Marinello Murder Trial," LaTonya Norton reporting, Gretna, LA, April 4, 2008. http://www.youtube.com/watch?v=XvXjCI_hNfE. Accessed October 14, 2014.

32. Paul Purpura, "Attorneys Ask for Another Delay in Trial; Marinello Defense Gets DNA Evidence," *The Times Picayune*, New Orleans, LA, May 8, 2008, AJ:1; "Marinello Prosecutors OK a Delay; New Report Prompts Bid to Postpone Trial," *The Times Picayune*, New Orleans, LA, May 9, 2008, B:1; B:3.

33. Nicholas J. Persich, "Memories Fade with Time" [Editorial], *The Times Picayune*, New Orleans, LA, May 17, 2008, B:4.

34. Paul Purpura, "Marinello's Murder Trial Postponed; New Date Uncertain After Storms Scuttle Plans to Start This Week," *The Times Picayune*, New Orleans, LA, September 14, 2008, A:1.

35. Paul Purpura, "Judge Upholds Marinello's Charge; Grand Juror May Be Witness to the Crime," *The Times Picayune*, New Orleans, LA, October 18, 2008, B:1.

36. WDSU-TV Channel 6 News Report, "Marinello Says It Was Impossible to Be at the Murder Scene," Richard Angelico reporting, New Orleans, LA, December 9, 2008. http://www.youtube.com/watch?v=9prIya BeqJ8. Accessed October 14, 2014.

37. Paul Purpura, "Testimony Begins in Trial of Marinello," *The Times Picayune*, New Orleans, LA, December 3, 2008, A:1.

38. Paul Pupura, "Radio Host 'Angry' Before Killing;—Testimony Explores Days Before Wife Died," *The Times Picayune*, New Orleans, LA, 4 December 4, 2008, A:1.

39. Pupura, "Radio Host 'Angry' Before Killing."

40. James Gill, "Strangely Carefree; Marinello Faces Justice," *The Times Picayune*, New Orleans, LA, December 5, 2008, B:7.

41. Paul Purpura, "Marinello Cell Phone Records Examined; Time of Shooting, Calls, Location Given," *The Times Picayune*, New Orleans, LA, December 6, 2008, A:1.

42. Purpura, "Marinello Cell Phone Records Examined."

43. Purpura, "Marinello Cell Phone Records Examined"; Robert McFadden, "Anthony Provanzano, Ex-Teamster Boss, Dies at 71," *New York Times*, December 13, 1988, B:16.

44. Purpura, "Marinello Cell Phone Records Examined."

45. Paul Purpura, "Marinello Ex-Lover Backs His Alibi; But Phone Call Used to Rebut Testimony," *The Times Picayune*, New Orleans, LA, December 7, 2008, A:1; A:25.

46. Paul Purpura, "Witness Tells of Beggar in Area Before Shooting," *The Times Picayune*, New Orleans, LA, December 12, 2008, A:1.

47. Paul Purpura, "Marinello Takes the Stand; He Explains Checklist, Gunshot Residue," *The Times Picayune*, New Orleans, LA, December 13, 2008, A:1.

48. Purpura, "Marinello Takes the Stand."

49. Paul Purpura, "Marinello Convicted in Wife's Murder; 'We're Drinking Champagne Tonight,' Victim's Mother Says," *The Times Picayune*, New Orleans, LA, December 14, 2008, A:1.

50. Purpura, "Marinello Convicted in Wife's Murder."

51. WWL-870 News Radio, "Marinello Murder Trial Special," hosted by Tommy Tucker, onterview with Debra Schmidt, jury forewoman in the Marinello Murder Trial, 16 December 2008.

52. WWL-870 News Radio, "Marinello Murder Trial Special," Tommy Tucker, Host,

Interview with Debra Schmidt, jury forewoman in the Marinello murder trial, December 16, 2008.

53. Paul Purpura, "Life Sentence Official in 2006 Killing; Marinello Shuffles Out of the Courtroom," *The Times Picayune*, New Orleans, LA, January 23, 2009, A:1; A:9.

54. WDSU-TV Channel 6 News Report, "Marinello Says It Was Impossible to Be at the Murder Scene."

Bibliography

Primary Sources

Anonymous. Interview with author, July 28, 2014, Metairie, LA, re: Liz Marinello.
Brown v. Board of Education of Topeka, Kansas, 347 U.S. 483 (1954).
Cassimere, Raphael, Jr., Ph.D. Interview with author, November 20, 2014, Kenner, LA.
Criminal District Court for the Parish of Orleans, No. 207, Case #10321, *State of Louisiana v. Louis Calire, John Gibson, and William Feehan*, Docket No. #1267.
Criminal District Court for the Parish of Orleans. Section "A," Judge Alfred Roman Presiding, Arraignment Hearing, February 21, 1888.
Federal Bureau of Investigation, *Huey P. Long File*, Item Nos. 49-12330-98-11623, www.paperlessarchives.com.
Fontanille, William A. Statement. February 25, 1984, Jefferson Parish Sheriff's Office, Homicide Unit, Gretna, LA.
Harry S. Truman Presidential Library. http://www.trumanlibrary.org/9981.htm. Accessed November 24, 2014.
Holliday, Winola. Interview with author, November 18, 2014, Kenner, LA.
Huey P. Long Assassination Collection, P1992-193. Louisiana State Archives, Dr. Florent Hardy, Archivist, William Stafford Asst. Archivist.
Jefferson Parish Sheriff's Office Crime Report. Sec. A, Item #B-14695-84, February 14, 1984.
LeBlanc, W. J. Interview with author, September 22, 2014, Kenner, LA.
Louisiana Legislative Acts of 1902, Act 160, Amending §2, §6, and §8 of Act 112 of 1890, pp. 305–306.
Louisiana Revised Statutes Title 14 § 30.1.
Myers, Janet. Autopsy Protocol. February 24, 1984, Dr. Richard E. Tracy, Medical Examiner.
Myers, Kerry. Statement. March 14, 1984. Jefferson Parish Sheriff's Office, Homicide Unit, Gretna, LA.
911 Transcript. February 24, 1984, Kerry Myers, Jefferson Parish Sheriff's Office, Operator 73.
Parish of Lafayette Criminal District Court Records. No. 2900, 2905, 2914, 2915, April 4, 1912, Louisiana State Archives, Dr. Florent Hardy, Archivist.
Passalaqua, Major Joseph D., Commander, JPSO Crime Scene Investigations Unit. Interview with author, August 14, 1991, Metairie, LA.
Report of Coroner's Inquest of Kate Townsend. November 3, 1883, p. 374, Orleans Parish Coroner Inquests and Views, New Orleans Public Library, Special Collections Division, Loyola Branch, Ms. Yvonne Loiselle, Head Archivist.
Report of the Findings to the Court of Psychiatric Evaluation of Clementine Barnabet. October 21, 1912, Records of the Lafayette District Court, in Federal Writers' Project, No. 45, Northwestern Louisiana University, Walton Memorial Library, Henry Research Center, Mary Wernet, Archivist.
Reports on Clementine Barnabet. Records of the Lafayette District Court, in Federal Writers' Project, No. 45, Northwestern Louisiana University, Walton Memorial Library, Henry Research Center, Mary Wernet, Archivist, p. 1.

Seal, Randy "Country," Washington Parish Sheriff. Interview with author, December 15, 2014, Franklinton, LA.
State of Louisiana v. Clementine Barnabet, Eighteenth Judicial District Court, Parish of Lafayette, State of Louisiana, Record No. 2900, October 16, 1912.
State of Louisiana v. Kerry Myers and William Fontanille, 545 So.2d 981 (La. 1989), 982.
State of Louisiana v. Myers, No. 90-KA-539 (Fifth Circuit Court of Appeals, State of Louisiana. 1991).
State of Louisiana v. Vince Marinello, No. 09-1260 (Ct. of Appeals, 3rd Cir. 2010).
Weiss Family Collection. Historic New Orleans Collection, Louisiana Digital Library http://louisdl.louislibraries.org/.

Newspapers

Associated Press
Belleville News-Democrat
Bellingham Herald (Bellingham, WA)
Bienville Democrat (Acadia, LA)
Bismarck Daily Tribune (Bismarck, SD)
Bryan Daily Eagle (Bryan, TX)
Columbus Daily Enquirer (Columbus, GA)
Daily Picayune
Daily States
Daily Telegraph (Monroe, LA)
Dallas Morning News
Fort Worth Star-Telegram
Gulfport Daily Herald
Idaho Daily Statesman
Kansas City Star
The Kingston Daily Freeman (Kingston, KY)
Lafayette Advertiser
Le Macébé (Lucy, LA)
Louisiana Weekly
Macon Daily Telegraph
Miami Herald (Miami, FL)
New Orleans Daily Democrat
New York Daily Mirror
New York Evening Journal
New York Herald Tribune
New York Times
Omaha World Herald
Philadelphia Enquirer
Rock Island Argus (Rock Island, IL)
St. Tammany Farmer
Salt Lake City Tribune
The State (Columbia, SC)
The Thunderbolt (Birmingham, AL)
Times Democrat
Times Picayune
True Democrat (St. Francisville, LA)
Washington Herald
West Feliciana Sentinel

Journals, Theses and Magazine Citations

Coxe, John E. *The New Orleans Mafia Incident*. Unpublished master's thesis, Louisiana State University, 1928.
Gardner, Jennifer. *The Murder of Patrick Mealey: Police Chief of New Orleans, 1880–1888*. Unpublished master's thesis, University of New Orleans, 2001.
Kurtz, Michael. "Organized Crime in Myth and Reality." *Louisiana History: The Journal of the Louisiana Historical Association* 24, no. 4 (Autumn 1983): 355–376.
Muller, Mary Lee. "New Orleans Public School Segregation." *Louisiana History: The Journal of the Louisiana History Association* 17, no. 1 (Winter 1976).
Schlesinger, Arthur M. "The Messiah of the Rednecks," in *The Louisiana Purchase Bicentennial Series in Louisiana History. Volume VIII: The Age of the Longs, 1928–1960*, ed. by Edward F. Haas. Lafayette, LA: Center for Louisiana Studies University of Louisiana at Lafayette, 2001.
Trotter, Michael C. "Huey Long's Last Operation: When Politics and Medicine Don't Mix." *The Ochnser Journal* 12, no. 1 (Spring 2012): 9–12.
Zinman, David. "The Meteoric Life and Mysterious Death of Huey P. Long." *American History Illustrated* 28, no. 3 (July/August 1993): 24–37.

Supplemental Media

"An Eyewitness in the Oneal Moore Case," *Injustice Files: Discovery Communications*, 2010, hosted by Ken Beauchamp. http://investigationdiscovery.com/tv-shows/injusticefiles/videos. Accessed September 9, 2014.

"The Lavoisier Reports: My Secret, My City: The Legend of Clementine Barnabet," http://ireport.cnn.com/docs/DOC-563081. Accessed June 3, 2014.

Shields, Alan. "Who Killed Who in the Louisiana House of Horrors?" *Startling Detective* 82, no. 2 (March 1992).

"Vince Marinello Trial Special," WWL-870 AM Radio, December 17, 2008, New Orleans, LA.

"Washington Parish Deputies Honored in Memorial," WDSU-TV, Heath Allen reporting, May 15, 2013.

WDSU-TV, Channel 6 News Report, "Change of Venue in Marinello Murder Trial," LaTonya Norton reporting, Gretna, LA, April 4, 2008. http://www.youtube.com/watch?v=XvXjCI_hNfE. Accessed October 14, 2014.

WDSU-TV, Channel 6 News Report, "Marinello Says It Was Impossible to Be at the Murder Scene," Richard Angelico reporting, New Orleans, LA, December 9, 2008. http://www.youtube.com/watch?v=9prIyaBeqJ8. Accessed October 14, 2014.

WWL-870 News Radio, "Marinello Murder Trial Special," hosted by Tommy Tucker, interview with Debra Schmidt, jury forewoman in the Marinello murder trial, December 16, 2008.

Secondary Sources

Asbury, Herbert. *The French Quarter: A History of the New Orleans Underworld*. Atlanta: Mockingbird Books, 1963.

Bartlett, Napier. *Military Record of Louisiana*. Baton Rouge, LA: Louisiana State University Press, 1964.

Campbell, Anne. *Louisiana: The History of an American State*. Atlanta: Clairmont Press, 2007.

Chandler, David. *Brothers in Blood: The Rise of the Criminal Brotherhoods*. New York: E.P. Dutton & Co., 1975.

Cometi, Elizabeth. "Trends in Italian Immigration." *Western Political Quarterly* 11, no. 4 (December 1958): 820–834.

Deutsch, Hermann. *The Huey Long Murder Case*. New York: Doubleday and Company, 1963.

Fairclough, Adam. *Race and Democracy: The Civil Rights Struggle in Louisiana, 1915–1972*. Athens, GA: University of Georgia Press, 2008.

Fineran, John Kingston. *The Career of a Tinpot Napoleon: A Political Biography of Huey P. Long*. New Orleans: John Kingston Fineran, 1932.

Gauthreaux, Alan G. *Italian Louisiana: History, Heritage, and Tradition*. Charleston, SC: History Press, 2014.

Harris, Thomas O. *The Kingfish: Huey P. Long, Dictator*. Baton Rouge: Claitor's Publishing Division, 1968.

Hogue, James K. *Uncivil War: Five New Orleans Street Battles and the Rise and Fall of Radical Reconstruction*. Baton Rouge, LA: Louisiana State University Press, 2006.

Hunt, Thomas, and Martha Macheca. *Deep Water: Joseph P. Macheca and the Birth of the American Mafia*. New York: iUniverse Publishing, 2004.

Jackson, Joy. *New Orleans in the Gilded Age: Politics and Urban Progress, 1880–1896*. Lafayette, LA: University of Louisiana Press, 1969.

Lonn, Ella. *Reconstruction in Louisiana After 1868*. New York: Russell & Russell, 1918.

Nelli, Humbert S. *From Immigrants to Ethnics: The Italian Americans*. Oxford, UK: Oxford University Press, 1983.

Powers, Madelon. *Faces Along the Bar: Lore and Order in the Workingman's Saloon, 1870–1920*. Chicago: University of Chicago Press, 1998.

Rable, George C. *But There Was No Peace: The Role of Violence in the Politics of Reconstruction.* Athens, GA: University of Georgia Press, 1984.
Rose, Al. *Storyville, New Orleans.* Tuscaloosa: University of Alabama Press, 1974.
Sacher, John. *A Perfect War of Politics: Parties, Politicians, and Democracy in Louisiana, 1824–1861.* Baton Rouge, LA: Louisiana State University Press, 2007.
Somers, Robert. *The Southern States Since the War, 1870–1871.* Introduction by Malcolm C. McMillan. Tuscaloosa: University of Alabama Press, 1965.
Tallant, Robert. *Ready to Hang: Seven Famous New Orleans Murders.* New Orleans: Pelican Publishing, 1952.
Tunnell, Ted. *The Crucible of Reconstruction: War, Radicalism, and Race in Louisiana, 1862–1877.* Baton Rouge, LA: Louisiana State University Press, 1992.
Wall, Bennett, et al. *Louisiana: A History* Arlington Heights, IL: Wiley-Blackwell, 1984.
Warmoth, Henry Clay. *War, Politics, and Reconstruction: Stormy Days in Louisiana.* New York: Negro University Press, 1970.
White, Richard D. *Kingfish: The Reign of Huey P. Long.* New York: Random House, 2006.
Zinman, David. *The Day Huey Long Was Shot, September 8, 1935.* New York: Ivan Obelensky, 1963.

Index